# How to Be Your Own Literary Agent

# HOW TO BE YOUR OWN

# LITERARY AGENT

*The Business of Getting a Book
Published*  REVISED AND EXPANDED

# RICHARD CURTIS

HOUGHTON MIFFLIN COMPANY   *Boston   New York*

For information about permission to reproduce selections from
this book, write to Permissions, Houghton Mifflin Company,
215 Park Avenue South, New York, New York 10003.

For information about this and other Houghton Mifflin
trade and reference books and multimedia products, visit
The Bookstore at Houghton Mifflin on the World Wide Web at
http://www.hmco.com/trade/.

Library of Congress Cataloging-in-Publication Data
Curtis, Richard.
How to be your own literary agent : the business of getting
a book published / Richard Curtis. — Rev. and expanded.
    p.  cm.
ISBN 0-395-71819-8
1. Authors and publishers — United States.   2. Literary agents
— United States.      I. Title.
KF3084.C87   1995
070.5'2 — dc20   95-40556   CIP

Printed in the United States of America
QUM   10  9  8  7  6  5  4  3  2  1

*This book was produced and directed*
*by my wife, Leslie, to whom*
*it is lovingly dedicated*

## Acknowledgments

My warmest thanks to Charles Brown, publisher of *Locus*, the newspaper of the science fiction field, who offered me the opportunity to test-fly the columns on which this book is based. To Seth McEvoy of Council of Writers' Organizations, Chris Steinbrunner of *The Third Degree*, Dale Walker of *Roundup*, and other editors of professional writers' newsletters who opened their pages to my columns. To Tom Hart, my Houghton Mifflin editor, for seeing this material as a book and helping me make it into one. To Clay Morgan and Lisa Sacks, my superb copy editors, who did not put their blue pencils down, thank goodness. And to Janet Silver, my Houghton Mifflin editor for this revised and updated edition, for pointing the way to the twenty-first century.

# Contents

# Introduction

If professionalism may be defined as mastery of the tools of one's trade, I have to wonder how many writers earning money from their work can truly call themselves professionals. After all, one of the most important tools of their trade is the publishing contract. Yet, of the thousands of writers I have known over the course of more than thirty years as agent, author, and lecturer, only a small percentage have had more than a superficial understanding of contracts and the negotiating skills associated with them. It is a sad irony that after struggling so hard for so long and at last achieving something worthy, a writer will then proceed to depreciate its value with a stroke of his pen on a publishing agreement.

I'm not sure I comprehend this reluctance of writers to understand and negotiate contracts. I know it's not necessarily a lack of legal sophistication. An editor friend of mine tells about the late Justice Abe Fortas of the United States Supreme Court, whom he signed up to write a book. The editor mailed off the firm's standard publishing contract, wondering what would be left of the document after so distinguished a jurist finished dismembering it. To the editor's astonishment it came back by return mail, signed without so much as one alteration. Appended to the contract was a note. "I haven't looked at it," scribbled Fortas, "but I'm sure it's okay."

Perhaps writers are apprehensive of contracts because they have something to do with being businesslike, a quality that some artists feel is not in keeping with the creative spirit. Many writers, particularly new ones, tend not to think of their work as having commercial or legal value. Not long ago an agent I know phoned a client to report he'd sold her first book. As expected, the author went slightly berserk with joy and hung up to share the news with her family. Fifteen minutes later she phoned back sheepishly. "Uh, I forgot to ask. How much are they going to pay?" Authors, it seems, are so grateful somebody wants to publish them that matters of money and contract become secondary.

The moment a writer receives his first offer for something he's written, however, he crosses the threshold into the business world. By endorsing that first check, he makes a legal commitment every bit as binding as a lease or a car-purchase agreement. Although lawyers and literary agents exist to interpret contracts for authors and conduct their business, rare is the writer who has not woken up one day to the realization that his appointed representative has not represented his interests as completely, as competently, as responsibly as was expected. Indeed, not a few wake up to realize their appointed representative has botched things up terribly. And that's just writers who do engage agents or lawyers; there are countless numbers who don't, and botch it without professional help.

Consonant with the creative spirit or not, then, it is every writer's responsibility to be businesslike, to feel comfortable with a contract, to understand what his agent or lawyer is trying to do for him, to understand what a publisher is trying to get him to do.

There are some wonderful works available on how to write, and this book doesn't pretend to compete with them. It assumes you're already writing or have written something and want to sell it, or have received an offer for it and want to negotiate a good contract. Despite its title, it is aimed as much at writers who have agents as at those who do not. Because agents are mortal and subject to errors, sometimes egregious and even fatal ones, no author is relieved from responsibility for his contractual commitments merely because he has an agent who is supposed to be an expert in such affairs. Quite the contrary, whether your agent is an expert or not, he has no liability whatever for legal and other problems arising out of documents he hands you to sign. My purpose for represented writers, then, is to help them understand and oversee their agent's work, to become informed clients.

I rest my authority on two qualifications. First, I have been a literary agent for over thirty years. Second, as author of more than fifty books I have committed just about every contractual blunder on record. Luckily, I am, I assure you, much better at representing others than I am at representing myself. But because of these experiences I feel compelled to state this book's bias candidly: I'm by no means certain a writer *can* be his own agent. The famous proverb of the legal profession, that the lawyer who represents himself has a fool for a client, may be apt for the writing profession as well. As my own client I tend to be impatient, to have no objectivity about my work, and to be so easily flattered that someone wants to publish me as to accept terms I would sternly reject if they were offered for one of my authors' properties. So this book is definitely a case of Do What I Say, Not What I Do.

Another bias of this book is that it's aimed at book, not magazine, writers. Most of the marketing, negotiation, and contractual strategies discussed in these pages can be utilized by magazine writers, however.

Because short stories, articles, essays, and poetry sales are so low-paying, most agents will not handle such material except as a courtesy to certain clients or in cases where the material clearly has the potential to sell to a high-paying market. My agency is no exception. But I'm not sure there's much an agent can do for magazine writers that they can't do for themselves. Magazine editors are much more responsive to unrepresented authors than book editors are, so it's easier for magazine writers to get a foot in the door. The price ranges of magazines are fairly inflexible, so there's not that much negotiating leeway for an agent. Magazine purchase agreements are less complicated than book contracts. All in all, magazine writers can survive without highly developed business skills; I don't think book writers can. Still, all writing paths seem to lead to books; at least I've never met a magazine writer who didn't have a book in him. Sooner or later, then, every writer will have to deal with the problems discussed here.

I wish to apologize to all women readers of this book for my use of the masculine pronoun when referring to authors and editors. Writing this work has certainly raised my consciousness about the way our language discriminates against women. At the same time I found that such usages as "he/she" didn't sit comfortably with me, and I was twisting sentences into cruel configurations by employing "they" or "you" or "one" all the time. So I've fallen back on the publishing tradition wherein, on all contracts, the masculine pronoun signifies writers of either sex.

Finally, a number of statements made in this book are critical of publishers. For these I will not apologize. But I would like to thank my publishers for tolerantly permitting me the freedom to make them. The opinions expressed herein are, I'm fairly certain, not necessarily those of the sponsor.

# How to Be Your Own Literary Agent

# 1 ✍

# An Agent Looks at the Market

In the beginning are the words: fifty thousand, seventy-five thousand, a hundred thousand or more. They comprise the book manuscripts that arrive at my agency's offices each day in sturdy gray canvas mail sacks or piled on the United Parcel Service man's creaking dolly. A few weeks ago, the day's batch was assigned to our readers for preliminary evaluation. Our readers are a congenial group of highly intelligent men and women who have all worked at publishing houses and are voracious consumers of literature, the kind who, after reading manuscripts all day for a living, love nothing more than to settle down with a good book at the end of the day. These people have excellent taste and well-honed commercial instincts, and they take great joy in discovering new talent, a joy made keener by the generous bonus I offer for any manuscript they recommend that goes on to get sold.

They have completed their appraisals of the manuscripts that came in two weeks ago, and written their reports and recommendations. If a recommendation was favorable, or even ambivalent, the manuscript was then routed to one of my associates or to me. Now, at 10:00 A.M., after filling our mugs from the coffee machine in our kitchen, my staff and I have sat down to talk about the manuscripts before us. As you are an agent-in-training, I would like to invite you to attend today's conference so you can be privy to the process by which the fate of those manuscripts is determined. And as you are also an author, and your own manuscript may be among those discussed this morning, I know you'll want to be there. How do you take your coffee?

You will hear a great deal of talk, because, like just about everyone else in the publishing industry, we are nothing if not articulate.

After all, our livelihoods, and our firm's reputation and credibility, depend on how accurately we express our feelings about what we read. Nevertheless, the essence of all that talk talk talk can be summarized in a brutally blunt three-word question: *Is it salable?* Cookbook, western, how-to, inspirational, thriller, juvenile — it doesn't matter what kind of book it is, the question is always the same. The issue is *not* how well the book is written, for the quality of writing is only one factor in the decision-making process, and not always the key one. A well-written book may be just as unsalable as a poorly written one; it just breaks your heart a little more to return it to the author.

Precisely what are the factors that go into the decision-making process? What criteria do agents apply when they review manuscripts? What do agents know, or think they know, that you don't know about the publishing market? Well, after more than three decades in the publishing field as both agent and writer, I've concluded, not without a great deal of sadness, that the decision to publish almost invariably boils down to a question of economics.

Someday, somebody a lot smarter than I will write a book showing how, throughout history, literature has been shaped by the prices of books. And I will tell everyone I know to go and buy that book. For I am convinced that inspiration, craftsmanship, creativity, and other authorly qualities are less important in determining what writers write and what publishers publish than such factors as lumberjacks' wages, the cost of a typesetter's home mortgage, the prime rate, and New York City's real-estate taxes. Irrelevant though these may seem at first, they constitute some of the economic forces that influence book pricing, and the price of books is *the* dominant factor in editorial decision making today, the unseen but dictatorial chairman of every publishing board.

This may be a painful pill for would-be Faulkners and Austens to swallow, and my last desire is to denigrate the miraculous processes by which raw inspiration is transmuted into literature. But I have to declare in all candor that no one interested in being published in our time can afford to be so naive as to believe that a book will make it merely because it's good.

Although inflation has driven the cost of everything up, it has particularly affected the way people dispose of discretionary income, and trade books (books of general interest, as opposed to text, professional, and other books for specialized markets) are definitely discretionary purchases. Book buyers who didn't hesitate to buy a hardcover novel in a bookstore for $14.95 a few years ago are now passing up comparable books at $24.95. Airline passengers who used to purchase three paperbacks at once for $1.75 each now carefully examine the racks and ultimately choose only one, selling for $5.95.

Because high prices have made book buyers extremely picky (I'm not even sure I'd pay $24.95 for my *own* novel in a store!), the publishing market has become very bestseller oriented, and the industry dominated by the blockbuster mentality, a mentality that seeks guaranteed profits through tried-and-true big-name authors writing in tried-and-true formulas. The pressures created by that mentality are exerted on writers, forcing them to write books of a certain kind or a certain length or a certain style, and in many cases forcing them out of the writing profession entirely. So I don't think it's far-fetched at all to imagine that a hike in lumberjacks' wages, which will in turn affect the cost of paper, might influence a publishing decision to raise book prices, leading in turn to a phone call from an editor to an author along the lines of, "Listen, Mr. Tolstoy, if we're going to hold the price of your book below $29.95, you'll have to do some judicious pruning in the 'Peace' section and get right into the 'War' stuff. Maybe you could trim that ballroom scene, edit some of Sonya's business, chop the prebattle chitchat, and for God's sake get rid of that peasant and his dog . . ."

These cynical observations won't win me many friends, and I certainly don't endorse the blockbuster mentality (unless the blockbuster happens to be by one of my clients), but I have to be completely frank with authors who seek publication in the general market: Whatever else your book may be, it must be profitable. And books that have little else to recommend them beyond being good are all too often marginally profitable, or not profitable at all.

There are four broad categories of books with commercial potential: backlist, frontlist, midlist, and genre. As we shall see, it's well-nigh impossible to define these categories narrowly, and they have a tendency to run into each other and blur at the edges. A frontlist bestseller may become a backlist classic that sells for decades; a genre western may be so extraordinary as to sell outside its traditional market and even make the bestseller list. A midlist author may at last write a book that hits the bestseller list, and discover publishers frenziedly bidding for the right to reissue his old, out-of-print genre books, to his embarrassment or amusement.

Let's look at these categories a little more closely.

**Backlist books.** Backlist books are books that sell over a long term. Their appeal for publishers is steady performance, predictability of market, and easy maintenance. Although it wouldn't be accurate to say backlist books sell themselves, they certainly don't require the special treatment demanded by books vying for a place on the bestseller list. As long as the overhead — printing, warehousing, servicing of orders, and so forth — doesn't get too high, the backlist can provide a publisher with his basic income and carry the firm over the roller-coaster ups and downs that attend the publishing of new books. Professional books, textbooks, cookbooks and other how-to's, classics, and juveniles fall into the category of backlist books. *Lost Horizon, Gone with the Wind, Catcher in the Rye, The Caine Mutiny,* and *Exodus* are examples of bestsellers that continue to sell briskly year in and year out after dropping off the list. Other books, such as *The Oxford Book of English Verse* or Paul Samuelson's textbook *Economics,* may never have hit the bestseller list, but move in enormous quantities over the long haul, and indeed over the long haul may outsell the blockbuster that struts and frets its hour upon the stage and then is heard no more. The Bible, of course, is always held up as the epitome of backlist books.

Unfortunately, the backlist has become harder and harder to maintain over the last few decades. The cost of printing and warehousing books that move too slowly, the cost of servicing and bookkeeping on single-copy orders, the cutbacks in library funding, the paperback revolution, the rise of the bookstore chains with their emphasis on fast turnover of merchandise, all these and other factors militate against profitability in backlist publishing. More and more, publishers want to get in with the books, get out with the profit, and the hell with posterity. So, like so much else in modern life, books have become more and more disposable — literally as well as literarily. They fall apart after a few years, or even after a few readings.

**Frontlist books.** The frontlist is a publisher's new releases, the books on which he pins his hopes for this season's success. Although not every book is expected or even intended to go on the bestseller list, it can safely be said that publishers do expect every new book at least to earn a profit; to hit a bestseller list, to become a solid backlist item, or just to burn brightly for a few months in the bookstores before being remaindered.

The apotheosis of the successful frontlist book is the bestseller, the book that appears on recognized lists such as those in the *New York Times Book Review* or *Publishers Weekly*. Other than that qualification, however, it's impossible to find many common denominators on any given list, short-term trends notwithstanding. As unclassifiably diverse as the books on any given bestseller list may be, there is one element running through almost all of them: At least 75 percent are by authors with previous bestseller track records. This fact cannot be overemphasized; with so many book buyers reluctant to pay high prices for books, the only way to lure them is with familiar, proven big-name authors. You will be more inclined to pay $25 for a book by the man who brought you *The Hunt for Red October* than you will be to pay the same money for one by someone who brought you three articles in the *Boston Globe*, a short story in *Redbook*, and a poem in the *Sewanee Review*. Oh, you might buy the latter if its publishers package and promote it as if it *were* by Tom Clancy, but such exceptions only underscore the rule, as is illustrated by a conversation I had with a paperback editor not long ago when I asked her how she intended to "position" a book I'd sold her.

"Well," she said, "I don't think it's strong enough to be our number-one leader for May, or even our second or third leader, but it might make a good fourth or fifth leader." ("Leaders" are a paperback publisher's big books for any given month.)

"Wait a minute," I said. "It sounds as if *all* the books you publish every month are called leaders."

"They are!" she exclaimed. "We have to publish every book as if it were a bestseller. If we don't feel a book has leader potential, we don't buy it."

The capital invested in acquiring, merchandising, advertising, and promoting books by brand-name authors is capital taken away from books by new authors, meaning that many a promising talent is frozen out of publishing at the entry level. It simply takes too long, and too many money-losing books, for most publishers to subsidize authors until their commercial potential is at last realized.

Oh, a certain number of books by such authors do find their way every year onto publishers' lists. Why? The reasons range from the deplorable — a publisher needs something, anything, to fill a slot — to the inspiring — a house establishes a policy of reinvesting its profits into the work of new writers, even if their books lose money. The publishing industry has a term to describe such work: "midlist."

**Midlist books.** These books are so called because they occupy the middle of a publisher's list between the blockbusters at one end of the spectrum and the backlist and genre books (mysteries, westerns, romances, and so forth) at the other. Midlist books are often sui generis, and possess neither the "legs" to become bestsellers nor the longevity to move steadily on a backlist.

If "midlist" sounds as if it has an opprobrious connotation — well, it does. The writing of midlist books, to quote a line Finley Peter Dunne used in another context, "isn't a crime exactly. Ye can't be sint to jail f'r it, but it's kind've a disgrace." Midlist authors are authors who have published *and* perished. They are easily identified at publishing parties, if they've been invited at all, as the people embarrassedly listing the titles of their books for listeners politely pretending to have heard of those books. Midlist authors are not failures, but they are not successes either. They are probably the most interesting type of writer, for they are generally intelligent, cultured, articulate, highly skilled craftsmen and craftswomen who care passionately about writing (their own and others') and bitterly resent the economic forces that have made publishing a branch of the entertainment industry and books the software of a word-processing medium. Nevertheless, many of them feel like losers, and, in the eyes of people who publish books, they may well *be* losers.

Which is why they don't stay midlist for long. Some drop out entirely; others shift to genre writing; and others gird their loins, apply themselves mightily, and produce the book that breaks them out of the midlist and vaults them to fame and fortune. Midlist authors who have "broken out" are easily identified at publishing parties, too. They're the guests of honor.

**Genre books.** Genre books come last in the publishing spectrum, but certainly not least, not in *this* agent's value system, anyway.

Genre books are popular books that fall into certain traditional categories: westerns, science fiction, mysteries, romances, male adventure, medical novels, occult thrillers, spy thrillers, and the like. Although the story lines of such books frequently follow formulas — the "tip sheets" (guidelines) issued by some romance publishers are intimidatingly elaborate, for example — the tendency among readers, publishers, critics and reviewers, and even writers themselves to oversimplify genre writing has created much confusion and not a little hypocrisy. Confusion because it is all but impossible to define what is and what is not a formula book; hypocrisy because the people who look down their noses at genre writing are often the same ones who profit from writing and publishing it, or secretly get a kick out of reading it.

Anyone attempting to define a genre too strictly will quickly find himself in deep trouble, for the best genre fiction, paradoxically, is not genre fiction at all. Is *The Ox-Bow Incident* a formula western? Yes and no. Is *The Spy Who Came In from the Cold* a formula spy thriller? Yes and no. Is *Murder on the Orient Express* a formula mystery novel? Yes and no. Did the Brontës, Robert Louis Stevenson, Balzac, H. G. Wells, Henry James, write formula fiction? They certainly did! They most assuredly did not!

On the bestseller list before me are represented such genres as mystery, occult thriller, adventure, romance, and family saga. Some of these books, and certainly parts of all of them, follow formulas. In fact, many of these and other best-selling authors got their start writing formula fiction at sweatshop rates.

Like a metallurgist sorting out rare metals from their baser kin, the agent weighs story line, characterization, and writing skill in each manuscript that comes before him, to determine whether a book fits into a very narrow category, or has the potential to break out of its category, as the above-named bestsellers have done. Indeed, many agents literally weigh their manuscripts. By merely hefting one and doing a rough word count, a good agent can often tell if a book is long enough to have big-book potential, for, with few exceptions, genre books of 50,000–60,000 words cannot attain the complexity and dimension necessary to make a nice juicy read.

Because it is so hard to define genre fiction, and because genre writing is the breeding ground for many best-selling if not classic authors, and because genre books pay the rents of all mass-market publishers, let those who do not profit from genre books cast the first stone. The terms *hack*, to describe genre writers, and *trash*, to describe the product of their labors, are not only offensive but inaccurate. If there are hack writers, there are also hack publishers and, for that matter, hack readers. No one in the publishing industry who knows what's involved in writing and publishing genre books calls them trash. Even the most formulaic of romances calls for highly developed skills, and while genre books are far and away the best means for aspiring writers to break into the book field, anyone believing he'll simply dash off a quickie paperback to raise a few thousand easy bucks is in for a rude surprise.

From year to year, genres go in and out of fashion. In the early 1970s, gothic novels were all the rage, then they suddenly fell from grace and were replaced by historical romances and family sagas. Then historical romances faded and were supplanted by glitzy contemporary romances. With the economic recession of the early 1990s, glitz lost some of its glitter and historical romances came roaring back bigger than ever. Male genres such as western and adventure, quiescent for much of the 1970s, came back strong in the early 1980s in the form of adult (ultrasexy, ultraviolent) western series, war and soldier-of-fortune series, spy thrillers, and the like. The end of the Cold War doomed some of these genres, depriving writers of many villains and story possibilities, and nothing notable has replaced them. Science fiction, which peaked with the *Star Wars* phenomenon, plummeted at the turn of the decade but has rebounded. Movie tie-ins, which may also have peaked after *Star Wars*, are at present moribund. Horror, whose demise has been predicted annually ever since *The Exorcist*, continues to be healthy, but seems to be moving away from occult and supernatural phenomena and toward psychological suspense. Mysteries, whose revival has been predicted for even longer, are finally alive and well.

Whatever the current trend may be, genres will always be with us, and genre writers will be the lifeblood of the publishing industry and, if I may be so bold, of literature itself. So here's my last word on genre writers. If I had room on my client list for only one more writer, and had to choose between one who's had a dozen solid but unspectacular genre paperback originals published and one whose first novel was a bestseller, I would be all but paralyzed with indecision, having seen so many of the former kind soar to wealth and glory, and so many of the latter fall ignominiously on their rear ends.

✍

Well, our meeting is over and the decisions have been made. The manuscripts have been sorted and we're ready to go into action. The rejected manuscripts are in this pile, the genre stuff in this, the books with midlist and backlist potential in that pile over there, and here, sitting on my desk like missiles poised on their launching pads, are the few we think can go all the way.

Which pile is yours in?

# 2 ✍

# Slush

W hen the nation was younger, and publishing still known as the Gentleman's Profession, most book publishers were happy to consider manuscripts submitted by unrepresented writers, and many a good book got published that way. But as publishing developed after World War II into big business, and literary agents rose to dominate the marketplace, publishers sharply veered away from unrepresented authors as significant sources of publishable material and began depending more and more heavily on agents to screen good properties from bad. At length, the conglomeratization of the industry, aided by permanent recessionary trends in the economy, completed the movement in that direction, and we are now at the point where very little unsolicited material is read by major trade-book publishers in the United States. For it is clearly cost-ineffective to retain editors to read "unagented" manuscripts when the ratio of acceptances to rejections is something on the order of one in ten thousand. (Unfortunately, *Webster's Unabridged* does not yet recognize the verb "to agent," but everyone in the business uses it, and so must you if you're going to be doing your own . . . um . . . agenting.) There are exceptions, but they only serve to prove the rule. *Ordinary People* by Judith Guest was plucked out of the unsolicited pile at Viking Press and went on to become a very big book and an even bigger movie. But according to the *New York Times*, it was also the first such manuscript accepted by Viking in twenty-seven years!

Manuscripts submitted to publishers by unrepresented authors are described by the depressing term *slush*, and slush they are, whether the work of a genius or the ravings of a lunatic. Insofar as any manuscript comes into a publishing company "over the transom" (uninvited), it falls under the official designation of Slush.

Although statistics are not available, and never will be (for few publishers will admit that they turn back unsolicited manuscripts without reading them), I would guess that most trade publishers today do not read slush. They return it with printed rejection slips, frequently with a statement that they read material only if submitted by literary agents. As I say, the reasoning is cold-bloodedly economic. Assuming a publisher gets 5000 unagented manuscripts in a year (a figure I'm told is on the modest side), and a skillful editor can read and judge four every working day, and figure 225 working days a year, that's less than 1000 manuscripts evaluated per editor per year. So you need four or five editors to plow through those 5000 manuscripts. Figure salaries for junior editors at this writing to be around $20,000 per annum, and you have an annual salary cost of $80,000 to $100,000 per year for the slush-pile staff. Then add fringe benefits and Social Security contributions. Recommended manuscripts must be read by senior editors, whose time must also be paid for. And what about the astronomical cost of returning all the rejected manuscripts whose authors have not included postage?

And so, if it is true that only one manuscript in thousands is worthy of acceptance by a publisher, you're talking about a cost of well over $100,000 to discover it, *not* including the cost of publishing it. With a bottom line like that, it had better be one helluva book! But because most publishers don't believe they will find such a consummate masterpiece under those bushels of over-the-transom submissions, they consider it more cost-effective to leave the sorting-out to the agents and spend the $100,000 where it can do more good — or at least where they think it can do more good. For this reason, it can be stated with some accuracy that a publisher will read the most dismal piece of junk submitted by a literary agent faster and maybe even more attentively than he will a good book that comes in on the slush pile.

I suppose you think I'm setting you up for a pitch for literary agents, right? Well, of course I am! You have to be slightly crazy to ignore those odds. The chances of culling a salable manuscript out of the piles of material submitted each week by nonprofessional authors are much better for an agent than they are for a publisher. The reason is that an author may write a perfectly publishable book but then submit it to a perfectly unsuitable publisher. If you turn out a nifty formula western and send it to Knopf, for instance, it most likely will never see the light of day. But if you submit it to an agent, that agent will say, "Of course it's wrong for them; they seldom publish that stuff. But it might be right for Berkley or Zebra or Bantam, publishers that have western lines." The agent, in short, has many more options with a given manuscript than a publisher does.

But *you* have a problem, and it's a fundamental one: You need an agent, but an agent may not need you. Despite a sharp surge in the last decade in the number of literary agents entering the field, few are so hungry for business that they will take on new clients indiscriminately. First of all, because they have been (unofficially, but effectively) vested by publishers with the responsibility for separating literary gold from dross, their reputations would quickly be ruined if they took on everything that comes their way. And second, they don't have time to read everything that comes their way, at least not without a staff of readers; and, as you now know, a staff of readers is a costly item.

Some agents charge reading fees to defray the cost of readers, but others simply return manuscripts unread, or cursorily read, with a printed note that says, in effect, "We can't accept you as a client until you have a track record."

Now, here's a pretty paradox: You can't get published without an agent, and you can't get an agent until you've been published! Where do you turn now? Is there no way an unagented author can get a foot, or at least a manuscript, inside the door of a publishing house?

I think there is. It calls for some work and expenditure of time and money, but if I were an unpublished author caught on the horns of this dilemma, here's how I would handle it.

**1. Study the market.** If you're going to be your own agent, you must learn who publishes what. The average reader is oblivious to the names of the publishers of the books he or she reads, but for the professional writer this knowledge is a must. Even a few minutes' browse in a bookstore will tell you that Knopf doesn't publish genre westerns, and that Dell doesn't publish deluxe editions of *Art*

*Treasures of the Louvre.* A few more hours there will reveal much more about the types of books published by different houses. Or you may send away for publishers' catalogues.

You should subscribe to professional writers' newsletters specializing in the field you're writing for, as these newsletters regularly run fairly up-to-date market reports and the names of key editors, price ranges and basic contractual terms, and special requirements ("We accept science fiction and fantasy, but no sword and sorcery"; "St. Martin's mysteries are sold extensively to lending libraries, so nothing too sexy and violent, please"; and so forth). *Writers Digest* frequently runs such reports and surveys, and the annual *Writers Market* published by the same company provides an excellent picture of market conditions. Above all, there is *Publishers Weekly*, the official trade publication of the publishing industry, which purveys thorough coverage of every aspect of the business.

**2. Address your submission to a specific editor.** Submissions aimed at specific editors will probably get prompter treatment than those not earmarked for anyone in particular or those addressed to the editor-in-chief or chairman of the board, who'll undoubtedly route them to the slush pile. Aside from the flattery implicit in this personal approach, the editor may well be sufficiently intrigued by your pitch letter to flip through the manuscript and read it himself, or at least turn it over to a trusted assistant, rather than condemn it to slushy exile. In fact, it might even be smarter for you to submit it to the trusted assistant, who is usually a bright, ambitious young person in whose heart simmers the strongest desire to discover authors whose success will sweep him into prominence, promotion, and decent wages.

The names of department heads and editor-specialists at each publishing company are listed in *Literary Market Place* (LMP), the publishing industry's official directory published annually by the Bowker Company. Unfortunately, high job turnover in the industry can make such listings unreliable and quickly out of date; by the end of each year, the emendations in my copy of LMP give it the appearance of a well-trampled game preserve after the rainy season. So always phone the publisher and find out the name and precise spelling of the editor to whom you wish to submit your manuscript.

Of all the advice I can give you about how to crack the market, this is far and away the most important. So I repeat it: *Address your submission to a specific editor.*

**3. Do a multiple submission.** For most literary agents the multiple submission is an important tool, and one that can be extraordinarily effective when applied with care and good timing. Until the 1960s, it was practically unheard of and was considered unethical and, indeed, scandalously improper. Publishers expected authors and their agents to make the rounds of houses one at a time. But that changed a few decades ago, as authors and agents grew tired of increasing (and increasingly long) delays and also recognized the enormous leverage inherent in competitive bidding. Today, multiple submissions are commonplace. But they are not used indiscriminately on every book an agent handles, for not all books require such special treatment. Some just aren't urgently timely; some aren't big-money properties; some appeal to specialized markets; and some simply aren't good enough for an agent to expend all that energy, credibility, and salesmanship. If an agent blitzes publishers with every manuscript he takes on, he'll soon get the reputation for being a hype artist, and the industry will begin discounting his judgment.

For the unrepresented author, however, the problem is the far more primitive one of survival: You're not worried about how much you're going to get for your book (yet); you're worried about whether the damned thing is going to get read. Submitting to one market at a time, you run the risk of delay, maybe three months or more per submission. I therefore see no reason whatsoever why you should not submit your manuscript to more than one publisher at the same time.

How many more than one? As many as you want. But you might hold some in reserve, perhaps a third or half of the potential market. Obviously these would be secondary publishers — the smaller or lower-paying houses, or houses that are ultraselective, or that are well inventoried, or that are undergoing turbulent shifts of editorial personnel that can paralyze the decision-making process. There are two good reasons for not shooting your entire wad on the first round of submissions. First, suppose you indiscriminately submit your manuscript to primary and secondary houses at the same time, and one of the poorer houses makes you an offer. You may get so excited you'll accept it (and who'd blame you?), only to be contacted by a better house a little later that *also* wants to buy your book! You'll kick yourself eternally. But by submitting to all top houses in the first campaign, you can feel confident that any publisher that makes you an offer is a good publisher, and you can accept it without qualms.

Another reason for reserving some publishers for a second round of submissions is that in case you decide, or are told, that your book needs revisions, you won't have exhausted the marketing possibilities with a flawed manuscript.

What's that you said? What happens if two or three or four editors start bidding for your book? My friend, that's what we call a *good* problem! We'll take it up when we discuss negotiation.

**4. Write a strong covering letter.** Nothing arrests an editor's attention more than a solid submission letter. Indeed, the fate of your manuscript may well hinge on the reception your covering letter gets when the box is opened. The pitch letter is nothing less than a seductive billet-doux inviting the wary, harried, jaded editor to sample the merchandise behind the curtain. So work on that letter as if your career depended on it; it probably does.

After a professional lifetime of both reading and writing submission letters, I think I can claim a pretty good sense of what lures an editor to step behind that curtain. Unquestionably, the key component is track record, and it should come first in your letter.

Track record breaks down into several subcategories that can be stated as follows:

- Have you had any books published?
- Have they been published by national (as opposed to regional, local, or subsidy) publishers?
- Have they been published recently?
- How many copies did they sell?
- Did they sell to any book clubs?
- Did they sell to any reprint publishers?
- Did they sell to any foreign publishers?
- Were they serialized in any major magazines?
- Did they sell to the movies or television?
- Were they well reviewed in significant media?

- Did they win any prizes or awards?
- Are you an expert or authority in a field related to the present manuscript?

Obviously, the more Yes answers you can furnish to these questions, the more attractive you and your book sound. Don't hesitate to toot your horn loudly about large printings, big sales, great reviews, high advances. Modesty here is fatal. Did I say seduce them? Hell, overwhelm them!

EXAMPLE:

I'm happy to enclose my science fiction novel *The 50th Moon of Saturn.*

I'm a physicist and radio astronomer connected with the Jet Propulsion Laboratory, but for relaxation I've been writing science fiction for the last ten years, my stories regularly appearing in *Fantasy & Science Fiction, Analog,* and other publications here and in England.

My first novel, *The 48th Moon of Saturn*, was published by Doubleday in 1994, was a Science Fiction Book Club selection, and was reprinted by Berkley. It was sold to publishers in England, Germany, Holland, Japan, and Italy. My second, *The 49th Moon of Saturn*, was published by Putnam's in hardcover in 1995, reprinted by Berkley, sold in six countries, and optioned by Steven Spielberg . . .

I challenge any editor to return that manuscript unread.

If your track record is less than overwhelming but still respectable, summarize it in a brief sentence or two, stressing anything that might catch the eye.

EXAMPLE:

After five years writing for astronomy trade magazines, I sold my first article to *Playboy* last year, and since then have sold two more to *Playboy* and been assigned by *Esquire* to write a piece about the Mars mission. The enclosed book manuscript is an expansion of my first *Playboy* article . . .

The opening sentence of this letter bespeaks the author's writing experience, field of expertise, and growth. The repeat sales demonstrate that the first *Playboy* sale was no fluke, and the *Esquire* assignment suggests he has attracted the attention of other national publications. The second line of his letter should make an editor say to himself, "Well, if it's good enough for *Playboy*, perhaps it's good enough for us." Certainly, the opening of this letter compels one to read further and explore the contents of the manuscript.

If you have no track record whatsoever, perhaps you can establish some other impressive credentials.

EXAMPLE:

I am Professor Emeritus of Renaissance History at Cornell University, and have always been amazed that the life of Irving de' Medici, Lorenzo's fourth cousin twice removed and an extraordinary adventurer, has never been adequately chronicled in fact or fiction.

Now there's one honey of an opening line! It establishes the author's authority, piques your interest in the subject, and guarantees that the material you are about to read will be fresh and original.

So much for track record. The second part of your letter will deal with the subject of your book. In fact, if you have neither track record nor any pertinent credentials, this part should be the opening of your letter.

Describing the book can be a tricky matter for an author, because both overstatement and understatement are called for. While you want to use the most enticing terms possible, you don't want to sound like a carnival barker. It's one thing for an agent to describe a book as unique, stimulating, enthralling, charming, shattering, but quite another for the author himself to do so. So you'll have to restrain your natural desire to tell the world what a great book you've written.

In describing a book, brevity is absolutely of the essence. Perhaps it's unfortunate that our world has become so slogan, jingle, and blurb oriented that we expect our books to be summarized for us in one pithy sentence. Nevertheless, that's what you have to do to rivet an editor's attention. Don't worry, editors and everyone else in the publishing business have the same problem. Editors have to "sell" the books they want to buy to their colleagues on the editorial board, or to sell the books they've acquired to book clubs, reprint houses, and other subsidiary markets. They also have to "sell" the company's salesmen on the books, get them fired up so they can go out and get orders from the bookstores and chains. With such a welter of material, the sales pitch must be a miracle of conciseness. Salesmen for book publishers will tell you they have less than thirty seconds to describe each book on their list to store buyers, so you may be sure they polish their spiel till it glows. What it comes down to, I'm afraid, is this: If you can't describe a book in a single sentence, people are going to wonder what's wrong with it.

Here are some one-liners from pitches my agency has made on our own clients' books:

"The true story of a brilliant English magician who applied illusion and deception to conquer the Nazis in North Africa" (*The War Magician* by David Fisher).

"A novel about divorced women that takes over where *An Unmarried Woman* left off" (*Female Complaints* by Leslie Tonner).

"A father, his son, and his grandson are locked in mortal combat over a family secret that touches on nothing less than the fate of the superpowers" (*Dynasty of Spies* by Dan Sherman).

"A scientist of the future desperately signals a colleague in 1962 to stop the future before it's too late" (*Timescape* by Gregory Benford).

We all know that truly good literature cannot, and certainly should not, be treated so glibly — "A boy and a slave challenge the father of waters and discover the meaning of brotherhood" (*Huckleberry Finn*); "A murderer is betrayed by his worst enemy: his conscience" (*Crime and Punishment*) — but, like a cockade or a décolleté gown, these one-liners command our attention instantly. So don't quarrel with the rules of the game; play by them, and learn how to compress the essence of your book into one coruscating gem of a sentence.

If, after declaring your track record and describing your book, you would like to add a line or two of personal background, it won't hurt, but try to make it brief, pertinent, and interesting, even charming or humorous. I don't know what others advise, but I for one have always been responsive to humorous touches, and think

I can vouch for most editors. For although publishing can be a deadly serious business, it is populated by men and women who fancy themselves reincarnated eighteenth-century wits, and a little comic relief is usually welcome if handled gracefully.

**5. Package your manuscript well.** The packaging revolution has proven that attractive presentation inevitably makes the critical difference for a consumer trying to decide between otherwise equal products. Yet I'm always surprised at the inattention paid by so many authors, and indeed some agents, to proper packaging of literary material.

Perhaps I'm a fanatic, but I will not allow a submission to leave our office if it is poorly typed or proofread, if the paper is old or stained or dog-eared or torn, or if its submission box (many agencies use special reinforced cardboard boxes designed for book manuscripts) is damaged. It's impossible to prove that neatness sells books, but I'm certain it helps, and I'm positive that sloppiness can kill a sale. Call it unfair if you will, but many editors unconsciously believe that the author who can't spell can't write. I know that's not true, as I represent some marvelous writers who couldn't spell their way out of the fourth grade, but they have the good sense to have their manuscripts professionally retyped. The real point is not that poor spelling betokens poor writing, but rather that it betokens lack of care.

For the purpose of submission to an agent for appraisal, a perfect manuscript is not necessary, but before you or your agent submit to publishers — clean up your act.

*Paper.* A heavy white bond not only looks handsome but gives the manuscript body and authority when it is hefted. Disdain erasable bond, because its waxy surface smudges and makes manuscripts slippery. It's been debated whether you should submit originals or photocopies to publishers. Obviously, if it's a multiple submission you have to go with photocopies. But for one-at-a-time submissions, there is nothing like an original for conveying the specialness of the work.

And for crying out loud, *never, never, never* submit your only copy of a manuscript, not even registered, certified, insured, guaranteed, or manacled to the wrist of a handpicked courier. Although the odds against loss may be 1000 to 1, you can almost bet your life that the one in a thousand lost will be the one of which there is no copy in the author's files. I once gave my only copy of a chapter to a man high in government for whom I was ghostwriting a book, and he promised to make a photocopy the next morning and hand-deliver it to me. He left the envelope in the trunk of his car. That night his car was stolen.

*Typewriter.* In the original edition of this book I stated, "An electric or electronic typewriter with a handsome typeface is all but mandatory," and word processors are "still beyond the means of 98 percent of professional writers . . ." How the world has changed in twelve years! Today, the computer is an all but essential tool of most professional writers, whose shop talk is peppered with references to megabytes of RAM, laser printers, and online uploading of text for transmission to publishers. Confronted with a typewriter, young writers are likely to exclaim, "What the heck is *that?*" Whichever device you choose, however, my advice about handsome typeface still applies.

A warning about computers: they are the enemy of editorial economy. I have become aware that, ever since the introduction of word-processing programs, manuscripts have grown grossly overweight. The reason is that authors think that editing their work on screen is sufficient. But they don't look over their hard copy and may fail to realize how verbose it is. This is truly a case of not being able to see the forest for the trees. The words may all be there, and correctly spelled, but there are just too many of them, and you cannot detect the problem unless you review the paper manuscript itself.

*Manuscript appearance.* Wide margins will give a nice border to your manuscript and can add bulk to a book that might be on the short side. By moving your left- and right-hand margins in by three or four characters each, you can extend the manuscript about one page for every ten.

Page numbers, or page numbers plus your last name, should go at the top right-hand corner of each page. I recommend against putting the book title on every page, because at some stage in the submission process you may decide on a better one, and you'll have to alter every page.

The manuscript must be perfectly, and neatly, copy edited before it goes out. The spell-checking feature of word processors has of course reduced spelling errors almost to zero. Almost but not entirely, for most spell-check programs don't recognize homonym errors. Thus, "We one the ball game" may be correctly spelled, but is a howling grammatical error. You must do eyeball reviews of your text and not leave it to your machine to find goofs. If you're a good speller and grammarian and can pick up your own errors, do it. But if you don't trust your spelling skill, have it read and copy edited by someone you know to be competent. Of all the compliments I've ever received as a professional writer, the one that made me proudest was paid by one of my editors: "When you read a manuscript by Curtis," she said, "you put your blue pencil down." Take the attitude that a typo could cost you a sale, because, as a matter of fact, it could.

Don't put your manuscript in any kind of binder. Editors and agents like reading manuscripts loose, from the box — or at least they're used to reading them that way. Don't bind the manuscript with a rubber band, as it can damage the paper when removed. Just place the manuscript in a typing-paper box.

On the title page put title and author's name, and, toward the bottom of the page, address and phone numbers, home and work. Copyright notices are unnecessary, as the manuscript is protected by common and statutory copyright law. Some authors, concerned about plagiarism or outright theft of their material, go through elaborate procedures of registering their material with the Writers Guild of America or other official or quasi-official agencies. I don't think these measures are necessary, and I've never seen an instance of a legitimate publisher ripping off an author's work, but if it helps you sleep at night, then register your work.

A few pieces of Scotch tape will hold the manuscript box closed, but some people go to incredible lengths to seal up their manuscripts, as if in anticipation that the parcel will be subjected to heavy bombardment. A cynical editor once observed that the more elaborately packed a manuscript is, the worse it is. Padded mailing envelopes are good, and can be stapled, taped, or tied. Place your manuscript with its covering letter in the typing-paper box, then enclose a stamped, self-addressed padded mailing envelope, seal up the bag, and send it either by priority (first-class) mail, registered if possible, or by United Parcel Service. Short of hand delivery, I'm not sure anything else is trustworthy for routine submissions. If you want to spend extra money for security and speed, the U.S. Postal and private express services are excellent.

I'm often asked whether, instead of a completed manuscript, one should submit just a portion and outline, or merely an outline, or nothing more than a letter of inquiry.

There are appropriate circumstances for each approach. If you are an authority in your field and have written, are writing, or contemplate writing a nonfiction book, you will certainly elicit responses with no more than a well-phrased query letter addressed to the editors of your choice. They may then ask you to detail the contents of your book or send some completed chapters or samples of your published writing, and on the basis of a partial manuscript or scarcely any manuscript at all they may offer you a contract. With nonfiction you can go further with less material, because publishers are predisposed to accept your authority and can quickly determine both the merit of and the market for your work.

No such predisposition exists with fiction unless you have a solid track record, and even then you will encounter resistance, because fiction is an inconsistent medium, and success in fiction an unpredictable event. If an astronomer with a track record of three successful books about black holes, red giants, and white dwarfs proposes a new book about binary stars, you can be pretty sure he'll capture a contract with little more than a letter of intent. But if a novelist with three successful works of fiction proposes a new novel, there is less guarantee that he'll be able to bring it off, and publishers will usually ask for more details, more material, more samples, before making a commitment to that next book.

And that's someone with a track record in novels. If you have none, or little, imagine the kind of resistance you're going to encounter if you send a letter or an outline or even a portion and an outline. Even half a manuscript, terrific as it may be, will meet with a guarded "Let's see the rest," because editors have seen too many novelists flag, flounder, or flop after turning in highly promising portions. Therefore, the rule for new novelists is, finish the book. Once you've sold it, you may be able to get a contract for the next one on the basis of a portion and outline or simply an outline.

✍

Okay, the manuscript is in the mail. How long should you wait before you can reasonably expect a response?

That's very hard to say, as it depends on so very many factors: the efficiency of the mails; the routing of the manuscript at the publisher's offices; the amount of work on the desk of the editor assigned to read your manuscript; the efficiency of the firm's procedures, such as scheduling of editorial meetings; and such other factors as vacations, illnesses, job turnover, and let's not forget garden-variety screw-ups.

My agency reviews its submission list biweekly; we are perpetually hounding editors for decisions, and our follow-up is as good as any in the business. Yet we know that despite all the pressure we exert, two months can slip by before we can finesse or force a decision, and I know from other agents that it is no better for them. When a book is hot, I can prevail on an editor to promise an overnight reading, with the understanding that in publishers' lingo, "overnight" means a week. (By the same token a week means a month, and a month probably means the manuscript is lost.) When we conduct an auction we can set a rigid closing date that publishers may ignore only at their peril.

Unrepresented authors can't conduct an auction, however, because they have no leverage. Their best weapon, then, is to play the odds by submitting their manuscript simultaneously to a large number of publishers. You are sending out a multiple submission to enhance the chances that your manuscript will reach some of the publishers without being pulped by postal machinery, that it won't be routed to the slush pile, that someone will find your covering letter provocative, that the editor will not be ill, on vacation, preparing for a semiannual sales conference, gallivanting off to this or that book fair, saddled with five emergency editing jobs, running around like a lunatic with four major auction closings in one week, having his company merged with a conglomerate, getting a divorce, quitting, being fired, or keeling over from a stroke.

I figure a month to six weeks is enough for you to wait before you begin follow-up on your submission, and at this point it would not be pushy for you to drop a line to the editors saying you're checking to see if your manuscript, submitted on such-and-such date, arrived safely, and, assuming it has, you look forward to a decision presently. You might even enclose a photocopy of your original covering letter.

And three weeks after that, you might venture a phone call. I recommend you call between ten and twelve in the morning or three and five in the afternoon, except Friday afternoons in the summer when all hands usually disperse early for the weekend. With luck you'll get the editor you submitted your manuscript to, or a secretary or assistant, and with a little more luck they'll be familiar with your manuscript and know at what stage of the editorial process it is. By politely but firmly pressing for a decision, you may very well be able to make one happen within a week or two. A little fib, or even a big one, might be useful here. "I'm going out of the country for a month and am trying to get all outstanding affairs wrapped up before I go." Or, "I've just gotten a call from another publisher I submitted my manuscript to, and he told me they're preparing an offer. So, before I begin negotiating with them, maybe you could let me know if you're interested, too." You can judge an agent by the quality of his lies, and I'm a great believer in creative fibbing. The creative part is not merely cleverness or credibility, it's designing a fib that doesn't backfire. If an editor calls you during the month you're supposedly out of the country, or ignores your bluff that another publisher is preparing an offer, your venture into creative lying will quickly come to grief. Still, as the publishing industry, perhaps like most industries, runs on polite little white lies (with a generous helping of gross falsehoods to keep things in balance), I wouldn't worry too much about the ethics of creative fibbing, God forgive me.

If you still don't have a decision, a phone call every two or three weeks is in order, with growing exasperation in your voice and increasingly mordant remarks to the effect that if a bank or brokerage house or our government were run as efficiently as publishers, the nation would go bankrupt even faster than it seems to be going now. You may reach a point where you're ready to bring in your lawyer or head for New York armed with a high-caliber repeating weapon. A better idea might be to call a friend or agent in New York and offer to pay his or her expenses for retrieving the manuscript and returning it to you.

I'm afraid I've painted the picture rather grimly, but I don't think it will help you to believe that an unagented author without a track record can take the publishing fortress with nothing more than a good manuscript and an honest face. It takes enormous energy, patience, persistence, confidence, and familiarity with the market and the people who run it, plus some other qualities you may not feel comfortable asserting, such as aggressiveness, guile, and ruthlessness. And finally, there is that unpredictable and uncontrollable factor, luck.

But then, just as the weight of discouragement seems to be snuffing the last embers of inspiration, enthusiasm, and pride that originally drove you to the typewriter to start, and continue, and finish that book, something unexpected happens. Something so wonderful, so thrilling, so incredible, your hands start shaking and your tongue and lips begin flapping stupidly as if you were under the influence of Novocaine.

An editor calls you and says, "We like your book. We'd like to discuss a contract."

The gray clouds part. The hot bright sun radiates down upon your happy face. Your heart swells to near-bursting. Your knees wobble. They like your book! They like your book! Slush no more! Oh joy! Oh rapture! Oh bliss! Oh . . . Oh Lord, what do you do now?

# 3 ✍

# *Negotiation*

Negotiation has been the subject of several best-selling books, and I'm happy to see the subject given its due in the public forum. Whatever our field of endeavor, even if we have none, we all negotiate something just about every day of our lives. Negotiation starts as soon as we express desire of any kind, for, generally speaking, to get along in civilized society you have to give to get, whether it be basic necessities like food and shelter, or profound abstractions like happiness and love. All of us are trained from our earliest days to trade off one thing for another, and so when it comes to negotiating something as sophisticated as a book contract, you cannot legitimately excuse yourself for making a bad deal on the grounds that you didn't know how to negotiate. Of course you know how! If you know how to say, "Please pass the butter," or "Give me a kiss," or "I'd like a raise," or "Lower your radio," or "Lend me some money," then you also know how to say, "I want an eighty-percent participation in translation rights with a pass-through on my share."

You see, when you say you don't know how to negotiate a contract, what you really mean is, you don't know what you're talking about. The terminology is less familiar to you than the terminology for negotiating a pay raise from your boss or a kiss from your love, but basically, terminology, not technique, is your problem. Terminology, then, is what the balance of this book will be concerned with, so that once the terms of a contract are familiar to you, negotiation becomes the simple application of a process you've been using all your life.

If we reduce negotiation to its most primitive level, we get the following dialogue between author and publisher:

"I want what you have."

"And *I* want what *you* have."

"Let's trade."

Ideally, the exchange should be even, with both parties feeling they've received value equal to what they've traded away. But in publishing, as in all other mercantile endeavors, this is seldom the case. In most instances, the party of the first part wants what the party of the second part has, more than the party of the second part wants what the party of the first part has. Therefore, the swap is usually uneven, and often inequitable.

The new writer is almost invariably on the rotten end of this equation, because he needs a publisher a lot more than a publisher needs him. That's called a buyers' market: The buyer has more power than the seller, and therefore controls the negotiation. At any given time there are a number of authors of such stature that they can dictate terms or at least neutralize a publisher's advantage, but for the most part it has been a buyers' market for years, and will continue to be for the foreseeable future. Stripped of excess verbiage, the dialogue between author and publisher in today's buyer-dominated market sounds something like this:

*Author:* "I want to be published so desperately I'll sign anything you hand me."

*Publisher:* "I'm glad to hear it, because if you don't like our terms, there are thousands of authors lined up behind you who will."

Armed with this coercive weapon, a publisher is able to place a dollar value on an author's eagerness to be published, and that value is not very high. Unless an author has some coercive weapons of his own — an extraordinarily good book, an agent, another publisher bidding for the property, a persuasive negotiating technique — he will have to accept that a disadvantageous deal is the lot of the newcomer, just as low wages are the lot of the new employee. One of my colleagues was recently asked by a young writer who'd been offered his first contract, "What should my negotiating posture be?" The agent replied, "Over a barrel with your buttocks bared."

That doesn't necessarily have to be your posture, and your first contract doesn't have to be the bitterly regretted, mistake-ridden experience that so many authors report. By taking time to bone up on your contractual terminology, you can add significant weight to your end of the scale, and hammer out an agreement that will serve your interests almost as well, perhaps *as* well, as one negotiated by the average agent.

That's all well and good, you say, but there's this publisher on the phone and he's about to make me an offer *now*. Am I supposed to put him on hold for a week while I bone up on my contractual terminology?

Of course not, though there's no harm in telling him, after hearing what he has to say, that you'll get back to him in a few hours. He knows you're virginal in matters contractual, and will certainly not take it amiss if you confess your inexperience and request a little time to recover from the shock and organize your thoughts.

But when he calls the first time, you need not worry that he's going to go over thirty or forty contractual articles with you. On the contrary, there are only some half a dozen items to be worked out immediately, and the rest can be dealt with in a leisurely fashion when the formal contracts have been typed up and submitted to you. The key aspects of a contract are called the "deal points." In a publishing contract, the deal points include such things as the primary rights, the territory, the advance, the payout schedule, the basic royalty percentage, and the control of, and participation in, subsidiary rights. Just about everything else is called boilerplate. "Boilerplate" is lawyer talk for the fine print that spells out terms that are supposed to be pretty standard. Of course a sharp author or agent, like a sharp lawyer, never takes boilerplate for granted, but my point here is that it isn't anything you have to address yourself to at once: It can wait till the contracts arrive. Only the deal points have to be resolved now, and to help you do that, I've summarized, in the appendix on page 284, what I consider to be poor, fair, and good terms. Although I will enlarge on these terms in the course of this book, you can at least get a thumbnail notion of how good or bad your deal is by referring to my summary.

As I say, the publisher won't be offended if, after hearing his offer, you tell him you want to mull things over for a little while, to talk them over with your husband or wife, to call a writer-friend you know for advice. Nor should it do any harm if you tell the publisher, "Offhand, from what I know about publishing deals, some of the terms you mention sound a little on the low side to me, but I'm sure we can work things out." That way you leave the door open for negotiation. Ask the publisher to run the offer down again to make sure you have it right, and carefully write down everything he says.

Having bought yourself a little time, there are a number of things you can do with it, at least after you've run out into the street in your bathrobe whooping maniacally that you're going to be published. You can, and should, mull things over, talk to your husband or wife about them, and call that writer-friend. You can study the pertinent chapters of this book. And you might want to call an agent.

I know, I know, I'm supposed to be telling you how to be your own agent. But I have to say that if ever there was a good time for you to contact an agent and request representation, this is it. Few agents will be unresponsive to an author who asks them to take over a negotiation; hell, most of them should be downright grateful. After all, half the job, and maybe the hardest half — marketing the manuscript — has already been done for them.

Believe it or not, many publishing companies urge the new author to get an agent, and prefer dealing with agents to negotiating directly with authors. Their reasoning is partially humanitarian: They don't want to take advantage of someone who doesn't know what he's doing. They're also being practical, however. It might cost them more money in the short run to negotiate with an agent, but in the long run they'll save money and headaches. For one thing, agents draw off any bad feelings that may arise out of a hard negotiation between an editor and an author. An editor may be furious at your agent but remain on the warmest terms with you, whereas if you're your own agent the editor's feelings toward you may be tainted. A second reason is that authors who have been exploited often sue, or give the publisher a hard time, when they wake up and realize they've been screwed. If a publisher refers an author to an agent, however, it's harder for the author to claim later on that he didn't have professional representation, or at least that the publisher didn't give him an opportunity to have it.

Because they don't want to be accused of favoritism, publishers will almost always give out the names of three or four agents, not just one, with whom they've had satisfactory dealings or about whom they've heard good things. At any rate, don't be surprised if, in the course of your first call from the publisher, he suggests or even insists that you contact some agents. If he doesn't, and you don't know of any, ask him for some recommendations. Whether you actually decide to engage one at this point or not, the publisher will respect you for considering that option, and, as some publishers distinctly do not like dealing with agents, your publisher may well become a little more accommodating at your mere mention of hiring one.

Occasionally an unrepresented author will call an agent not to engage him but to ask his advice on a contractual negotiation in progress. Most agents, like most doctors or lawyers, will give you a minute's free phone consultation, but as a minute is not going to satisfy you, and as there's nothing in it for them anyway, I would advise against it. But you might, if you're within traveling distance, offer to pay an agent a fee for an office visit, or, better, suggest a meal or a drink outside the office, so that there are no interruptions. Then pick his brains to your heart's content. If his fee comes to less than the commission you'd have to pay him if he officially represented you, you'll have made a good bargain — at least ostensibly. As you lack the agent's skill and experience, there's no guarantee that you'll apply his crash course in agenting as effectively as you'd like to, and your mistakes may in the long run prove more costly than his commission. Still, a coaching session with an agent is an option open to you, if you can find one agreeable to this arrangement.

If your book is on submission to other publishers besides the one who's made you an offer, you may want to call them to tell the editors that you do have an offer and ask them if they want to make one, too. As it's unlikely that they will be able to marshal their procedures and personnel on such short notice (even though they may have had your manuscript for six months!), they will undoubtedly ask you for a little more time. Because one of their competitors has made an offer, their interest in your book will be heightened, and because they don't want to hang you up they'll try to move on your submission fast. But it is extremely unlikely they'll be able to get back to you the same day, or even the next day or two, because of the complex nature of editorial decision making. You must be very, very careful not to allow too much time to pass, because if your original publisher begins to think you're playing games, he can withdraw his offer. Most agents are adept at stalling a publisher while contacting others to ascertain their interest in a book, but the author who fools around is fooling with fire. So if you've told your publisher you'll let him know your answer tomorrow afternoon, then you must be strict in giving the other publishers until tomorrow afternoon to decide. They may woo you with very persuasive arguments ("We can top that offer, I'm sure," "We're a much better house than the one that wants to buy your book," and so on), but they are still birds in the bush as far as you're concerned, so don't let them tempt you beyond your deadline.

If another publisher or two or three (if you're going to dream, dream big) do make offers, then you have what is known as a bidding situation. The rewards in terms of getting the best publisher, getting the most money, and generating the most excitement are undeniable. But the risks are so great, and the mistakes to be made so numerous, that I do not feel I would be serving new authors well by advising them how to conduct their own auctions. I'm not talking about making poor deals or offending feelings; I'm talking about provoking lawsuits. Unless you set rigid rules for bidding, and strict definitions of terms, you may very well get yourself in trouble far beyond anything you imagined. Even many agents are loath to auction off properties, because they know that when things get intense, tempers are likely to flare and the consequences can be catastrophic. So if you want to arrange an auction, call in an agent; pay the commission. (See Chapter 21.)

If you've decided against hiring an agent and wish to go it alone, and you've armed yourself with information and advice, it's time for you to flutter your fledgling wings and try out your negotiating technique. But not on your publisher. Find someone with worldly experience, with a business or law or even publishing background, and rehearse with that person the things you're going to say. It may be wife or husband, parent or child, brother or sister or friend, just someone who can intelligently play the devil's advocate and test your negotiating skill. You might then switch roles and yourself take the part of your publisher, strenuously arguing as to why you cannot possibly budge on any of the terms originally offered. Assuming the character of the person on the other side of the negotiating table can help, because the more you know about how a publisher thinks, the easier it will be for you to overcome his resistance to your bargaining tactics.

A word about attitude. Although publishers' and authors' interests are not always harmonious, and indeed are sometimes antagonistic, it is not in your best interest to approach negotiations with a publisher as if you were enemies. Yes, your publisher will probably try to take advantage of your inexperience and eagerness to be published, but that doesn't necessarily mean he's out to skin you alive. He's simply attempting to exploit your weaknesses to make the best bargain for his company. Your goal is essentially the same as his, and you know perfectly well that if *he* were inexperienced and eager to publish *you*, you'd exploit his weaknesses to make the best bargain for yourself.

So don't take it personally or feel paranoid if the publisher tries to drive the best bargain he can at your expense. It's strictly business!

Don't worry about your publisher's attitude; worry about your own. Your own will be dictated by the value you set on your property. Before you enter into negotiations, set in your mind the rigid limits to which you will be pushed before walking away from the negotiating table. Rehearse these in your own mind, then rehearse them with your partner. Establish your first offer, your fallback position, and your last position on each deal point. Decide in advance what you're prepared to trade off, what would be a fair compromise, and what you would consider a "deal breaker," a demand so onerous that your honor compels you to refuse to sign the contract.

Once you have some sense of these limits and feel comfortable with them, you can enter negotiations with a certain degree of quiet confidence. Your tone and manner should say, "I'm grateful that you want to buy my work and I'm eager to work things out with you. You'll find me cooperative during these discussions, and I'm willing to hear your viewpoint and accommodate it to the greatest extent possible. But there are some aspects of your offer that, if I accepted them, would be so disadvantageous to me as to make it impossible for me to live with myself. So I hope you'll be able to accommodate me on those points."

Despite certain adversarial aspects of publishing, it is essentially a cooperative venture, with each party needing what the other has in order to bring forth the final product, a successful book. If you approach negotiations as a kind of joint undertaking in which both you and your publisher have the same basic goal in mind, then you should be able to work out a deal whereby if one of you profits, both of you profit.

If, however, you make a bad bargain, you can take comfort in two thoughts. The first is that an agent might not have been able to do much better. Unless the work is extraordinary, a first sale is a first sale, and the negotiating parameters aren't very wide whether it's the author who's doing the talking or an agent. The second consolation is that there's always the next book. Assuming this is not the only book you're ever going to write, the day will come when the value of your talent has risen to a point where it can command terms it cannot command now. Publishers appreciate that, and the wise ones are inhibited from taking flagrant advantage of the new author by the realization that one day the tables could turn. Agents have long memories, and so do authors. What you lose today, you'll gain tomorrow.

And because publishers do have a vested interest in long-term relationships with authors, their terms may be more flexible than you think. In fact, they often build some "budge" into their budget and fully expect you to try to dislodge it. So let's not disappoint them. Having determined in your mind the limits of your own negotiability, you must now probe those of the other guy.

Here are some thoughts on how to formulate and execute your negotiating strategy.

**Do your homework.** If you've kept up with the marketplace, subscribed to newsletters in your particular genre, and consulted with agents or other writers, it will be hard for an editor to take advantage of your ignorance — because you won't be ignorant. You can tell him that you happen to know that he's giving a better royalty to other authors doing the same kind of book, or that other publishers are paying higher advances for similar material, or that a

50–50 split with a publisher on movie rights is a poor deal by industry standards. An editor will deal respectfully with an author who knows what he's talking about, or at least sounds as if he does.

**Find common ground with your publisher.** When you coldly analyze a publishing deal, you realize that author and publisher have already agreed on almost everything before they start negotiations. You both like the book, you both want to see it published, succeed, and make a profit. You've both agreed that 95 percent of the contract is boilerplate that doesn't have to be discussed right away.

Of the remaining 5 percent — the deal points — there may be some terms that each party is willing to concede without a fight, or with a negligible one. Establish those right away, so that it all comes down to a mere one or two or three items to be resolved. Then ask yourself, Are they really unresolved, or are we both talking about the same thing? By discussing these matters with your publisher, hearing his reasoning and presenting yours, you may realize that his demands aren't as incompatible with yours as either of you thought. Notice that I call him "your" publisher; I've already assumed that he is. So has he. If you try to make the assumption too, and talk to him not as an adversary but as a teammate with whom you are trying to solve a mutual problem, you may dissipate his resistance.

**Assume that everything is negotiable.** Out of every ten items on a publisher's negotiating agenda, perhaps seven are easily negotiable, two are negotiable with difficulty, and one is non-negotiable. The same is true of the items on your own agenda. Unless both of you are non-negotiable on the same point, you have the makings of a deal, and it's just a matter of discovering the common ground. Even non-negotiable items don't necessarily have to break deals; you can trade yours for his. If the advance is not open to discussion as far as the publisher is concerned, and the handling of movie rights is not open to discussion as far as you're concerned, you may still make a match by trading off.

**Support your position with cogent arguments.** Discovering common ground is the essence of negotiation, and often the differences are semantic and will yield to effective verbalization of one another's viewpoints. As I said at the outset, this is something we do every day in our social relations, and the methods are as varied as human personality itself: One can plead, coax, charm, threaten, ma-nipulate, lie, reason, and so forth. You must select the mode or modes that feel most comfortable to you. Style aside, however, there are really only two fundamental techniques for negotiating: argument and leverage. The first is a means of getting your way by skillful reasoning; the second, by coercion.

Let's consider the latter first. Agents are sometimes in a position to force publishers to accept terms unwillingly. By threatening to move a valuable author to another publisher, let's say, or to stop submitting to a house, some powerful agents can impose terms on a publisher that that company would ordinarily find unacceptable and non-negotiable. (When I say "threaten," I don't necessarily mean pounding fists on tables; in the gentlemanly world of pub-lishing, a word to the wise is usually sufficient. An alert publisher can detect the rattle of an agent's saber with very little difficulty.)

For the first-sale author, scarcely any leverage is available. If he has a second publisher bidding for his book he might have some, or he might threaten to bring in a tough agent or lawyer. But such tac-tics on the part of someone who isn't sure of what he's doing can prove harmful. A publisher will respond to an author who leans too hard on him by walking away from the negotiating table and not coming back, unless the author's book is a hot property. I men-tioned attitude earlier, and a poor attitude can be a significant if un-seen factor in the negotiating equation: "Is the profit we're going to make on the book worth putting up with this hostile, obnoxious au-thor?"

So, for most authors on their own, application of leverage and pressure is not the answer. Far better is the use of effective argu-mentation.

For each improvement in terms you ask of your publisher, you must have a strong supporting argument, and preferably more than one. There are weak arguments and there are strong ones. A weak argument is one that appears to be good for the author but not for the publisher. "I want a higher advance because I need money to build an addition to my house" is a poor argument because your addition to the house doesn't do anything for your publisher.

Strong arguments promise benefits to the publisher as well as to the author. These benefits may be expressed in terms of time, money, or energy saved by the publisher, or by larger profits earned. "I need a higher advance so I can quit my night job and finish the book in half the time it would otherwise take me" is a stronger argument, because it's usually to a publisher's advantage to get a book into production quickly.

Select your arguments judiciously and rehearse them assiduously, taking the publisher's side so you can be prepared for anything he may throw at you. And if he's any good, he'll throw everything at you. "I'm sorry," he might say, "we can't go higher than a six-percent paperback royalty. If we do, we'll lose money."

Analyze that argument and ask yourself, Is there any common ground here? Obviously not. But maybe by exploring his definition of "lose money," you can discover something that will help you. "How many copies of my book do you have to sell before your firm breaks even on its investment?" you might ask.

"Oh, one hundred thousand copies," he says.

"And at what point would you be making a big profit — you know, really shoveling the money in?"

"Let's say two hundred thousand copies," quoth he.

"Okay, then," you reply, "I'd like to propose that when sales reach two hundred thousand copies, the royalty scale goes from six percent to eight percent."

Your publisher will be hard put to argue with your proposal, because it was he who suggested the 200,000-copy breakpoint, and you've put him in a position of admitting that if he doesn't raise the royalty, his firm will be making an excessive profit on sales beyond 200,000 copies.

But no — he has another argument up his sleeve. "We can't raise our royalty even at two hundred thousand copies," he says, "because inflation will have increased our production costs."

It's not a great argument, but unless you anticipated it and have a counterargument at your disposal, he may well leave you speechless. How about this: "If inflation raises your production costs, you can raise the price of the book, and there'll be money to spare for its author."

Nice going! I'll bet he didn't expect you to say that! But don't congratulate yourself too quickly. "We're loath to raise the price of our books because people will be reluctant to buy them," he comes back.

"A good point," you admit, "but I think what I've said makes sense, too. Is there some way we can compromise on this?"

"Yes," he says. "You did make some very good points. So I'll tell you what: I'll split the difference with you and go to seven percent after two hundred thousand copies."

Congratulations! Break out the champagne! You are now a bona fide negotiator!

**Respect your publisher.** Although he may seem to be trying to take advantage of you, many of his arguments are genuine explanations of problems and realities he, like every publisher, has to cope with. Listen to these with an open mind and don't be too quick to dismiss them. The publishing industry does suffer from many serious problems, and by giving your publisher a sympathetic ear and an occasional break, you can establish strong ties that will benefit you in negotiations to come.

Just don't lose sight of the fact that you have to pay rent just as he does.

**Get it in writing.** All understandings, agreements, and modifications should be stated in writing. After you've closed your basic deal, ask your editor to send you a brief memo confirming his offer, subject to the issuance of a formal contract. Upon your receipt of this memo — assuming it conforms to the verbal understanding you reached — send a memo of your own (keep a copy for yourself), stating that you agree to the terms of the letter and look forward to receiving the contract. You now have a document that has legal weight in case your publisher tries to cancel the deal or alter terms reached verbally.

Occasionally a publisher will agree to something but because of company policy will be unable to stipulate it in a contract. In that case, he may not object to putting it in a "side letter," which carries some legal weight and does bind his company somewhat. For instance, a minimum advertising budget, which most publishers are loath to put into contracts, may be promised in a side letter. Such a letter is particularly valuable if he leaves the company and his successor wants proof that his predecessor did agree to something.

·And of course any modifications of the agreement should be stipulated in writing, either as amendments or exchanges of memos. Remember Sam Goldwyn's immortal aphorism: "A verbal agreement isn't worth the paper it's written on."

## A Typical Publishing Contract

On the next few pages is a contract issued by a paperback publisher, unaltered except for omission of the publisher's name and address. Although I'll be using its provisions as a starting point for discussion of contractual features, its use here is not intended to imply criticism. It's not a bad contract; it's not a terrific one, either. If you want a terrific contract, you'll have to negotiate one. In the material that follows, I'll tell you how.

### ———————————— CONTRACT ————————————

**Agreement** made this ____ day of _____ , 19 ____ , between [name of publisher], a corporation organized and existing under the laws of the State of New York and whose principal office is at [address] New York, New York (referred to as the "Publisher") and _____ whose address is _____ and who is a citizen of and resident of _____ (referred to as the "Author" and designated by the masculine singular pronoun) with respect to a work provisionally entitled _____ _____ (referred to as the "Work").

**1. Rights and Royalties**
**A.** The Author hereby grants and assigns to the Publisher the following exclusive rights in the Work during the terms of copyright and all renewals and extensions thereof in any country in the World, and the Publisher shall pay to the Author or to his duly authorized representative an advance of $ _____ against all the Author's earnings under this Agreement payable as follows:

  **(a)** $ _____ within thirty (30) days of the signing hereof.

  **(b)** $ _____ within thirty (30) days of the acceptance by the Publisher of the manuscript of the Work and as is later provided.

  **(c)** $ _____ within thirty (30) days of publication of the Work and as is later provided.

**B.** It is expressly agreed and declared that all rights and benefits of whatever nature granted to the Publisher by this Agreement shall extend to and may be exercised by the Publisher's wholly owned subsidiaries or affiliate companies.

**Rights**

**A.** To publish and market the Work throughout the world directly or through a wholly owned subsidiary or affiliate company at retail prices to be determined by the Publisher.

**B.** To license or sublicense others to manufacture, print, publish, distribute and sell the Work in whole or in part, in paperback and/or hardcover editions, throughout the World, at prices to be determined by the Publisher, prior to or simultaneous with publication by the Publisher.

The terms "License" and "sub-License" shall not include nor apply to any publication by a wholly owned subsidiary or affiliate company of the Publisher, nor shall include _____ Publishing Company Limited of Ontario, Canada, which for the purpose of this Agreement shall be considered an affiliate company of the Publisher.

**C.** To license the publication of the Work in Braille or to be photographed or microfilmed for sale to the physically handicapped.

**D.** To sell, license or dispose of all rights, property and uses in the Work (other than book publication) including but without limitation for dramatic, dramatico-musical, motion picture, radio, television video, videodisk, phonographic or audio reproduction, multimedia, interactive, or commercial exploitation (toys, games, posters, etc.) purposes and for newspaper and magazine publication.

**Royalties** *(Compensation for items A–D below corresponds to Rights A–D above.)*

**A. (1)** The Publisher or its wholly owned subsidiaries or affiliate companies may distribute copies on a fully-returnable basis and royalties shall be based upon net retail sales to the public less reasonable reserves against returns.

**(2) "Publisher's Editions"** means any, or all, editions published by the first publisher of an edition, whether such first publisher be the Publisher, or its wholly owned subsidiaries, affiliate companies, successors or assignees. If such first publisher is the publisher of a hardcover edition licensed by the Publisher, then in that case "Publisher's Editions" means all other editions published by the Publisher, its wholly owned subsidiaries, affiliate companies, successors or assignees.

**(3)** For each **racksize paperback** Publisher's Editions sold in the United States:

**(a)** 6 percent of the cover price on the first 150,000 copies; and

**(b)** 8 percent of the cover price on all copies in excess of 150,000.

**(4)** For each **trade paperback** Publisher's Editions sold in the United States:

4 percent of the cover price

**(5)** For each **hardcover** Publisher's Editions sold in the United States:

**(a)** 10 percent of the cover price on the first 5,000 copies;

**(b)** 12 ½ percent of the cover price on copies in excess of 5,000 and up to 10,000; and

**(c)** 15 percent of the cover price on all copies in excess of 10,000.

**(6)** On each **paperback, trade paperback,** and **hardcover** Publisher's Editions sold in Canada, and in foreign countries:

⅔ of the prevailing domestic royalty rate calculated in Canadian dollars or the applicable foreign currency on the Canadian or foreign cover price of such edition.

**(7)** For copies of "Publisher's Editions" published and sold for use as **premiums,** 20 percent of the proceeds of such sales less the Publisher's direct expenses and cost of manufacture.

**(8) No royalty** shall be paid on copies distributed for review, advertising, publicity, Author's promotion, sample or like purposes, or sold below or at cost including expenses incurred, or furnished gratis to the Author, or sold to the Author for author's personal use or resale.

**B. (1)** For **paperback** editions sold in the United States: 50 percent of the net royalty received by the Publisher for such editions.

**(2)** For **hardcover** editions sold in the United States: 50 percent of the net royalty received by the Publisher for such editions.

**(3)** On any **book-club paperback** editions: 50 percent of the net royalty received by the Publisher for such editions.

**(4)** For **trade paperback** editions sold in the United States: 50 percent of the net royalty received by the Publisher for such editions.

**(5)** On any **book-club hardcover** editions sold in the United States: 50 percent of the net royalty received by the Publisher for such editions.

**(6)** On any **foreign language** translations of the Work sold in the United States: 50 percent of the net amount received by the Publisher for such editions.

**(7)** On each **paperback, hardcover, book-club paperback, trade**

**paperback, book-club hardcover** editions or **foreign language** translations sold in foreign countries: 50 percent of the net amount received by the Publisher for such editions.

(8) For any **magazine or newspaper serialization** prior to, or after, any publication of the Work (whether hardcover or paperback editions): 50 percent of the net amount received therefor by the Publisher.

C. No payment of royalties or other compensation to the Author.

D. (1) 50 percent of the net amount received by the Publisher or its wholly owned subsidiaries or affiliate companies or any assignee of the Publisher after deducting the expenses of such sales, licenses, or disposition of rights and the collection of the proceeds including reasonable attorneys' fees.

(2) The Publisher or its wholly owned subsidiaries or affiliate companies or any assignee shall not be required to sell, license or dispose of any such rights, uses or licenses in and to the Work.

## 2. Author's Representations and Warranties

A. The Author represents and warrants to the Publisher as follows:

(1) that he is the sole author of the Work;

(2) that the Work is original and does not infringe upon any existing common law or statutory copyright or upon any common law right, proprietary right, civil right, or any other right whatsoever, and that no part thereof was taken from or based upon any other literary, dramatic or musical material, or any motion picture;

(3) that the Work is innocent and contains no matter that is scandalous, obscene, libelous, or violates any rights of privacy, or of publicity, or is otherwise contrary to law; and statements in the work asserted as facts are true or based upon reasonable research for accuracy;

(4) that the Work has not heretofore been published in any form;

(5) that the title of the Work may be legally used by the Publisher in the exercise of all or any of the rights herein conveyed;

(6) that he is the sole and exclusive owner of the rights herein conveyed to the Publisher; that he has not heretofore assigned, pledged or otherwise encumbered the same; and that he has full power to enter into this Agreement and to make the grants herein contained; and

(7) that the representations and warranties of the Author contained in this Agreement are true at the date of signing and shall be true upon the date of publication of the Work, and thereafter, and the Publisher

may rely upon them in dealings with any third party relating to the Publisher's rights under this Agreement.

**B.** The Author agrees to hold harmless and indemnify the Publisher against any claim, demand, action, suit or proceeding, recovery or expense of any nature whatsoever arising from any claims or infringement of copyright or proprietary right, or claims of libel, obscenity, unlawfulness or invasion of privacy or based upon or arising out of any matter or thing contained in the Work; or any breach of warranties or representations herein contained.

**C.** The Publisher shall promptly notify the Author of any claim, demand, action, suit or proceeding which may relate to the warranties or representations of the Author under this Agreement, and the Author agrees to cooperate fully in the defense thereof. The Author shall indemnify the Publisher against all expenses in connection with such defense and shall comply with and pay any judgment, decree or fine, penalty or settlement made in relation thereto. The Publisher shall have the right to extend the benefit of the Author's representations and warranties to its distributors, subdistributors, vendors, licensees and sublicensees, and the Author shall be liable thereon to such distributors, subdistributors, vendors, licensees and sublicensees, to the same extent as if such representations and warranties had been originally made to them. The Publisher shall have the right for itself, its distributors, vendors, licensees and sublicensees and on behalf of the Author, to effect any settlement of such claim, demand, action, suit or proceeding which, in the opinion of the Publisher's counsel, shall be reasonable and proper in the circumstances.

**D.** In defending any such claim, demand, action, suit or proceeding, the Publisher shall have the sole right to select counsel. The Author may at his own cost and expense select separate counsel to act on his behalf.

**E.** These warranties, representations, and indemnities shall survive the termination of this Agreement.

**F.** During the pendency of any claim, demand, action, suit or proceeding the Publisher may at its option withhold all or part of the amounts due to the Author under this or any other Agreement with the Author, until such sums in respect of which the Author has agreed to indemnify the Publisher, its distributors, subdistributors, vendors, licensees or sublicensees, shall have been paid in full. The failure by the Publisher to withhold all or part of such amounts shall not prejudice any other right or remedy which the Publisher may have against the Author.

**G.** The representations, warranties and indemnities contained in this paragraph 2 shall not extend to drawings, illustrations, or other material not furnished by the Author.

### 3. Author's Name and Likeness

**A.** The Publisher shall have the right to use the Author's actual or legal name, or any pseudonym which the Author may use or has used or by which he may hereafter be known, irrespective of the name under which the Author may enter into this Agreement.

**B.** The Publisher shall have the right to use the Author's name or pseudonym as provided in sub-clause (1) together with the Author's likeness in a reasonable manner to advertise and promote the sale of the Work.

**C.** The Publisher may authorize a licensee or a sublicensee to use the Author's name and likeness in connection with the promotion of any licensed or sublicensed rights, provided the licensee or sublicensee specifically agrees (i) that it will take all necessary steps to protect the copyright in the Work, and (ii) that the Author's name or likeness will not be used to promote or sell any commercial product or service except that a licensee or sublicensee shall be entitled to use such name or likeness on the front and back cover of paperback editions of the Work sold by such licensee or sublicensee to commercial firms for use or resale by them in connection with the promotion of their own products.

**D.** In the case of the licensing of motion picture rights in the Work, the Publisher may authorize a licensee or sublicensee to publish excerpts or summaries not to exceed 7,500 words of the motion picture version of the Work, for the sole purpose of advertising and promoting such version.

### 4. Appearances of Author

The Author agrees provided that the same shall not interfere with his regular employment or business matters in which he is then engaged, and provided that the Author is not then in such poor health as to prevent cooperation, the Author shall give, without charge (unless the Publisher, or its licensee or sublicensee shall be enabled to obtain a fee for the same), any and all newspaper and/or magazine interviews, and will make such radio and/or television as well as book and department store appearances as the Publisher, its licensee or sublicensee may be enabled to arrange in connection with the promotion and sale of any edition of the Work. Any fee which the Publisher or its licensee or sublicensee shall be able to obtain for such interview and/or appearance shall belong and be paid to the Author. If the interview and/or appearance shall be out of the city or town in which the Author shall then reside, reasonable travel costs (and hotel accommodations, if necessary) required to enable the Author to fulfill the engagement shall be paid by the Publisher or its licensee or sublicensee.

## 5. Delivery of Manuscript

**A.** On or before _____ the Author shall deliver to the Publisher two complete copies of the Work in final form in double spaced typing on white paper on one side of the paper only in satisfactory order for printing. At the same time the Author shall, at his expense, furnish all drawings, charts, designs, photographs and other illustrations that the Publisher deems requisite to the Work. If requested by the Publisher, the Author shall also supply, at his own expense, an introduction, a foreword, a table of contents, an index and a bibliography, all ready for publication. The manuscript of the Work shall be deemed satisfactory and acceptable only when actually accepted in writing by the Publisher. If the Author fails to deliver the complete material within the specified time, the Publisher shall have the right, unless it extends the delivery date in writing, to decline to publish the Work, terminate this Agreement, and recover any and all amounts that it may have advanced to the Author.

**B.** If the Publisher does not deem the manuscript satisfactory, it shall notify the Author in writing within sixty (60) days after receipt thereof, specifying in detail the reasons for the Publisher's dissatisfaction. The Author shall then have ninety (90) days within which to revise the manuscript in order to render it satisfactory to the Publisher.

If at the conclusion of such ninety (90) day period the Publisher still deems the manuscript unsatisfactory then the Publisher at its sole option may **either**

(i) give notice in writing to the Author that this Agreement shall forthwith cease and terminate. In such event all rights of every kind herein granted by the Author to the Publisher shall revert to the Author, and the Author shall be obligated to return one half of the advance received from the Publisher; **or**

(ii) give notice in writing to the Author that the Publisher elects to complete the Work, or render it satisfactory. If within thirty (30) days after such notice the Author shall not have delivered to the Publisher a completed or revised manuscript satisfactory to the Publisher, then the Publisher may employ a writer or writers to complete or revise the Work to the Publisher's satisfaction, and in any publication or use of such completed or revised Work, the Publisher may use the name or pseudonym of the Author as Co-Author of the Work with such writer or writers.

**In such event**

(a) any advance payment made by the Publisher to the Author shall be deemed to be a fixed and final advance of royalties, of any kind, due under this Agreement.

(b) the Author shall not be entitled to any further amounts due under any provision of this Agreement unless such amounts exceed the payments made by the Publisher to such writer or writers as Co-Author.

(c) the Author shall not be liable for any matter not contained in the original manuscript and inserted therein by or at the instance of such writer or writers as Co-Author.

## 6. Loss and Return of Manuscript

**A.** The Author shall prepare his manuscript in triplicate, and all drawings, charts, designs, photographs and other illustrations in duplicate, and shall deliver to the Publisher two copies of the manuscript and one copy each of the drawings, charts, designs, photographs and other illustrations as is provided by paragraph 4 hereof. The Publisher shall use due care in safeguarding the same. If the originals are lost or destroyed from any cause whatsoever whilst in the Publisher's or the printer's possession, the Publisher shall not be liable therefor, and the Author shall thereupon deliver to the Publisher the copy of the manuscript previously retained by him together with the second copy of each of the drawings, charts, designs, photographs and other illustrations.

**B.** After publication, and on the written request of the Author, the Publisher agrees to return to the Author one copy of the original manuscript and/or galley and page proofs thereof, with the printer's corrections. If the Author does not request such return in writing within one month following the date of such publication then in such case the Publisher may destroy such manuscript and/or galley and page proofs.

### 7. Publication of Book

**A.** The Publisher may at its own expense publish the Work within ____ months following the delivery by the Author of the complete manuscript thereof in an edition of not less than 10,000 copies embodying the Work in whole or in part.

**B.** In the event of any delay from causes beyond the Publisher's control, the publication date may be postponed until the next spring or fall season immediately following the cessation of the cause of the delay.

**C.** The Publisher shall have sole discretion to determine the style, type, manner and all other matters relating to production and printing of all editions, the fixing and modification of list, wholesale and retail prices of all editions, and all matters relating to distribution and sale.

**D.** The Publisher shall have sole discretion to change the title of the Work and to make deletions, revisions or additions to the manuscript or any edition, and to use the name of the Author as Author of such varied Work but the Author shall not be liable for any matter not contained in the original manuscript.

### 8. The Copyright

**A.** Upon first publication of the Work, the Publisher shall duly register it for copyright in the name of the *Publisher/Author* in the United States of America under the Universal Copyright Convention, and shall insert the requisite copyright notice in all copies of the Work that are distributed to the public. The Author shall furnish the Publisher promptly with any authorization or other document necessary for this purpose.

**B.** The Author authorizes the Publisher at the cost and expense of the Publisher to make the Author a co-plaintiff with Publisher in any litigation against a third party for infringement of the copyright on the Work, but the Publisher shall not be liable to the Author for its failure to take such action. If the Publisher shall fail to take timely action then the Author may do so in his own name and at his own cost and expense. Any recovery from such litigation shall be applied first to reimburse such cost and expense in connection therewith, and the balance shall be divided equally between the Author and the Publisher.

**C.** The Author agrees that if the present copyright law of the United States of America or of any other country in which the Work is protected by copyright shall be amended or changed or a new copyright law be enacted so that the term of copyright is extended or the benefits thereunder enlarged, the Publisher shall forthwith automatically become entitled to all of such enlarged benefits thereby conveyed for such extended term.

## 9. Permissions
If the Author shall include in the Work any material, either of his own or of any other writer, composer, or artist, whether or not previously published, and not in the public domain, then any permissions required for such inclusion shall be obtained by the Author at his own expense.

## 10. Submission of Proof
Upon the written request of the Author, the Publisher shall submit galley and page proofs of the Work to the Author. Subject to the provisions of sub-paragraph 7D hereof, such proofs shall be set up in conformity with the final manuscript submitted by the Author. The Author shall correct and return the proofs to the Publisher within seven (7) days of receipt thereof. The Publisher shall have the right to charge against the Author's royalties, or to require payment in cash, of the amount of expense incurred by it because of the Author's deletions, revisions and additions (other than corrections of the printer's or the Publisher's errors, and deletions, revisions or additions made at the Publisher's instance), in excess of fifteen (15%) percent of the original cost of composition, provided that (a) an itemized statement of such charges is forwarded to the Author within thirty (30) days after the date of publication; and (b) the corrected proofs are made available for inspection by the Author or his duly authorized representative, on request, at the Publisher's office.

## 11. Statements and Payments
A. The Publisher shall render to the Author semi-annual royalty statements commencing one year after the publication of the first or any subsequent or reprinted edition, accompanied by a remittance of the amount shown to be due thereon, subject to a reasonable reserve against returns, on or before

(i) May 31 of each year covering the last six months of the preceding year

(ii) November 30 of each year covering the first six months of the year.

All royalty statements shall set forth in detail the various items for which royalties are payable and the amounts thereof, including the number of copies sold in each royalty category.

**B.** If the total royalties due are less than $100.00 the Publisher may defer the rendering of statements and payment of royalties until at least $100.00 are due.

**C.** If the Author shall have received amounts in excess of the royalties due under this Agreement, then the Publisher may recoup such overpayment from any further royalties payable to the Author for the Work or due under any other agreement between the Author and the Publisher for any other work.

### 12. Examination of Accounts

The Author shall have the right upon written request to have his accountant examine the Publisher's books of account insofar as they relate to the Work. Any such examination shall be conducted at the place where the Publisher maintains such books of account. It shall be conducted during reasonable business hours in such manner so as not to interfere with the Publisher's normal business activities. A true copy of all reports made by the Author's accountant shall be delivered to the Publisher at the same time such respective reports are delivered to the Author by such accountant. In no event shall an audit with respect to any statement commence later than twelve (12) months from the date of dispatch to the Author of such statement nor shall any audit continue for longer than five (5) consecutive business days nor shall examinations be made hereunder more frequently than twice annually, nor shall the records supporting any such statements be audited more than once. The expenses of such examination shall be borne by the Author, unless errors of accounting of 10 percent or more of the total sums paid to the Author shall be found to his disadvantage, in which case, the expenses thereof shall be borne by the Publisher. All royalty statements rendered under this Agreement shall be binding upon the Author and not subject to objection for any reason unless such objection is made in writing stating the basis thereof and delivered to the Publisher within twelve (12) months from delivery of such statement, or, if an examination is commenced prior thereto, within thirty (30) days from the completion of the relative audit.

The Publisher shall not be required to retain supporting records after any statement of royalties has become binding upon the Author.

### 13. Publisher's Contracts with Others

**A.** Whenever the Author's share of the proceeds thereof is $100 or more, the Publisher shall promptly inform the Author of the terms of any contract into which it may enter or any license or sublicense it may grant with respect to the Work hereunder. The original of such contract or license shall be exhibited by the Publisher to the Author or his representative at the Publisher's office, and a copy thereof shall be furnished to the Author upon his written request. The Publisher shall account for and remit the Author's share of any moneys received under such contract, license or sublicense in the manner and at the time provided for the payment of royalties hereunder, subject always to the provisions of sub-paragraph 11C.

**B.** The provisions of this paragraph shall not apply to any contract, license, or sublicense between the Publisher and its wholly-owned subsidiaries or affiliate companies.

### 14. Author's Copies

On publication of the first Publisher's Edition, the Publisher shall give twenty-five (25) free copies to the Author, who may purchase further copies for personal use at a discount of forty (40%) percent from the retail price.

### 15. Conflicting Publications

The Author agrees that during the term of this Agreement he will not without the written permission of the Publisher, publish or permit to be published any material in book, magazine, pamphlet, or newspaper form, based upon the material in the Work, or which is reasonably likely to injure its sale.

### 16. Option for Next Work

The Author agrees to submit to the Publisher his next book-length work before submitting the same to any other publisher. The Publisher shall be entitled to a period of six (6) weeks after the submission of the completed manuscript, which period shall not commence to run prior to one month after the publication of the Work covered by this Agreement, within which to notify the Author of its decision. If within that time the Publisher shall notify the Author of its desire to publish the manuscript, it shall thereupon negotiate with him with respect to the terms of such publication. If within thirty (30) days thereafter the parties are unable in good faith to arrive at a mutually satisfactory agreement for such publication, the Author shall be free to submit his manuscript elsewhere, provided, however, that he shall not enter into a contract for the publication of such manuscript with any other publisher upon terms less favorable than those offered by the Publisher.

### 17. Termination upon Bankruptcy and Liquidation

If (a) a petition in bankruptcy is filed by the Publisher, or (b) a petition in bankruptcy is filed against the Publisher and such petition is finally sustained, or (c) the Publisher makes an assignment for the benefit of creditors, or (d) the Publisher liquidates its business for any cause whatever (but expressly excepting from each of the foregoing provisions any reorganization proceeding by or against the Publisher under the United States Bankruptcy Act or any similar state statute) then, the Author may

(1) revoke the Publisher's right to publish the Work if it has not then been published;

(2) require that the Publisher cease further publication of the Work but if the Work has been published then the Trustee, Receiver or Assignee shall be permitted to sell those copies of the Work already printed or actually in the process of being printed;

(3) revoke such other rights granted to the Publisher under this Agreement which have not then been exercised or otherwise disposed of by the Publisher;

(4) and thereupon all rights granted by him hereunder shall revert to the Author together with any existing property originally furnished to the Publisher by the Author or at his expense but subject to any contract, sale, license or other disposition of any rights, uses or property in the Work which the Publisher has made or granted prior thereto.

### 18. Non-Publication and Out of Print Provisions

**A.** If the Work shall not be published as is provided by paragraph 7, or, sixteen years from the date of first publication of the Work, it shall no longer be in print and for sale, then the Author may give written notice to the Publisher of his desire to terminate this Agreement, and in such event the Publisher shall declare within sixty (60) days in writing whether or not it intends to print or reprint or cause the Work to be printed or reprinted in an edition of not less than 10,000 copies. If the Publisher or any of its wholly-owned subsidiaries, or affiliate companies, declares its intention to do so, such publication shall take place not later than six (6) months from the giving of such notice. If the Publisher shall within sixty (60) days declare in writing that it does not intend to print or reprint nor cause the Work to be printed or reprinted, or if the Publisher within such time declares that it does so intend, but within six (6) months publication does not take place, then all rights granted hereunder shall terminate and revert to the Author at the end of such sixty (60) days or six (6) month period, as the case may be, provided the Author is not then indebted to the Publisher for any sum owing to it under this Agreement.

**B.** The Work shall be deemed to be in print if it is on sale by the Publisher or any of its wholly-owned subsidiaries, or affiliate companies, in any form permitted hereunder, or, if it is under option or if any license or sublicense granted by the Publisher, is outstanding.

**C.** Nothing contained in this Agreement shall obligate the Publisher or any of its wholly-owned subsidiaries, or affiliate companies, to exercise any or all of the rights granted hereunder, or to publish or to cause to be published hardcover or paperback editions of the Work, or to distribute, market, or exploit the Work anywhere in the World.

### 19. Assignment

**A.** The Author may not assign his rights or obligations under this Agreement without the prior written consent of the Publisher.

**B.** The Publisher may assign all or any of its rights or obligations hereunder without restriction.

**C.** If the Publisher shall assign any or all of its rights or obligations contained in this Agreement, the Publisher shall be under no obligation to the Author to pay to him all or any part of the consideration received by the Publisher for such assignment provided that, either

(a) the Publisher remains liable to make payment to the Author of the royalties set forth in paragraph 1B; or

(b) the assignee agrees (as if it were the Publisher) to make payment of such royalties to the Author out of the net proceeds of sales made pursuant to licenses or sublicenses granted by the assignee and received by such licensee or sublicensee.

## 20. Force Majeure

The Work shall not be deemed out of print nor shall the Publisher be liable because of delays caused by war, invasion, insurrection, blockade, embargo, riot, flood, earthquake, act of God, fire, strike, breakdown of market distribution facilities, shortages of labor or material, government or governmental agency, interference of civil or military authorities, or other causes of a like kind beyond its control.

## 21. Survival

Subject as is otherwise herein provided this Agreement shall bind the parties hereto and their respective administrators, executors, successors and assigns.

## 22. Arbitration

**A.** Any claim or controversy arising among or between the parties hereto pertaining to those matters contained in this Agreement shall be settled by arbitration in the City of New York by three (3) arbitrators under the then prevailing rules of the American Arbitration Association.

**B.** In any arbitration involving this Agreement, the arbitrators shall not make any award which will alter, change, cancel, or rescind any provision of this Agreement, and their award shall be consistent with the provisions of this Agreement. Any such arbitration must be commenced no later than ninety (90) days from the date such controversy arose.

**C.** The award of the arbitrators shall be binding and final, and judgment may be entered thereon, in any Court of competent jurisdiction.

## 23. Notices and Service of Process

Service of notice of arbitration and of process and of any and all documents and notices required to be made or given under this Agreement shall be delivered personally or sent by either Certified or Registered Mail, Return Receipt Requested, addressed to any party at the address first above stated. Any notice required to be made or given under this Agreement shall be deemed to have been made or given five (5) days after the date upon which it is received, without regard to the date the same may have been mailed by the sender.

## 24. Interpretation

This Agreement shall be governed and interpreted by the laws of the State of New York.

## 25. Waiver

No waiver or modification of any of the provisions of this Agreement or of any of the rights or remedies of the parties hereto shall be valid unless such change is in writing, signed by the party to be charged therewith. No waiver of any provisions of this Agreement shall be deemed a waiver of any other provision.

## 26. Entire Agreement

This Agreement constitutes the entire agreement between the parties and may not be terminated, altered, or amended except by a writing executed by all the parties hereto sought to be charged therewith.

## 27. Additional Documents

The Publisher and the Author and each of them agree that they will execute and deliver to each other at any time all and any documents reasonably necessary to fulfill the terms of this Agreement including but not limited to application to secure copyright upon the Work.

## 28. Counterparts

This Agreement may be executed in two or more counterparts, each of which shall be deemed an original, but all of which together shall constitute one and the same instrument.

## 29. Appointment of Literary Agent

The Author hereby authorizes his agent _____
to collect and receive all sums of money payable to him under the terms of this Agreement and the receipt of such agent shall be a good and valid discharge in respect thereof. Such agent is authorized and empowered to act on behalf of the Author in all matters in any way arising out of this Agreement.

**In witness whereof** the parties hereto have duly executed this Agreement the day and year first above written.

**Publishing Corp.,**
(Publisher)

By:

_____
(President)

_____
(Author)

_____          _____
Social Security Number                      Date of Birth

# 4 ✍

# *The Basic Deal*

P in a publishing contract to a wall and throw a dart at it. I guarantee that the clause you hit will be a potential source of contention between you and your publisher. There is scarcely a word anywhere in a contract that has not at one time or another been the source of a quarrel or, worse, a lawsuit between publisher and author. Yet, surprisingly to many people not familiar with the publishing business, few controversies stemming from book contracts have ever been litigated to the limits of the judicial system. Instead, they are usually settled by negotiation within the framework of tradition and convention that has been established over many centuries, a framework so unique that it has led many lawyers to throw up their hands in frustration.

Because ignorance of these traditions and conventions can lead to heartache for an author, or, worse, to a royal shafting, it is absolutely essential for writers today to familiarize themselves with them. Although literary agents can guide authors through the shoals of indemnity and warranty clauses, royalty schedules and termination provisions, not all authors have agents, and not all authors who do have agents have good ones. Thus the author who cavalierly tells his agent, "Just show me where to sign," is the author who, I can safely predict, will one day wake up and say, "I've been screwed." So it is incumbent on writers to educate themselves in matters contractual, to arm themselves not merely against abuse by publishers but against the frailties of those they've charged with representing their own interests.

As we have seen, almost all of the provisions of a publishing contract are "boilerplate" and need not be negotiated at the time the basic deal is struck. Some of them need not be negotiated at all. But all of them bear significance and the potential for mischief, or they wouldn't be in the contract to begin with. A word, a phrase, can substantially affect the meaning of a provision, and if it can affect the meaning it can affect your interests, sometimes profoundly. Take the words "or any other." This innocuous phrase, inserted in the proper place in a contract, can cost an author untold money and grief. Thus:

> Any sums due or owing from Author to Publisher, under this (or any other) contract, may be deducted from any sums which are or may become due from Publisher to Author under this (or any other) agreement between Publisher and Author.

Thanks to those three little words, any profit you earn on one book you've written for your publisher may be applied to make up a loss on any other book you've written for your publisher. Many an unwary author has accepted this language unquestioningly and therefore signed away precious earnings.

Not all contracts have such dangerous pitfalls, but every contract does have its traps, and the material in the following chapters is aimed at helping you find and avoid them.

According to common law, when you write a book you not only produce a literary work, you also create rights to that work that make it entirely and exclusively yours. Those rights are generically known as the copyright, and the mere act of writing your book is sufficient to protect your work from misappropriation. You don't have to hire a lawyer or apply to any government agency to register the copyright at this point; it exists from the moment the words exit your brain and make their appearance on paper.

It is when you decide to publish your work that common law protection leaves off, and you have to undertake certain procedures prescribed by statutory law if you want continued protection. Copyright law is a federal matter, and the statutes defining it are described in congressional copyright acts. These acts are made to conform to the copyright laws of other nations, so that work published in one country is also protected in those countries that subscribe to the copyright treaties known as conventions.

When you sell your work to a publisher you convey some or all of your copyright. The terms by which you convey it are described in a contract. The contract stipulates to whom you convey the rights, the financial compensation you receive for doing so, the permissible uses of the material, the length of the term of the license, the languages and territories in which the material is to be printed and distributed, the format in which the work is to be utilized (mass-market paperback, magazine serialization, film adaptation, and the like), and other details concerning the work's exploitation. The contract also stipulates which parts of the copyright you wish to keep in order to license them to entities other than the publisher. These parts are called the reserved rights.

A contract can be quite simple; you can convey your entire copyright to one entity, a publisher or producer, say, in all forms and languages in perpetuity, for a flat sum of money, reserving no rights and allowing the purchaser to do anything he wants with it — an "outright sale." Or the contract can be extraordinarily complex, with many reserved rights and every term spelled out in exquisite detail. Most publishing contracts fall between the two extremes. They are printed forms expressing the publisher's interpretation of a fair arrangement between publisher and author but leaving room for changes, additions, and amendments. Most publishers furnish the author with several unexecuted copies of their contract — one each for author and publisher, and one for the author's agent, if any. Negotiated changes are made on the contract, and then the author initials them and signs the last page of each copy. The publisher counterinitials them and countersigns the papers and returns one set to the author, along with any financial consideration called for upon execution of the documents. And that completes the formalities.

Your publishing contract distinguishes between primary and secondary rights. The primary rights are the essential ones defining your publisher's rights to print, publish, distribute, sell, and license the work. This includes the form the work is to take, the language it's to be published in, the territory in which it may be sold, and any subsidiary rights to be placed under the publisher's control.

Although there is no "standard" deal, most publishers acknowledge that there is a traditional or typical arrangement between authors and themselves, and they call *it* a standard deal. It can be described thus:

**Form.** The author grants the publisher the right to print, publish, distribute, sell, and license the work in *book* form. The contract may specify the form of the book, such as "hardcover trade edition," "trade-sized paperback edition," or "mass-market paperback edition," and in many cases the contract embraces all three types of book. Some contracts specify maximum or minimum list prices for each edition, to help define them further.

**Language.** The language in which the book is to be published or licensed is English.

**Territory.** The territory exclusively reserved to your publisher is, traditionally, the United States, its territories and possessions, the Philippine Islands, and Canada. Excluded (despite a court ruling prohibiting the practice) are the United Kingdom and members of the British Commonwealth of Nations such as Australia, New Zealand, and South Africa. These are reserved for your eventual British publisher. Sometimes these British rights are conveyed to your American publisher as part of your basic deal, in which case the contract will grant the publisher "world rights in the English language," allowing him to export your book to, or license the rights in, England and member countries of the British Commonwealth.

In addition to the exclusive territorial rights described above, you also grant your publisher the nonexclusive right to distribute his edition in the so-called open market. This is the area outside of the territories reserved strictly for your American and British publishers. In this area both publishers are free to sell their editions of the same book simultaneously and competitively. Germany, France, Holland, Spain, and Japan, for instance, are open-market territories where you might find both the American and British editions of your book in the same English-language bookstore. I stress English language: The right to publish your book in other languages, such as German, French, Dutch, Spanish, or Japanese, is a separate right that is reserved by the author in the so-called standard deal.

**Subsidiary rights.** The contract says "license" as well as "distribute." That means that instead of publishing and distributing the book, or certain editions of the book, your publisher has the right to license another publisher to do so. For instance, a hardcover publisher may want to see a book published in mass-market paperback form but lack the printing or distribution capacity for such an edition. So, for a financial consideration, the hardcover publisher will license the mass-market rights to an outside firm.

Besides reprint rights, the primary subsidiary rights include book-club rights; second serial rights (magazine or newspaper rights after publication of the book); the right to include selections, abridgments, and quotations in other books; and nondramatic mechanical-reproduction rights. The latter means that the book can be recorded in the form of a reading on radio, television, film, tape, or record, but it cannot be adapted into a stage play, or a radio, motion picture, or television play.

These, then, are the primary rights an author grants to his publisher. All other rights may either be reserved by the author or granted to the publisher. Secondary subsidiary rights, on the other hand, include first serialization rights (for publication in magazines or newspapers before book publication); rights for dramatization for radio, stage, motion picture, or television; British Commonwealth rights; foreign translation rights; and commercial rights (the right to produce or license commercial products related to the book). The author is free to market and sell those rights. If, however, the author doesn't know how to exploit subsidiary rights and doesn't have an agent, he may wish to convey them to his publisher, in effect making the publisher his agent for those rights.

✍

There are two forms of income to be made from publication of a book. The first is royalties, a percentage of the retail or wholesale price of the book; the other is licensing fees, a percentage of the publisher's receipts deriving from the licensing of certain primary or subsidiary rights.

Against the revenue anticipated from these sources, the publisher pays the author an advance. Earnings from royalties and subsidiary income are applied toward the advance, and when they reach a total equal to the advance, the advance may be said to have earned out. Thereafter, the excess royalties and subsidiary income are paid to the author in semiannual installments, accompanied by renderings of the account known as royalty statements.

Let's delve into royalties, subsidiary income, and advances a little more deeply.

## Royalties

Every publishing contract, except for those calling for outright sales for flat fees, itemizes the basic royalty the author is to receive, and some five to ten variations applicable to special conditions. Most writers approach royalty schedules with approximately the same awed respect with which the devout approach a shrine. Only after years of experience do they realize that these percentages are not chiseled in stone. Unfortunately, by that time they may have lost a lot of money, for even the minutest differential in a royalty scale can have a tremendous effect on earnings, one way or the other.

I'm not sure how exciting I can make royalty schedules, discounts, and the like sound. I happen to be one of those nuts who takes pleasure in calculating that a difference of one-half of one percent royalty on 150,000 copies sold of a $7.00 paperback will mean $5250.00 to an author. If you happen to be one of those nutty authors who likes $5250.00, then hang on for a short survey flight over the terrain of publishing accounting.

There are two fundamental ways in which publishers calculate royalties. The first is to base them on the list price of the book — the price described in the catalogue or printed on the cover or dust jacket of each copy. The second is to base them on the net receipts collected by the publisher after the publisher has discounted the book or deducted other costs of doing business such as shipping charges or sales commissions.

Trade publishers — publishers of general works of fiction and nonfiction — generally apply their basic royalty rate to the list price of their books, but use a net-receipts approach for books sold under certain specific conditions. Business, technical, art, professional, and other specialty publishers may also use a list-price approach, but frequently base their standard royalties on the *net* price of their books — the price they charge to bookstores, distributors, jobbers, and so forth.

All publishers discount their books to retailers and wholesalers, and often the discounts offered by trade and specialty publishers are the same. But the difference between a royalty based on the list price and one based on the discount price is, obviously, quite pronounced. It can be vividly illustrated by the following example.

Suppose Publisher A buys your novel, offers you a royalty of 10 percent of the list price, and publishes it at $15.00. That's $1.50 per copy to you. But suppose Publisher A offers you 10 percent of the *net receipts*. That means your royalty would be based on what Publisher A collected after discounting the book to a wholesaler or retailer. Now, suppose further that the publisher gives a 40 percent discount, meaning he collects 60 percent of $15.00, or $9.00 per copy. Your royalty would be 10 percent of $9.00, or $0.90 per copy. The difference between the two methods of calculating royalties is $0.60 a copy. On a sale of 5000 copies, that's $3000!

There's nothing inherently wrong with a royalty based on net receipts as long as you're aware that it *is* based on net receipts and you negotiate to compensate for the difference. In the above example, in order to earn the same $1.50 per copy, you'd have to get a 16.67 percent royalty on the net proceeds to achieve parity with a royalty of 10 percent of the list price. All too often, though, authors don't understand the difference between the two systems, and the results can be catastrophic. On the other hand, that 10 percent royalty based on net receipts may not always be unfair. If a book is expensive to produce and market, the publisher's profits may not be that large, and 10 percent of net might well be equitable.

Another area of confusion for many writers is the difference between the royalty from the sale of copies of a book and the revenue derived from *licensing the right* to sell copies of that book. Publishers frequently find themselves with a choice of selling their book in a certain market or licensing another publisher to sell it in that market. For instance, Pocket Books might export copies of a certain title to England; or it might license an English publisher to publish and distribute the book in that same territory. In the first instance, Pocket Books would pay the author a royalty for each copy sold through export. In the second, it would pay the author a share of the licensing fee it charged the English publisher. Since both modes of accounting are expressed in percentages (say, 4 percent royalty on copies Pocket Books sells through export or 25 percent of the revenue derived from the licensing of the rights to another publisher), it's important for you to keep this distinction firmly in mind when you read the royalty schedule of your contract. In the material that immediately follows, we'll be discussing only royalties on copies sold. Subsequently, in our discussion of subsidiary rights, we'll take up percentages of licensing revenue.

Now, what types of royalties are there, and what are considered fair ones?

**The basic royalty.** This is the percentage that applies, or is supposed to apply, to most books sold in traditional consumer markets — bookstores and newsstands — and it's the only one you need to negotiate when you make your original deal. It is usually expressed as a percentage of the list price of the book, and assumes a normal or traditional discount between publisher and distributor, bookstore, or other sales outlet. In trade publishing, for instance, the traditional discount is 40 percent; that is, the publisher will sell a $10.00 book to a store for $6.00, and if the store sells it at list price it will make $4.00 a copy over its purchase price.

When the discount is normal, the publisher can afford to pay the author a normal royalty. In American hardcover trade publishing, that royalty has generally emerged as 10 percent of the list price of the first 5000 copies sold, 12 ½ percent of the next 5000 copies sold, and 15 percent thereafter. On a $10.00 book, the author would thus get $1.00 a copy up to 5000 sold, $1.25 on the next 5000, and $1.50 on all copies sold thereafter.

In mass-market (rack-size) and trade (oversize) paperback publishing, the discounts, and therefore the royalty scales, are not quite so rigidly fixed in tradition, so there is more range in both types. Mass-market royalties start at a low of 4 percent and go as high as 12 percent, 15 percent, or even higher. The "breaks," the points at which the royalty percentages escalate, are normally fixed at hundreds of thousands of copies sold. Thus a typical mass-market paperback deal might call for a 6 percent royalty on the retail price of the first 150,000 copies, 8 percent on the next 350,000 copies, and 10 percent thereafter. In trade-paperback publishing the rates usually start at a low of 6 percent and top out at 10 percent, with escalations based on sales in the tens of thousands. Thus: 6 percent of the retail price on the first 10,000 copies sold, 7 percent on the next 15,000, and 8 percent thereafter might be a typical trade-paperback royalty schedule.

The variations, exceptions, and complications arise because publishers don't always sell their books at normal or traditional discounts. Historically, publishing contracts have always made allowances for bigger-than-usual discounts, and there is nothing inherently unfair about that. As in any other merchandising enterprise, large discounts *should* be offered to buyers who take large quantities. So if a contract stipulates a decreased royalty on a book sold at a high discount, the author doesn't necessarily have cause for complaint. Because even if he's making less money per book, he's selling more copies.

Book merchandising, however, has changed radically in recent years, and big discounts are becoming more the rule than the exception, thanks to the rapid growth of big bookstore chains like Barnes & Noble that have fantastic buying power. Where a 50 percent discount for mass-market paperbacks was average for publishers only a few years ago, it is commonly exceeded today. And because it is, authors who don't understand the relationship between discounts and royalties are getting hurt, and sometimes badly. Let's see why.

Suppose you have a contract with a mass-market publisher that calls for a 6 percent royalty on your $6.00 book, or $0.36 per copy, but the contract says that if your book is sold at more than 50 percent discount your royalty will be reduced by half, to 3 percent, or $0.18 per copy. Well, a few years ago such a reduction was only a marginal possibility. Today, however, it's more like a probability. You may therefore find yourself getting $0.18 a copy when you were expecting twice that amount! That's a loss of $18,000 for every 100,000 copies sold.

You must, then, when you negotiate your contract, try to make sure that your royalty rate won't be cut back at too low a discount rate. In the above example, if you could arrange it so that your royalty isn't reduced until the publisher's discount reaches, say, 55 percent or better, you might save yourself some or all of that $18,000.

In many publishing contracts the royalty doesn't drop quite so sharply, but is graduated to conform with graduated increases in the publisher's discount. In a typical hardcover contract I have before me, the publisher stipulates that if the book is sold at a discount of more than 48 percent, the author's royalty rate will drop one-half of one percent for each percent of discount. Thus, if your normal rate on a hardcover book is 10 percent of the list price on normally discounted sales, your royalty will go down to:

- 9 ½ percent if the discount goes to 49 percent
- 9 percent if the discount goes to 50 percent
- 8 ½ percent if the discount goes to 51 percent and so forth . . .

Such an arrangement isn't unfair in theory, but some publishers' contracts leave the matter open-ended, so that presumably your royalty rate could go down to zero. Therefore you should set a bottom limit on your royalty and insist that in no event will it be reduced to less than one-half of the basic royalty, unless the books are sold at or below cost, in which case you are not entitled to any royalties.

**Reduced royalty on small reprintings.** Publishers, at least hardcover publishers, commonly stipulate in their contracts that if they go back to press for a small printing (2500 copies is the traditional figure) just to keep the book in print, they may reduce the royalty paid on books sold out of that printing. The idea is to help the publisher keep the book available to the consumer for as long as possible, and, because small printings are more expensive per unit than large ones, the publisher asks the author to help subsidize the printing by accepting a lower royalty. To reassure authors that these small reprintings aren't a ruse to beat them out of royalties, publishers usually stipulate in their contracts that they won't invoke the small-reprintings royalty for a certain period of time subsequent to publication, such as two years.

Authors and agents used to appreciate publishers' efforts to keep their books in print. That appreciation seems to be diminishing, however. For better or worse, the trend in publishing is away from keeping books in print for a long time. Authors and agents prefer to recover the rights to a book whose sale is marginal, so that they can resell it or simply hold on to the rights until such time as there's a surge of demand for it — when the author becomes famous, for example. And the Internal Revenue Service's 1980 ruling applying the *Thor Power Tool* decision of 1979 to publishers' inventories, which adversely affects the way publishers account for their backlist inventories, has made it expensive for publishers to keep books in print for a long time.

Paperback publishers seldom have contract clauses referring to small printings; indeed, they seldom have clauses referring to any printings at all. If they wish to keep a book in print, they just go ahead and print more copies, and leave it to the author to find out how many copies were printed and when.

**Canadian and export royalties.** Traditionally, American publishers buy from authors the exclusive right to distribute their books in the United States, Canada, the Philippines, and United States territories and possessions; and the *non*exclusive right to distribute the books elsewhere in the world (the so-called open market) with the exception of the British Commonwealth, which includes Australia, New Zealand, and South Africa.

Because of the higher cost of selling books outside the United States, publishing contracts call for a reduced royalty on such sales, ranging from two-thirds to one-half of the basic royalty. Many contracts, particularly hardcover ones, call for a reduced royalty on exported "sheets." Sheets are unbound books. Sometimes a publisher prefers to ship sheets to a foreign market, where they're bound by a publisher at the other end. An English publisher, for instance, might find it too expensive to set type on a book he buys from an American author or publisher. So he'll import the sheets of the American edition, print his own front matter (English copyright information, logo, list price expressed in pounds, and so forth), and bind them all together in England. The royalty your American publisher pays you for this "sheet deal" shouldn't differ too greatly from the one he pays you for bound books exported to the same territory.

**Royalties on cheap editions, library editions, deluxe and other special editions.** Your publisher's contract generally gives him the right to publish variations on your book within a certain price range. If, praise the Lord, it becomes an enduring classic, he may want to bind it in leather with gilt lettering, printed on fine rag stock. Your royalty percentage on this book may drop, but it shouldn't drop too far from your basic one; your publisher's costs will be higher, yes, but so will his price and profit per copy. The same goes for library editions (which are more strongly bound to withstand the intensive handling of schools and libraries), large-print editions, and the like.

Hardcover contracts often give publishers the right to issue "cheap" editions. These are still hardcovers, but the print may be smaller, the paper pulpier, the cover lighter, the binding less elaborate, and there may be no dust jacket. Such editions are usually designed for students or others who wish to own a hardcover but can't afford the full-dress version, and the contract generally stipulates a minimum price below which the publisher cannot sell the book — otherwise it'll compete with paperback reprints.

"Cheap" editions seem to be a dying breed, however, because publishers now prefer to issue trade-paperback editions of their hardcover books when they wish to reach the market that buys cheap editions. The trade, or "quality," paperback is printed with the same plates as the hardcover edition, but a soft cover is substituted for the hard. Where a contract does call for a cheap edition, your royalty will usually be reduced. Do be sure that the publisher's minimum price on such an edition is not so low as to ruin the book's chances for a reprint sale. When I came into the business, a publisher could safely establish the price of a cheap edition at $2.50. Now, with mass market paperback prices at this writing hovering in the $6.00 to $7.00 range, it would be sheer madness to allow a hardcover publisher to issue a cheap edition for $2.50 or even thrice $2.50.

**Mail-order royalties.** Some types of books lend themselves to sale through mail order — the kind in which you clip a coupon out of a newspaper or magazine and send it in with your check, or where you receive a solicitation through the mail. Royalties on books sold in this fashion are generally lower than the basic one because of the higher cost of marketing them. Newspaper and magazine ads are expensive, mailing lists and printed solicitations are costly, and shipping and handling costs are high, too. A royalty of no less than 5 percent of the retail price is normal and not unfair.

**Royalties on sale of overstock and remainders.** If a publisher finds himself with too many copies of a book in the warehouse, but wants to retain enough to meet routine demand and keep the book in print, he will sometimes sell off the overstock. Overstock usually goes to a jobber on a nonreturnable basis at a large discount. In such cases the author's royalty is reduced, generally to something like 10 percent of the publisher's proceeds on a discount of 65 percent or more.

This royalty is not unfair, but authors might gain a measure of protection by requiring that the publisher not sell off any overstock before the expiration of one year from publication. They should also stipulate that they have the right of first refusal to buy the overstock. This will enable them to stock their libraries as plentifully as necessary, for once a book goes out of print, the author will never again have such an opportunity. One of my clients, a writer-lecturer, claims to earn over $20,000 annually by selling, after his lectures, copies of his book purchased dirt-cheap from his publisher's overstock.

Overstock and remainders aren't the same thing. Remainders are the balance of a publisher's inventory of a book, sold off when the publisher decides to allow the book to go out of print. Remainders are usually sold at or below cost, and have no royalty value to authors. But again, authors should have first claim on remainders.

Authors who see their books piled up in remainder bookstores are quick to conclude that the books have been remaindered; but the piles may only be overstock. Since the shedding of overstock by a publisher is often a prelude to remaindering, however, the author desirous of recovering his rights should begin inquiring regularly about the in-print status of his book — say, every six months.

**Other royalties.** No royalties are payable on copies furnished gratis to the author, or for review, advertising, samples, publicity, promotion, or like purposes, or on copies destroyed by fire or water, or on copies sold below the cost of manufacture.

## Primary Subsidiary Rights

Among the rights you convey to a publisher when you sell him your book is the right to license others to publish different versions, editions, and adaptations of the work. These are the subsidiary rights, and they are divided into two groups: primary and secondary. This doesn't imply that the former have more value than the latter; often the opposite is true. It means that in most cases the primary subsidiary rights automatically go to the publisher, whereas the secondary ones are up for grabs, sometimes going to the publisher, sometimes being reserved by the author, and sometimes being split between them.

The primary subsidiary rights are:

- Book club
- Reprint
- Second serialization
- Selections and abridgments
- Nondramatic mechanical and electronic reproduction

The secondary subsidiary rights are:

- First serialization
- Dramatization for stage, screen, radio, and television
- British Commonwealth
- Foreign translation
- Commercial exploitation
- Multimedia versions

I'll save the secondary "sub" rights (as subsidiary rights are often referred to in the trade) for chapter 10, and concentrate here on the primary ones.

As I say, these are almost invariably granted to your publisher in the package of rights permitting him to publish, *and license others to publish,* your book. The licenses of these sub rights are restricted to the same language — English — and territory as the ones in which your publisher is allowed to distribute. If you granted your publisher the right to publish in the English language, in the United States, its territories and possessions, the Philippines, and Canada, but *not* in the British Commonwealth, then anybody who licenses subsidiary rights from your publisher must restrict exploitation to the same areas.

Let's examine these rights in detail.

**Book club.** There are several major book clubs in America, and a number of lesser ones. The major book clubs include Book-of-the-Month, the Literary Guild, and Reader's Digest Condensed Books. Some of the smaller ones are the History Book Club, the Military Book Club, the Travel Book Club, the Science Fiction Book Club, and the Mystery Guild.

The purpose of the clubs is to sell copies of selected books at a discount to members in exchange for a guaranteed purchase of a minimum number of selections annually. The clubs are aimed at people who may not have access to good bookstores, or time and patience to shop for books, or who simply want to save a few dollars on the books they buy. Some clubs print their own editions of a selected title, while others buy copies in bulk from the publisher, who may print the club's logo on the books before going to press.

Before publication, publishers submit manuscript or proof copies of their books to the clubs, where committees of readers judge the books' merits and try to anticipate what club members will want to buy and read. If the judges feel the demand will be strong, they make an offer to the publisher in the form of an advance against royalties, or perhaps a flat fee for a fixed number of copies printed or purchased. The money can be very big, as in the case of the $1.75 million reportedly paid for James Michener's *The Covenant* by the Literary Guild. Often, however, the price comes to only a few thousand dollars, and the chief value of having a book selected is not the money but prestige and publicity.

**Reprint.** When you sell your book to a publisher, you transfer to him the right to make arrangements with outside publishers to reproduce your book in a variety of editions. Although we've come to think of reprints as mass-market paperback editions of hardcover books, reprints come in all shapes, sizes, formats, and prices: hardcover editions, deluxe editions, large-print editions, and trade-paperback editions, to name some, as well as the usual rack-size paperback. So if you sell your book originally to a mass-market paperback house, your contract will probably permit that publisher to make a deal with a hardcover publisher to do a hardcover edition. Such deals don't happen very often, for a hardcover publisher can make little profit by buying a book to which he doesn't control paperback rights; but it has happened. A notable example is *The Exorcist*, which Harper & Row bought from Bantam. In such cases, a paperback firm, believing that a book it has bought directly from an author might benefit from the prestige and review attention it would get if done in hardcover (reviewers in general still don't take original paperbacks seriously), will offer it to hardcover publishers along with some sort of incentive, such as a small royalty on paperback sales plus a contribution to their advertising budget.

For the most part, however, we think of a reprint as a paperback edition of a hardcover book. At some point after a hardcover publisher has bought your book, he will offer it to the paperback reprint publishers, in hopes of making a deal with one of them. The timing and nature of such deals depend on a great many factors. If the publisher thinks he has a hot property — perhaps he's made a big sale to a book club, early reviews are raves, and the movie and foreign rights have been snapped up — he may try to auction the paperback rights from manuscript or bound galley proofs, capitalizing on the mounting excitement. If the book is more routine, the publisher may wait until it's been published, in hopes that good reviews, strong hardcover sales, publicity, or some other piece of good fortune will arouse a paperback publisher's interest.

Up until a few years ago, news of big reprint deals and spectacular paperback auctions was an almost daily occurrence, fueling the public's growing image of publishing as a glamour industry. The competition for reprint rights was so intense that books of only average merit were being acquired at auction for tens or hundreds of thousands of dollars. Except for a few Jeremiahs, no one thought the carnival would end. But around 1979 the reprinters began to evince signs of sluggishness, and within a year or two the pulse of the reprint market had slowed to a moribund rate.

A number of trends had converged at once. Inflationary increases in book prices, coupled with the advent of a deep economic recession, had made consumers extremely picky about what they paid three, four, or five dollars for. The growth of paperback originals undercut the reprint market, as paperback publishers realized that instead of paying $500,000 for reprint rights to a hardcover book, they could hire a writer for $10,000 to write a similar book, spend $50,000 to promote it, and sell almost as many copies as they would have sold of the reprint, while saving hundreds of thousands of dollars in the bargain. Another factor was that after spending millions to acquire reprint rights to some hardcover bestsellers, which of course meant further huge outlays to advertise and promote their paperback editions, they just didn't have enough money to get involved in the next paperback auction, or the one after that. And last but not least, many houses took baths on reprints for which they had overpaid.

Today, the reprint market remains a shadow of what it was in the boom time of the 1970s. The paperback publishers husband their reprint money for the proven big-name best-selling authors, so that we still do hear from time to time of seven-digit deals. But they are few and far between, and for the foreseeable future most authors should consider themselves lucky if their hardcover books sell to the paperback companies at all, let alone for five or six or seven digits.

I have made this depressing digression for two reasons. The first is to help you put into perspective any fantasies you may entertain about big reprint action on your hardcover book. The other is to introduce you to a hybrid of the publishing industry, the hard-soft deal.

In a hard-soft deal, the same publishing company acquires both hardcover and paperback reprint rights to a book simultaneously. Since the paperback reprinter is part of the same corporate entity as the hardcover publisher, the paperback royalties are not split between hardcover publisher and author, as they are when a hardcover house sells reprint rights to an outside paperback company. In a hard-soft deal, a full hardcover *and* a full paperback royalty go to the author.

The hardcover-softcover combine is the result of a process that has been going on in publishing for some time, but seems to be rising to prominence today, and perhaps dominance tomorrow. Paperback publishers have been marrying hardcover ones through acquisition or merger, and in several instances paperback firms have created their own hardcover divisions. The advantages to both hard and soft companies are many: Acquisition and production costs are decreased; marketing, advertising, and promotion are better controlled and coordinated; hardcover books that deserve paperback reprint, and paperbacks that deserve hardcover treatment, all get their due.

For the author there are advantages and disadvantages. The disadvantage is that by selling hard and soft rights at the same time, he eliminates the possibility of a big paperback reprint auction. The advantage is guaranteed publication in both hardcover and paperback, plus full royalties from both editions.

If you don't hear about big reprint deals much these days, it may well be because paperback rights are going to the same companies that buy hardcover rights. If such a deal is offered to you, consider it seriously. Make sure your contract stipulates that hardcover publication is guaranteed, though, for contracts often state that the publisher has the *right* but not the *obligation* to publish a hardcover edition.

**Second serialization.** Publication of your book may attract magazines and newspapers interested in utilizing some or all of the material. That utilization might take the form of a condensation in one or more issues; or excerpts; or publication of the entire book in one issue or several. Your book publisher handles second-serial sales — that is, sales after book publication. Magazine or newspaper serialization before publication is a sub right that may be reserved by the author. If that's the case with your book, and you do place first serial, make sure the serialization comes out no later than publication date of your book, otherwise you could get into trouble with your book publisher.

**Selections and abridgments.** Your publisher has the right to publish these himself, or license them to other publishers. Another publisher may want to use a part of your book in an anthology, or create a shortened version of it for a condensed-book club or book digest. Obviously, these rights sometimes spill over into book-club and second-serial areas.

**Nondramatic mechanical and electronic reproduction.** This gives the publisher the right to record, or arrange for others to record, your book on phonograph record, film, audio- or videotape, or other mechanical and electronic recording devices now in existence or to be developed in the future. This clause frequently ruffles authors' feathers, because it suggests the right to produce theatrical or television motion-picture adaptations from their books. That is not the case, because your contract distinguishes between dramatic and nondramatic recordings — or at least it should. If someone wants to record somebody reading your book page by page, that would be governed by this clause of your contract; if someone wants to make a radio, stage, television, or movie play out of the material, that's quite something else. I suggest, then, that you make sure that the word *nondramatic* is used in this clause; but you might try to strike the clause out entirely, because even something as innocuous as a videotaped reading of your book could jeopardize a movie or television deal.

**Electronic rights and multimedia.** These are special situations that we'll be discussing at length later in the book. At this writing, and for a long time to come, electronic rights are being hotly contested by publishers, authors, and agents. There seems to be a consensus that publishers are entitled to retain the right to reproduce verbatim the text of a book for use on personal computers or other electronic reading devices. That makes this application of your book a primary right to be ceded to your publisher.

There is another form of electronic rights, however, that allows publishers to enhance your text by means of audio, still pictures, animation, video, and music. Your text may be rearranged nonsequentially, enabling a computer user to interact with it or to "access" any part of it in the same way you can jump to any passage on your music CD. Such enhancements may be made in some cases without your approval.

Many publishers are fighting to make these multimedia versions part of their primary rights package, whereas writers and agents feel that they should be reserved for authors, or at least that ownership should be subject to negotiation. The issue is of particular concern when the work is fiction, because it may well be said that a multimedia adaptation of a work of fiction is called — a movie! And movie companies are fighting just as hard to acquire multimedia rights to properties as publishers are.

When your publisher sells one of the above subsidiary rights, he makes a contract with the purchaser. Although most agents and lawyers would argue that it's the author's right to see such contracts, such is seldom the case. The reason (though publishers won't say it) is that the author, or his agent or lawyer, would be inclined to meddle in the sub-rights negotiations if allowed to review the contract, and thus have the power to kill deals. And, frankly, who knows but that this might be true? On occasion an agent is able to secure for an author the right to approve reprint deals, but that's unusual. Publishers do report subsidiary deals, and furnish summaries of the terms to authors and agents, but the reliability of such reporting varies from publisher to publisher.

The traditional division of proceeds from the licensing of these principal subsidiary rights is 50–50 between publisher and author. The publisher's 50 percent goes into his own bank account; the author's 50 percent goes into the author's royalty account. If the royalties and subsidiary income in the author's account exceed the advance paid him by the publisher, the excess will be released to him in the semiannual statements rendered by the publisher. At least it's supposed to be, but often the publisher holds a reserve against returned books — a subject we'll take up in the chapter on royalty statements.

Is the 50–50 split on subsidiary income negotiable? Not very often, but sometimes the division can be tilted in the author's favor. Stay tuned to the end of this chapter and I'll explain how.

## The Advance

As a down-payment against royalties and the author's share of subsidiary-rights income, publishers usually pay an advance. Usually but not always. University presses often do not because they don't have the money; and technical, business, and professional publishers frequently offer no-advance contracts, their justification being that contributors to their enterprises aren't as concerned with money as garden-variety authors are. Also, publishers of general material often buy a writer's services for a flat fee — no royalties or subsidiary income. This occurs when the publisher controls the copyright and is in a strong position to dictate terms. Whenever possible, fight for some kind, any kind, of royalty or share of subrights income. Shortly after starting out as a free-lance writer, I was asked to write a novelization of a dreadful movie, and allowed myself to be talked into doing it for a flat fee, on the grounds that the book would come and go as quickly as the film. Well, the film came and went, but my book went through several printings here and abroad. Take heed from this example.

In theory, the advance represents the publisher's reasonable estimate of the minimum revenue an author can expect to earn from his book. For example, if a publisher is paying a 10 percent royalty on a $10.00 book, and anticipates selling a minimum of 5000 copies, it would seem likely that the author could count on a $5000 advance — 5000 copies × $1.00-per-copy royalty. To this add anything the publisher expects to earn from the author by way of subsidiary income. If he is certain there will be a paperback reprint sale for no less than $10,000, which he'll split 50–50 with the author, he would add the author's $5000 share to the $5000 advance, bringing to $10,000 the amount he can presumably afford to pay as an advance.

In practice, the advance may be substantially less — or substantially more. For one thing, publishers' profits and losses aren't calculated the same way authors' earnings are. For the author in the above example, 5000 copies of his book have to be sold before he recoups a $5000 advance. But for the publisher to recoup his investment, he may have to sell 10,000 copies, or maybe 30,000 copies. Royalties, you see, are only one of a publisher's many costs; there are also the costs of paper, manufacture, editorial salaries, warehousing, distribution, advertising and promotion, overhead, depreciation, the cost of money, and other expenses. After weighing these against anticipated revenue from the sale of books, publishers project how many copies they will have to sell in order to break even, and the number they come up with may have nothing to do with the number of copies necessary for the author's advance to earn out.

Your publisher may want to spend a lot of money advertising your book, creating an additional burden on his budget and raising his break-even figure to 15,000 copies sold. To defray that expense, he'll try to make the advance as low as possible. Maybe he can get the author to accept $2500. In that case, it will take only 2500 copies sold for the author to recover his advance and begin earning royalties; but it will take 15,000 copies sold for the publisher to recoup his investment. Of course, if the publisher can count on some subsidiary money, such as a guaranteed reprint sale, then his investment will be defrayed by that much, and he can afford to pay a higher advance.

Another factor, much harder to calculate, is enthusiasm. If a publisher adores the book and absolutely must have it and knows, just *knows*, the book is going to be a big hit, he may chuck his profit-and-loss calculations out the window and agree to an advance that is way out of line with anything sensible his business advisers urge him to pay. This is the part of publishing that makes it, still, an art and not a science. Editors who use their instincts and play their hunches are a dying breed in this age of conglomeration and bureaucratic overmanagement in publishing; still, from time to time an editor or a company will go temporarily mad with enthusiasm, and that's what engenders the headline-making advances that seem to have no correspondence to reality.

Advances may be paid either in one lump or in installments. Because money costs so much these days, publishers try to hold on to it as long as they can, and therefore they stretch out the payout schedule over as long a term as traffic will bear. If the book you sell your publisher needs no editorial work, and the advance is low, you may be able to collect the full sum on signing the contract. But if the book needs work, or the advance is high, or the book was purchased on the basis of a partial manuscript, then the advance will surely be payable in installments. The first installment is paid on signing the contract, the second is due on delivery and acceptance of the completed or revised manuscript, and there may be further installments on publication or even later.

On bigger deals, publishers and agents often work out bonus advances or "escalators" payable when certain contingencies occur, such as the appearance of the book on the bestseller lists (which lists, which position on a list, and length of time on a list are negotiable), national release of a movie based on the book, or other desirable events that enhance the book's value. These sums are added to the advance, so that a $25,000 bonus paid for a book that makes the bestseller list, when added to an original advance of $50,000, means the book must earn a total of $75,000 in royalty and subrights revenue before the author will see further income from the book.

Under normal circumstances, each book you sell to a publisher should have its own accounting, and money earned or lost on one book should not be applicable to money earned or lost on another. When a publisher does apply royalties earned on a profitable book to make up for royalties lost on an unprofitable one by the same author, he is using a procedure known as joint accounting. (It's also known as general accounting, basket accounting, and cross-collateralization.) References to joint accounting are often quiet little sentences buried deep in the boilerplate of a contract, but, as I pointed out earlier, the harm they do may be inordinate if one of your books is a big winner and another is a big loser. So I urge you to search out and destroy anything in your contract suggesting that the publisher has the right to jointly account your books.

There are occasions, however, when an author will voluntarily agree to a joint accounting arrangement with a publisher. This usually occurs when a deal is made for more than one book at a time and the advance is substantial. It's easier to swallow joint accounting when your publisher is offering you $250,000 for your next two books than it is when he's offering you $10,000 for the two. The best thing to do is resist joint accountings no matter what, but if you have to accept them, try to limit the number of books that fall into the basket arrangement so that it's not open-ended. For instance, I have a paperback series with one publisher who insists on tying the royalty accounting on each new book he buys to the accounting on books in the series already purchased. At that rate the author might never see any royalties; every time he was supposed to, the advance on his new book would raise the total advance that had to be earned out. So we've compromised by limiting the joint account to groups of three books: books 1, 2, and 3 form one jointly accounted set; books 4, 5, and 6 form another, and so forth. In this way, once the first package of three earns back its joint advance the author will see royalties — those royalties won't be applied to the unearned advance on books 4, 5, and 6.

Are advances refundable? It depends on the conditions. Once a finished manuscript has been accepted by the publisher, the advances paid on signing and acceptance should not be refundable. If an author fails to deliver a manuscript or revision on time, the publisher has the right to request a refund of any advance paid to date. Usually publishers are not strict to the minute if an author is late (they couldn't afford to be, considering how many authors *are* late), but if the manuscript is flagrantly overdue, or if the publisher *must* have a manuscript by a certain date (to tie in with release of a film, for instance), then the publisher's request for a refund may be justified because the publisher could lose money for publishing late.

Most contracts have (and all should have) a clause stipulating the period of time within which the publisher must publish the author's book. This period generally ranges from twelve to thirty-six months. If the publisher fails to publish within this term (barring acts of God or such unforeseen and uncontrollable events as strikes, riots, wars, and the like), the author may reclaim his rights and the publisher forfeits any advances paid to date. Also, most contracts have (and again, all of them should have) a provision for reversion of rights to the author after the book has gone out of print. Some publishers slip a line into their contracts saying that the rights will revert at that time *if* there is no unearned advance outstanding. That means that in order to get his rights back, the author must repay whatever part of his advance is unearned by royalties and sub-rights revenue. That line should be struck out of the contract.

The most controversial contractual stipulation revolving around refund of advances has to do with the publisher's rejection of completed manuscripts or revisions. Most contracts stipulate that in the event the author delivers an unacceptable or unacceptably revised manuscript, the author must refund the on-signing portion of the advance. The decision as to what is acceptable rests solely with the publisher, and obviously the possibility of arbitrary rejection is deeply disturbing to authors and agents. In actuality most such rejections, at least those that my agency has been involved in, have not been unjustified. But that's not the point. The point is whether it's fair for the publisher to expect a refund.

A publisher's down-payment on an uncompleted or problem manuscript represents his investment in an author, not a refundable option on his work. If the author turns in an unacceptable completion or revision (and most contracts give authors an opportunity to revise in such a case), the publisher must consider the investment lost, the same as an oil company whose drill fails to strike oil.

Because a growing number of authors, agents, and authors' groups have protested the way most acceptance clauses are framed, many publishers have modified theirs so that the author has to refund his advance only if and when he sells the rejected book to another publisher. This is scarcely better, as he still has to refund the first publisher's down-payment, wherever the money to do so comes from. Whenever I can, then, I strike such references in the acceptability clause of a contract.

## Trading Off Advances, Royalties, and Subsidiary Rights

Just how negotiable are the elements of the basic deal? As I said earlier, negotiability is usually a matter of who's holding the higher cards, and, for the new author, that's usually the publisher. Using some of the approaches we've discussed, however, the author can improve his position. Then, through discussion and negotiation, both parties can ascertain where they stand and trade off the things that are most or least important.

For instance, if a publisher tells you he simply can't pay a higher advance because the company has cash-flow problems, you might be able to counter by saying, "Fine, I'll accept that low advance in exchange for a higher royalty." The publisher might go for this exchange, because he figures (1) he's saving money up front, where he needs it most, and (2) if the book does well, he won't mind paying a higher royalty, because both he *and* the author will be making a profit.

Or, if you can't budge the publisher on advance or royalty, request something that doesn't cost the publisher anything, such as a bestseller bonus or movie escalator. For a publisher, such contingency payments are no-lose situations. If your book doesn't go on the bestseller list or become a movie, the publisher doesn't have to pay the bonus. If your book does, your publisher doesn't mind paying, because he knows he'll make the money back on increased sales generated by these happy developments.

Sometimes there are tradeoffs on the subsidiary rights. An author's biggest cards are his secondary subsidiary rights: first serial, performing, British, foreign translation, and commercial exploitation. As these potentially lucrative rights are traditionally reserved by the author, your publisher might cast a covetous eye on them and be willing to give you something in exchange for a piece of that action. (I've detailed such negotiations in the chapter on ancillary rights.)

Harder to swap are the primary subsidiary rights — book club, reprint, and so forth — for they are vital to publishers and it's hard to envision how they could give up much in that department. It does happen sometimes, however. For example, when I sell a paperback original, I sometimes try to reserve the hardcover rights if the paperback company has no expectations of bringing out or licensing a hardcover edition. Although few hardcover firms will buy a book to which paperback rights have already been sold, there are some who do library or deluxe editions and don't care about paperback revenue; they make their profit strictly on hardcover sales.

Although the 50–50 split on primary subsidiary rights is ironclad in most instances, occasionally one can wangle a division of proceeds in favor of the author, say 60–40, or an escalating split that might look like this: 50–50 on the first $50,000 of paperback revenue collected by the publisher, 55–45 in favor of the author on the next $50,000, and 60–40 thereafter. A publisher might do this in exchange for a lower advance, and he can afford to do it because it's a no-loss situation. If the paperback rights go for less than $50,000, the publisher gets his traditional 50 percent; but if they go for more, he doesn't mind giving a little more than half to the author because there's so much more profit to spread around.

To sum it all up, there is little in a publishing deal that is immutable. Once you know what a publisher wants most, and he knows what you want most, the scene is set for that historic handshake.

# 5 ✍

# Warranties and Indemnities

Lawyers are fond of saying that anybody can sue anybody for anything. This is as true in the book world as it is in any other field of endeavor. You may be fanatically meticulous about checking your facts, disguising names, dates, places, events, and identities, obtaining releases, securing permissions, paraphrasing other people's writing, and getting legal readings by nit-picking attorneys, only to find yourself hauled into court by some nut who thinks he recognizes himself, or by some litigious crank hoping to pressure you into paying him a settlement.

So if, when you turn a manuscript in to your publisher, you wonder if there's anything in it you can be sued for, the answer is an unequivocal *yes*. There is, indeed, scarcely anything you *can't* be sued for. This chapter addresses itself to what some of those things are, and how contractual language is structured to handle claims and lawsuits brought against authors and publishers.

In this respect, the pertinent provisions of publishing contracts are the warranty and indemnity clauses, which respectively describe the author's responsibility for making a manuscript as lawsuit-proof as possible and his obligation to repay or contribute to his publisher's costs and losses if a lawsuit is brought against that publisher over claims arising from his book.

Few things frighten publishers more than lawsuits. Aside from the obvious reasons of the heavy cost of defending them and the disastrous expense of losing or settling them, publishers harbor a strong sense of the injustice of having lawsuits brought against them simply because as corporations they have more money than authors do. Why, they reason, should they take the rap for an author who didn't do his homework? The answer is that they have an obligation to do their own homework, and they must accept the wages of risk equally with the author. To make an author totally liable for, say, plagiarism is by no means unreasonable, for plagiarism is a misdeed perpetrated without the knowledge of the publisher. But when a publisher is fully cognizant and a witting participant in a potentially provocative publishing act, such as bringing out a book that invites a libel or invasion-of-privacy suit, the publisher should be required to share the costs of defending that action, and the expense of damages or settlement, if any, with the author.

But few publishers see it this way, and most place the responsibility for their protection from lawsuits squarely on the shoulders of authors. This burden is always heavy and usually outrageously unfair, and although you can negotiate some of the contractual language some of the time with some of the publishers, many authors and agents have learned that it is easier to alter the course of the planets than the phrasing of a warranty and indemnity clause. I'll have some proposals at the end of this chapter, but my advice is that you expend your energy making sure your manuscript doesn't breach its warranties, rather than tilt with the implacable minions of a publisher's house counsel. If you're concerned in the slightest that your manuscript has actionable elements in it, and you don't want to be sued, go over it with a fine-tooth comb, have an attorney read it with the eyes of a devil's advocate, and eliminate anything you think may be legally provocative.

I say "don't want to be sued" because there is an odd and perverse species of author who says, "Hell, I hope I *am* sued! Think of the publicity that'll create for my book!" Such people have a very unrealistic notion about both the legal *and* the publishing professions, for, even in the unlikely event that their publisher would knowingly permit legally provocative material to be published, they soon discover that after the first headline (if there *is* a headline), the process of litigation is enervating, depressing, and impoverishing. And even if the suit engenders tons of publicity, the book sales thus stimulated seldom do the author much good, for by virtue of the warranty and indemnity provisions of the publisher's contract with the author, *the publisher has the right to freeze all those royalties and use them to defray legal expenses and/or pay damages or settlements.* Engrave this fact on your mind and you'll be well on your way to lowering the odds of having a lawsuit brought against you.

What warranties are you required to make when you sign a publishing contract? Let's examine some typical ones:

**That you are the sole author of the work.** That is, that no one else will come forth to claim to be the author or co-author of the work. "Sole author" does, however, also apply to two or more authors who collaborate on a book and sign the contract. If you hire someone to write parts of the book for you, then that person must sign a release acknowledging you to be the sole author and waiving any claim against you in that regard.

Tied to this first warranty is usually some wording to the effect that you own the rights you're granting the publisher, that the work is free of liens and encumbrances, and that you have full power to execute the agreement. This means that you haven't assigned your ownership of the copyright to another party, that you haven't made a contract with another publisher to publish the book, that if your book was previously published, the previous publisher has terminated the contract and given you a formal reversion of rights, and that there isn't a legal judgment against you that might interfere with a publisher's freedom to publish and profit from your book.

**That the work is original with you and does not infringe statutory copyrights or common-law literary rights of others.** "Original" obviously refers to plagiarism. Lifting the work of another author is, needless to say, a mortal sin. But there are some gray areas, such as paraphrasing someone else's work, which may or may not get you into trouble. If you have thus paraphrased, it's a good idea to show your lawyer, or your publisher's lawyer, the material in question, so that steps may be taken to disguise or eliminate potentially actionable similarities.

Plagiarism is also covered by the second part of the above warranty, which refers to infringement of statutory copyrights or common-law literary rights, for plagiarism is as flagrant an infringement as can be found. But the infringement provisions also apply to improper use of copyrighted material, such as quoting a published book, article, song lyric, or other source without permission. This is a violation of *statutory* law, for copyrights are established by government legislation; but there is also a body of *common* law governing certain authorial rights, such as an author's proprietorship over material as soon as it is committed to paper. Thus, unauthorized use of an unpublished manuscript may be considered a violation of an author's common-law literary rights.

**That the work has never been published.** This is clear-cut enough, but there are some gray areas here, too, such as prior publication of part of the work in a magazine. Or the book may indeed have been published and gone out of print. In such cases the exception must be noted in the contract.

Frequently a phrase is attached to the above warranty to the effect that the work is not in the public domain. We generally think of the public domain as the repository for books whose copyrights have expired. Books published before the revised copyright act were given twenty-eight-year copyrights, renewable for another twenty-eight years, after which they fell into the public domain, meaning anyone could publish them without obligation to the author or the original publisher. (The present copyright law protects a work published after January 1, 1978, for fifty years past the death of the author.) There are other ways a work can fall into the public domain, however. An American author who first publishes his book in a foreign country must take out an interim copyright that protects it from being pirated in the United States until the author can properly sell it to a publisher here.

**That the work is not obscene or scandalous.** Over the last fifteen or twenty years, legal standards of morality have taken such a beating that it has become all but impossible to define obscenity or scandal. Legal action taken against books and authors has been restricted to local prosecutions, where the work violates community standards. But such actions are usually doomed to failure, either defeated by liberal elements within the community or overruled on appeal to higher jurisdictions.

For this reason, references to obscenity and scandal in the warranty clauses of publishing contracts seem to be disappearing, and even where they still appear, publishers have softened their resistance to striking them from the catalogue of authorly transgressions printed in their contracts. Nevertheless, if we take the position that anything we can knock out of a warranty clause will enable us to sleep easier, it's worth knocking obscenity and scandal out of yours, however remote the odds that a claim on those grounds will be made against you.

**That the work does not defame, libel, or violate the rights of privacy of other persons.** This provision usually applies to nonfiction books, but works of fiction, particularly the variety known as *roman à clef* (novels whose fictional characters and story lines are based on real ones), may also be subject to invasion of privacy, defamation, or libel proceedings.

Under a long tradition of common and statutory law, the privacy of individuals is afforded a reasonable amount of protection. The First Amendment does permit writers some freedom to expose the private lives of individuals, but the rule of thumb seems to be that the less well known the person, the more he is entitled to privacy. As one begins to achieve public prominence — by becoming, say, a movie or sports star, a politician, a criminal, a captain of industry or finance, a best-selling writer — one becomes more and more vulnerable to scrutiny of one's private life by the media. And the more famous you become, the more lenient the law is toward those who rake over the details of your personal affairs, the position being that if you didn't want the exposure, you shouldn't have chosen to become a celebrity.

Furthermore, the more famous you become, the more lenient the law is toward those who *inaccurately* rake over the details of your personal affairs — that is, defame or libel you. Although libel law is grounded in the attitude that a writer's best defense against libel and defamation suits is the truth, there is wide latitude in the interpretation of "truth." Everyone may know that Joe X is a mad-dog killer-rapist-robber-arsonist-burglar, but if he's never been convicted, you may very well lose a libel suit (to say nothing of your kneecaps) by calling him a criminal in print. Nevertheless, the more prominence one achieves, the greater the right of journalists, critics, and biographers to criticize one's character and behavior; and the law affords them wide First Amendment protection even when they write arrant nonsense, yea, even when they write scurrilous lies. The law usually draws the line at the point at which it is no longer a question of sloppy research or misguided zeal, but of genuine malice.

When writing about real people you must take the above factors into account. But in view of the dictum that anybody can sue anybody for anything, you have to realize that no amount of scrupulous research, no amount of felicitous phrasing, no amount of disguising and fudging of personalities and events, will prevent a determined plaintiff from going after you and/or your publisher. For example, though the law clearly states that a deceased person cannot be libeled, the families or descendants of deceased persons have been known to attempt to sue biographers or publishers they felt wronged their late lamented. Or, despite the rule of thumb that the truth is a writer's best defense against a libel suit, there is nothing to prevent a party who believes himself libeled from forcing a writer and his publisher to go to tremendous expense to support that truth. Even the author of a *roman à clef*, as a landmark case (*Bindrim* v. *Davis*) demonstrated, is not necessarily guaranteed victory in court just because certain names, places, dates, or events are obscured by a fictional screen.

These, then, are the representations you make to your publisher when you sign a contract. It should be clear how easily a litigious individual can take advantage of them, and how thoroughly your royalties may be tied up and actually dissipated by a publisher defending you, and itself, from the most specious and asinine of claims. Even more disquieting is the fact that the warranty and indemnity provisions survive the termination of your agreement, meaning that if, long after your book is out of print, someone sues your publisher for something you said in that book, your publisher may still hold you liable. Furthermore, your contract usually gives your publisher the right to extend the umbrella of your warranties and indemnification to other persons or firms. Suppose a person believing himself injured by your book not only sues your publisher but sues the publishers of the German, French, Italian, and Japanese editions to whom your publisher licensed translation rights. *Their* costs and damages, too, may be laid off on you.

Pretty grim, huh? It certainly is, and that's why, as you write or review your manuscript, you should use all the common sense you can muster, err on the side of caution, and, when in doubt, consult a lawyer. Where a book is potentially lawsuit-provoking, ask your publishers to get a reading by *their* lawyers, too. Publishers have a contractual right to require authors to change legally offensive material, and, if an author doesn't cooperate, to cancel the contract and get their money back from him. But sometimes a publisher doesn't know that a book is potentially lawsuit-provoking. In a recently settled case, an author included a girl friend's name in a novel, thinking she'd be flattered. She wasn't, and sued. The publisher in turn sued the author on the grounds that it isn't a publisher's responsibility to go over fiction manuscripts the way it goes over nonfiction ones — it's assumed that the names have been changed to protect the innocent. In my opinion, the publisher was right.

The indemnity provisions of a contract cover a publisher's procedures for recovering from the author the costs, losses, or damages arising out of the author's breach of his warranties. Taken together, the warranty and indemnity clauses menace every author's peace of mind like a pair of snarling guard dogs. Just how successful you can be in muzzling these beasts is a hard question to answer; some of the toughest negotiations I've ever conducted have involved attempts to modify those provisions. As I've said, authors are best advised to do everything in their power to make their manuscripts lawsuit-proof, rather than hurl themselves against the well-fortified legal departments of publishing companies. But for those who want to try, I'll offer some negotiating tips at the end of this chapter.

To review, a typical warranty clause stipulates that:

- You are the sole author of the work.
- The work is original with you and does not infringe statutory copyrights or common-law literary rights of others.
- The work has never been published and is not in the public domain.
- The work is not obscene or scandalous.
- The work does not defame, libel, or violate the rights of privacy of other persons.

Although some of these warranties are ambiguous, and it's easy to imagine claims arising out of something in a book that is not only *not* the author's fault but is clearly the *publisher's* fault, publishers are obdurate about placing the responsibility for any lawsuit upon the shoulders of the author. And, as they have access to the author's royalties, they are in a position to seize them to pay some or all of the expenses and/or losses engendered by a lawsuit. How this is done is described in the indemnification clause of your contract. By indemnifying your publishers, you assume all responsibility and liability and some or all of the expenses and damages they incur in defending themselves.

Here are some typical articles in an indemnification clause:

- The publisher has the right to defend itself against any claim, suit, or action, using counsel of its choosing.
- The publisher usually has the right to settle any such claim, suit, or action on such terms as it deems advisable. Some contracts say "with the author's consent," others don't.
- In the event a final judgment is entered against the publisher, the author shall be liable for, and shall pay the publisher the full amount of, the judgment, and reimburse the publisher for any and all expenses incurred in the action, including counsel fees. Some contracts specify that the author has to pay in full for the publisher's expenses incurred in fighting any claim or allegation, whether it results in a final judgment or not.
- In the event of a settlement, the author is liable for, and must pay the publisher for, some or all of the costs, including attorneys' fees and expenses.
- The publisher has the right to withhold and apply any royalties or other sums due the author under this or any other agreement as security for the author's obligations as described above.

Quite clearly, the indemnification provisions of a publication contract are slightly less fair than a rental agreement with a particularly venal landlord. Do you have to accept them, or is there leeway for negotiation?

The answer is, it depends. It depends on the publisher, the importance of the author, and the nature of the book. If you're a big-name astronomer writing a book about lunar craters, the chances are you'll be able to persuade your publisher to strike references to obscenity in your warranty clause. But if you're taking an intimate look at the sex lives of the current administration's cabinet ministers, then (assuming your publisher is actually willing to publish such a book) you can be quite sure your publisher isn't going to want to alter a jot of your warranty-indemnity clause. Anything you can remove from that clause is one less thing you have to worry about in this parlous life, so, meaningless though it may be, try to remove the obscenity reference in your contract for the book on lunar craters.

Some authors try to insert the phrase "To the best of my knowledge" at the beginning of their warranty clause, so that to the best of their knowledge the book doesn't infringe on anyone's copyright or invade anyone's privacy. Few publishers will buy it, however, because it so vitiates the stern intention of the warranty as to make it meaningless. "To the best of my knowledge the gun wasn't loaded, your honor." See what I mean?

The most important modification you can try to effect has to do with whether or not a claim, allegation, or action taken against your publisher is successful. As stated above, many contracts make the author liable for a publisher's costs in combating a mere *claim*, whether the claim is validated by a court judgment or not. This is patently unfair, particularly if you have exerted all reasonable care in making your book lawsuit-proof. Publishers attract lawsuits by mere virtue of their size and apparent wealth. Why should an author be the fall guy (or gal) for a publisher in a nuisance suit aimed strictly at forcing a settlement? If, therefore, you can work into your indemnity clause some wording to the effect that the author shall be liable for a publisher's costs and damages *only* if a claim against the publisher results in a final judgment entered against the publisher (after appeals), you'll definitely put your legal relationship with your publisher on a fairer basis.

Another sentence you may try to work in states that your indemnity doesn't apply to any material inserted in your book by the publisher. From time to time a publisher will add text, or in editing alter the meaning of the text, or insert illustrations that violate one warranty or another. Surely the author shouldn't be liable for such material over which he had no control.

Authors should have some say about who is selected to defend the publisher, what the legal fee is, and how the defense is conducted. Some wording indicating that the publisher will consult with the author on such matters would be helpful. The Authors Guild recommends wording that the author may, if he chooses, defend a suit against his publisher "with counsel of his own choosing, at his own expense; provided that if he does, Publisher may nonetheless participate in the defense with counsel of its choosing and at its own expense."

It may be possible for you to work into your indemnification clause something requiring the publisher to pay a percentage — ideally 100 percent and realistically 50 percent — of the cost of a settlement. Settlement of a suit doesn't acknowledge liability, so you shouldn't have to pay the publisher's share of a settlement when you haven't admitted liability and no judge or jury has found you liable. Of course, if an author doesn't consent to his publisher's decision to settle, and wants to carry the suit forward on his own, that's a different matter entirely, and all costs and losses then become rightfully the author's.

Although indemnification clauses traditionally give the publisher the right to hold an author's royalties against damages, costs, or settlements, you may be able to rule out the deduction of royalties from contracts other than the one that is the subject of the suit. You may be able to curtail the length of time the money is held, or put a ceiling on the amount set aside. You may be able to effectuate the holding of only a percentage of your royalties, so that some of them are passed through to you while the rest are put in escrow to pay for the lawsuit.

You may be able to write into your contract that when you turn your manuscript in, the publisher will secure a legal reading from its house counsel or an outside law firm, at the publisher's expense. By doing so, however, you put yourself into the position of binding yourself to any recommendations the publisher's lawyers make. If you don't go along with them, the publisher has the right to cancel the contract and demand its money back from you. If you cooperate with the attorneys and alter everything to their satisfaction, however, it seems logical that the publisher should then waive your liability. It'll never happen — but it does seem logical!

If you're really nervous about a lawsuit, there's always libel insurance. All publishers carry it, and the reason they are so adamant about refusing to modify their warranty and indemnification clause is that (so they claim) they are worried that their insurance company will not settle their claim if the wording of that clause has been altered. Libel insurance for individual authors is difficult to obtain and very expensive, but as a last line of defense it may be worth it. Viking Press and some other publishers made headlines when they offered to take out, and foot the bill for, libel insurance for their authors.

But, to be shamelessly repetitive, the first line of defense is care and caution, not only in reading and rereading your manuscript but in reading and rereading your contract. Your agent may have done his or her level best to negotiate good warranty and indemnity provisions — but maybe not. When the lawsuits start flying, they'll be aimed at *your* head and your publisher's, not your agent's, for agents are not signatories of publishing contracts and they aren't, therefore, liable for any disasters arising out of their sloppiness, inexperience, or negligence. Thus when push comes to shove, you're on your own. A lawsuit can push and shove you into bankruptcy. So for God's sake, be careful!

# 6 ✍

# Permissions

If the ratio of fiction to nonfiction submitted to my agency is any indication, I'm probably safe in assuming that readers of this book are primarily fiction writers. So when you sign a publishing contract, you may not dwell for very long on the clause requiring the author to deliver photographs, drawings, maps, charts, tables, indexes, and other illustrative material, suitable for reproduction, at his own expense, and to obtain permission, again at his own expense, for any copyrighted material by others that is used in his book. In the garden-variety novel such material isn't employed.

The odds are fairly high, though, that sooner or later you will find yourself having to deal with this contractual provision. You may, for instance, write a nonfiction book in which you quote other authors extensively; you may write a juvenile novel or some other book that lends itself to illustration; you may be asked to edit an anthology, or asked permission by someone else to quote from your book in his work; you may wish to use someone else's photographs or illustrations, or perhaps use some of your own; you may want to quote someone else's song lyric or poem, or borrow a few lines from an article, essay, short story, or other book.

Invariably the use of such material is going to cost somebody money. If you don't anticipate that fact and provide for it in your negotiations, that money will come out of your pocket. The amount can be substantial.

Consider illustrations. In most cases, author and publisher are in agreement at the outset as to whether the book is to be illustrated. But not always. After the author delivers the manuscript, his publisher may call him and say, "We think a couple of maps would help the reader visualize the battle scene in chapter six," or, "We think we could reach a larger audience if the book were illustrated with line drawings." If illustrations were not part of your original bargain, the responsibility and cost should be assumed by the publisher. Don't be surprised, however, if your publisher says to you, "We've got the world-famous artist Morty DaVinci interested in doing the illustrations, but he wants a royalty, and if we pay it to him we'll lose money, so could we prevail on you to reduce yours so we can make this a profitable proposition?" You will then have to decide whether your reduced royalty will be offset by the sales generated by this august artist's illustrations.

In cases where it's agreed at the outset that your publisher will furnish an artist for your book, that artist's royalty will be included in the royalty provisions of your contract. Authors' royalties for illustrated juvenile books, for instance, are generally lower than they are for nonillustrated books, because the publisher has to reserve some of the royalty for the illustrator. But if you can determine that your publisher is paying only a flat fee and no royalty to the artist, then your own royalty should be higher. Or if you are doing your own illustrations, then the full royalty should come to you, plus whatever additional advance your publisher had budgeted for an artist or photographer.

One of the commonest and most unfortunate scenarios develops when an author, after signing a contract calling for him to provide graphics, finds that he has underestimated the cost of an artist's or photographer's services, or the cost of materials or permissions. These costs can completely wipe out your profits, so you must research them thoroughly before striking a deal with a publisher. Suppose, for instance, you agreed to furnish twenty illustrations for your book, and negotiated a contract with your publisher calling for a $5000 advance for text and illustrations. You might then discover that the minimum charged by good illustrators for the kind of artwork you have in mind is $250 per picture. Thus you might come perilously close to breaking even or losing money — not even counting your agent's commission.

The answer, then, is to evaluate your costs before you submit your project or accept any offers. Work out terms with your photographer or artist, then build them into your negotiations with your publisher. If possible, make allowances for cost overrides, because in this, as in any other enterprise where subcontractors are involved, if something can go wrong it will.

The cost of illustrations and other copyrighted material does not necessarily have to come out of your advance and royalties. Because publishers reserve some of their production budget for the cost of illustrating books, it's not unreasonable for you to ask that in addition to your advance the publisher pay you a sum of money for graphics, a sum not to be recovered from royalties. This fee might simply be turned over to you for disbursement as you see fit (as is usually done with editors of anthologies), or it may be paid to you only upon presentation of invoices. Occasionally such invoices are paid directly to the artist by the publisher.

Sometimes you can get the publisher to share the cost of permissions fees paid for art, photos, quotations, or other copyrighted material, and you can even work things out so that the publisher advances your share of the permissions costs. Suppose the publisher agrees to pay you a $5000 advance for writing the text of an illustrated book, but wants you to provide illustrations, and acknowledges the fairness of contributing 50 percent of your payout for permissions. The contract would thus state, "Publisher shall pay 50 percent of any permissions fees for material copyrighted by others (to a limit of $ _____ total permissions fees). Publisher shall also advance Author's share of said permissions fees, but shall be entitled to deduct said share from royalties or other earnings payable to Author." And sometimes you can even get the publisher to help clear the permissions as well as pay for them.

Many of the warranties you make to your publisher about the text of your book apply to the illustrations, too: that the artist controls the rights to the material and has the right to license them; that the illustrations don't infringe the rights of others or violate anyone else's privacy; and so forth. You may be required by your publisher to provide releases or signed permissions or copies of your contracts with illustrators, in case claims against the publisher arise.

Usually the illustrations you furnish must be camera-ready, but occasionally, where maps, charts, graphs, and the like are provided by you in rough form, the publisher will agree to engage a professional artist to render finished illustrations or accurate mechanical drawings at the publisher's expense. But if you originally agreed to provide finished, camera-ready work, and the work you turn in is less than acceptable, the publisher may claim the right to redraft it and deduct the cost of doing so from the acceptance installment of your advance, or from future royalties.

Questions frequently arise about who owns the original art after the publisher is through with it. This matter should be settled at the very outset. Is the artist selling you (or your publisher) the painting or drawing or photograph, or only the right to reproduce it? Many commercial artists stipulate that they are to recover their originals when the publisher has finished production of the book, leaving them free to sell or otherwise dispose of them or even resell the reproduction rights to another publisher. Original art can be extremely valuable, so make sure everyone knows where he stands on this issue.

Indexing is another cost that lurks unseen in the fine-print thicket of a publishing contract, and you may not even realize you've been bitten by it until you get your first royalty statement and discover a deduction of several hundred dollars for the index prepared by a free-lance indexer. Publishers offer authors the option of doing their own indexes or allowing the publisher to farm the job out to such a specialist. Depending on your time, the complexity of the job, and your fondness for such work, which for high drama is every bit the equal of counting pennies, you may or may not want to undertake it. If you don't, it'll be assigned and your account will be debited.

Song lyrics, poetry lines, and prose quotations may have to be paid for, and, even if they don't, it's both wise and courteous to ask for permission, and to acknowledge the source and include copyright information in your book. The current copyright law is less than precise about fair use, and a survey I conducted of rights and permissions editors at several publishers revealed a great deal of uncertainty about how much one can quote without permission before one may be said to have infringed someone's rights. The rule of thumb, then, is Better Safe Than Sorry.

When you do request permission to quote, be certain what it is you're requesting permission *for*. Will the quotation appear only in a hardcover book? What happens, then, if that book is sold to a paperback reprinter? Will you have to pay again? Is your book to be published only, say, in the United States and Canada? Then what happens if a German publisher wants to translate the book? Do you have to pay again for that right?

If you anticipate subsidiary sales of your book, you can build provisions for them into the permissions requests you furnish to the copyright holders. There are many formulas. For instance, if your book is going to be published in the United States and Canada but there's a possibility it will sell foreign rights, then you might offer the copyright owner X dollars for the primary (United States and Canada) territory, and a fraction of X for every sale to a foreign publisher, or a fraction of the advance paid by each foreign publisher. In the case of anthologies, the fraction is determined by dividing the total number of words in the anthology by the number of words in each selection, and paying the copyright owners in that proportion for subsidiary income (less the anthologist's share, of course).

By anticipating costs for illustrations, quotations, and other copyrighted material, you will not only save yourself time and money but sleep as well, for there are few things as insomnia-producing as the realization that out of a $5000 advance paid to you by your publisher you've incurred $10,000 in expenses.

# The Option Clause

Among the most treacherous pitfalls in publishing contracts is the option clause. Essentially, the option clause defines the means by which a publisher may acquire an author's next book or subsequent books. The spirit of the clause is plain. The publisher who is willing to invest in your book should have the right to maintain an exclusive relationship with you for as long as that relationship is mutually profitable and satisfactory.

Few would say that this principle is unfair. But there are many unfairly framed option clauses, and many occasions when it is distinctly undesirable to have one at all. The misfortunes, some bordering on the nightmarish, that can befall the author who does not think his option clause through to its logical consequences can be illustrated in the following horror stories:

Joseph L sold his first novel to a publisher. He'd been marketing it for over a year, during which time he'd written a second. No sooner was the ink dry on his contract than he submitted the second novel to his publisher. "I like it," his editor said, "but the company wants to see how your first book does before committing itself to the second. Our contract says we don't have to begin considering your next manuscript until four months after publication of the present one." Joseph felt a sickening sensation in the pit of his stomach. "When will you be publishing the first one?" he asked. "Well," said the editor with a remorseful shrug, "our contract gives us up to two years."

Judy G, a science-fiction writer, was a little smarter than Joseph L and negotiated an option clause stating that negotiations on her next book could start as soon as her present one was accepted. So she submitted the new one. Unfortunately, her editor was fired and the firm launched a debate about whether it was feasible to continue its science-fiction program. The debate lasted six months, and Judy was powerless to get a decision on her book, because the contract did not specify a time limit for decisions. Nor could she offer the book elsewhere, because her present publisher's option was still in force.

Bob D was totally disgusted with his publisher for numerous reasons and had been approached by a house where he would be well treated and well published. So when his publisher offered him a $10,000 advance for his new book, Bob went to the other publisher and got an offer of $15,000, and informed the first house that he was leaving. "Uh-uh," his publisher said. "Our option clause gives us the right to retain your next book if we match the offer you get from another publisher. And we've decided to match the fifteen thousand dollars. Welcome back."

When and why does one modify the option clause? As a rule of thumb, prolific writers are going to experience more complications with their options than are their slower-producing colleagues. That's because it's not usually sound publishing, or in the author's best interests, to bring out more than one or two books a year by the same author. Thanks to a perversity in human nature, frequent exposure of popular authors often cheapens their value in the eyes of their readers, and so publishers try to restrict the flow of new works. But what if the author is capable of writing three or four books a year, or more? Or, in addition to those popular books, wants to write material that the publisher doesn't like, or doesn't publish, or doesn't publish well?

One answer is pseudonyms. Some writers maintain their exclusivity with one publisher by writing under one or more pen names in addition to their real one. All too often, however, that arrangement is impractical or undesirable, and the author must seek other markets for his excess output. In such cases, the phrasing of the option clause becomes critical. Many an author has been impaled on an option clause that required an incredibly long delay before the publisher was obligated to consider his next manuscript.

Therefore, when examining your option clause, you should ask yourself exactly what kind of books you write (or want to write) and how frequently you can turn them out. If there is any question of your loading your publisher up with more books than it can absorb, or books the publisher won't like or doesn't do well with, then you should narrowly define your future books. Thus, instead of

The Author grants the Publisher the right to publish his next book-length work . . .

you might stipulate

The Author grants the Publisher the right to publish his next book-length work of fiction written under his own name . . .

or

The Author grants the Publisher the right to publish his next book-length work of fiction featuring the hero Thor, written under the pseudonym Peter Pater.

As I say, some option clauses are structured so as to frustrate an author who produces a new book (or outline) before his last book has been published. Publishers would prefer not to negotiate for a new book until they know the sales results from the previous one. Thus they stipulate something like:

Negotiations on said option work shall not commence until four months after publication of the Work that is subject of this agreement.

Think about it. A publisher may be permitted by contract to take between twelve and thirty-six months to bring out your book (and some publishing contracts omit publication deadlines entirely!). To this add those four months called for in the option clause. You may have written four or five books or more while waiting for the red light of your option clause to turn green. So you must amend that clause to read:

Negotiations on said option work shall not commence until *thirty days* after *acceptance* of the Work that is subject of this agreement.

Another tricky item in some option clauses calls for negotiations on the author's next work to commence after "delivery to Publisher of a completed manuscript." Some authors do prefer to complete a manuscript before turning it in to their publishers. Many, however, cannot afford to write books without a down-payment, or need editorial guidance in the development of their books from outline to final draft. Therefore, it is important to insist that the option clause be keyed to delivery of a *detailed outline*, or perhaps a detailed outline and two or three chapters.

When negotiating your option clause, it is important that you limit the time your publisher takes to consider your material and make a deal with you. Otherwise, again, you may be hung up indefinitely. I try to ensure that negotiations commence within thirty days of delivery of the manuscript or outline. And furthermore, I stipulate that if agreement on terms has not been reached thirty days after commencement of negotiations, the author is then free to negotiate with another publisher.

Many option clauses state that if the author is unable to reach terms with his publisher and begins negotiating with another publisher, he may not make a deal with that other publisher on terms less favorable than the ones offered him by his present publisher. Thus if the author's present publisher offers him a $10,000 advance against a straight 10 percent royalty and he turns it down, then goes to another publisher and (all other terms being equal) accepts $7500 against an 8 percent royalty (because, say, the second publisher is more prestigious than the first), then he may be in violation of his option clause.

The phrase restricting an author from making a deal elsewhere on terms less favorable is designed to prevent authors (and their agents) from capriciously jumping from publisher to publisher — for, yes, authors are also capable of abusing their option clauses. But, to use a motto popular among agents, options are made to be broken. If your present publisher offers you $10,000 against a 10 percent royalty and promises to publish your book in two years, while your new publisher offers you $7500 against 8 percent but promises to publish your book in six months, who is to say which of the two publishers has offered you more favorable terms?

Some option clauses state that if your present publisher rejects your new manuscript or outline and you can't sell it to another publisher, then the publisher's option remains in effect, and you are obliged to show your publisher your next work after the one that didn't sell to anybody. This is another safeguard against authors breaching the spirit of their option clauses, for many an author, in order to sever relations with a publisher, has said, "Oh, well, I'll just submit any old piece of trash out of my trunk, and when it's rejected I'll be free to sell my work elsewhere."

Perhaps the most onerous condition attached by some publishers to their option clauses is one that permits the publisher who has failed to reach an agreement with you on your option work to match any offer you may secure from another publisher, and thereby acquire the property. Such a clause might be framed like this:

> If Author and Publisher cannot agree upon terms for said next work, Author shall be free to negotiate with other publishers, provided that the Publisher shall have the option to obtain the right to publish said next work by matching terms which the Author shall have obtained elsewhere.

Here again, theoretically, the publisher is seeking to prevent the author from taking the option clause too lightly by, say, selling the property to another publisher for $1.00 more than the original publisher offered. In practice, however, things can go very badly for the author whose property is hobbled by such a condition. Unless the book or author is extremely hot, many publishers are reluctant to consider a project which, after the editorial board has gone through the elaborate deliberations that characterize publishing decisions these days, they can lose even if they make an offer substantially better than the one made by the original publisher. So this stipulation should be eliminated from your option clause if possible. If your publishers make you their best offer, and it's not good enough for you, and someone else makes a bona fide higher one, your work should go to the highest bidder without your having to refer that offer back to your original publisher.

There are some other angles that must be carefully thought out when you consider the option clause of your contract. One calls for an option on your next *two* works, and is phrased in such a way that even if your first option work is rejected, your publisher still has an option on the work after that. This is unacceptable, for once you move to another publisher, that new publisher will demand a continuing option on your work and will be justifiably upset to learn that your old house can get you back on your next book.

Some option clauses grant the publisher the right to your next work "on the same terms and conditions" as those paid on the present work, or on the same terms and conditions "except that the amount of the advance and the royalties shall be subject to negotiation." This condition too must be eliminated from your option clause, for, as you become more sophisticated about contractual matters, you will, from book to book, want to improve or modify not merely the advance and royalties but other contractual terms as well. In fact, it could be argued that the above terminology provides the publisher with an infinite option on your work. Therefore, your option clause should grant the publisher the right to acquire your work merely "on terms and conditions to be negotiated."

Now, assembling all the elements we've discussed, we may be able to design an ideal option clause — that is, one that is fair and reasonable to both publisher and author. I've attempted this below. As I am an author's representative and don't want to be overly fair to publishers, however, I've bracketed language that, if eliminated, will give the author a better break:

> The Author grants the Publisher the right to publish Author's next book-length work *(here give detailed description of type of work and byline)* on terms and conditions to be negotiated. [Publisher shall not be required to consider said option work until Work which is the subject of this agreement has been accepted.] Publisher shall commence negotiations with Author on option work no later than thirty days after Author delivers to Publisher a detailed outline of said option work. If Author and Publisher cannot agree upon terms and conditions within thirty days after commencement of negotiations, Author shall then be free to sell said option work to another publisher [but only on terms and conditions no less favorable than those offered by Publisher. In the event Author has not, within one year subsequent to termination of negotiations with Publisher, sold said option work to an-

other publisher, then Publisher's option on Author's next work shall remain in effect].

Among the horror stories authors tell me, a great many revolve around poorly written option clauses. Don't become a victim of one. Read yours carefully and fight hard for wording that covers the contingencies I've discussed in this chapter.

# 8 ✍

# *Termination and Reversion of Rights*

O ne of the most remarkable changes I've witnessed in the three
decades that I've been in the publishing business is the shrinking of the life span of books. When I entered the field in the 1960s, a
book of any quality at all could be expected to be available to consumers for several years. Today, we project the age of many books
in weeks. If you put a recently published book and a recently
picked tomato side by side on a shelf, there's a good likelihood that
the book will rot first.

The change has triggered a pole-reversal in our attitude toward
books. Whereas the thinking of authors used to be, "How can I keep
this book in print as long as possible?" today it is, "How quickly can
I get the rights back?" This shift is reflected in pressure exerted by
agents on publishers to install language in their contracts enabling
authors to recapture their rights the moment their books are removed from the marketplace. Hardcover publishers, too, fight to
curtail the term of license they in turn grant to paperback reprinters. The idea is for the rights owner to take the dead or dormant
property away from a publisher that is not exploiting it and resell it
to one that will put it back into play.

Although one can get very nostalgic about the good old days
when writers wrote for posterity, it would be foolish not to play by
the rules that govern the modern-day game. If a publisher is committed to a book and works to keep it available to buyers, there are
usually contractual provisions for retaining the rights or extending
the term. But if a publisher can't or won't support that book, it
stands to reason that the property should be recovered and recy-
cled.

Most often a new author is so excited about selling his first book to a publisher that he seldom looks beyond publication date when he contemplates its fate. He cherishes the perfectly understandable fantasy that it will remain in print for years and years and will be available in bookstores for the foreseeable future. That it might go out of print one day, considering it isn't even *in* print yet, is a matter of very remote concern to him. And that the book might go out of print within a year or less after publication is so shocking to him that his first impulse is to dismiss the suggestion with a (nervous) laugh. Most books, however, do go out of print eventually, few being relegated to the status of deathless classics. Even more disturbing, an increasing number of them go out of print in a distressingly short time.

The reason for this lies in the ferocious competition among publishers for shelf space in bookstores. Thousands of books sweep into the stores every month, enjoy their moment in the sun, and are swept out again on the tide of next month's releases. None but the hardiest survive the deluge. Though you may receive royalty statements for years, the actual activity of your book can often be measured in days. The "sales" reported to you every six months may not really be sales at all, but merely released reserves — sales revenue held by your publisher until it is clear that the books shipped will not be returned for credit. Although your publisher lets a little of that money go every six months, it may actually have been collected during the first few months of your book's existence.

One day, then, you may wake up to the realization that your book has had it. After a suitable period of mourning, your thoughts will turn to recovering the rights to it, in the hope that one day you can sell them to another publisher. It is wise to try to recover them, for if you are normally ambitious, assiduous, and talented, you are going to become popular if not famous, and your earlier books will be in demand. They can be an asset of tremendous potential, and so you are well advised to look hard at the out-of-print and termination provisions of your contract when you are negotiating it, however difficult it is to conceive that you will need them.

Most publishers have some such provisions in their contracts as a matter of course. In some instances the termination clause calls for automatic termination of the contract and reversion of rights after a fixed period, generally three to seven years. From an author's viewpoint this is highly desirable, as it completely eliminates debate over the definition of "out of print," a debate that can hang you and your book up for years. Naturally, if something is highly desirable to an author, there must be something seriously wrong with it from a publisher's viewpoint, and that is the case here. The way a publisher sees it, even if a book is long out of print there is no telling when the author may be exalted to bestseller status with some future book, at which point those dormant early books take on tremendous value. The publisher will therefore try to bargain for an ambiguous out-of-print clause that will enable him to hold on to the rights for as long as possible. Something along these lines:

> The book shall be considered in print if it is on sale by Publisher or under license granted by Publisher as provided herein, or if any contract for its publication is outstanding.

In other words, your book will be considered in print as long as it is available to the consumer in any edition controlled by the publisher, including its own and those licensed to other publishers such as reprint houses, book clubs, and foreign publishers. But the above wording raises more questions than it answers. What does "on sale" mean? Copies in the bookstore? Copies in the warehouse? Three copies in the bookstores? Ten copies in the warehouse? And what about those licenses to other publishers? Does your publisher have adequate termination provisions in his contract with the book's Turkish publisher? And how do you ascertain the number of copies in stock, anyway? Visit your publisher's warehouse? Visit your *Turkish* publisher's warehouse? The nightmare potential here is very high.

One creative way to resolve the ambiguities of the phrase "out of print" would be to apply to American contracts a technique some agents use in their dealings with foreign publishers; namely, to specify that the book will be in print for as long as the publisher reports X copies sold every year or pays the author Y dollars annually. This becomes a sort of annual rent on your property, and gives your publisher the right to hold on to your book as long as he pays you a fair rent.

As this solution is imaginative and simple, I cherish little hope that it will be adopted by American publishers. Therefore you will probably have to focus your negotiating efforts on honing the language in your termination provisions until they have something of a cutting edge. Here are some suggestions.

**Pin down the publisher as to how soon you may ask for a reversion.** Ideally, your termination clause would read that you may ask for a reversion of rights "if the publisher fails to keep the work in print," meaning that you could literally ask for a reversion within months after publication. Obviously this is unacceptable to most publishers, so they generally try to stipulate a minimum time before you can terminate your contract, to wit: "If after seven years from date of publication the work is no longer in print . . ." Seven years is far too long. Try for one year, and, after your publisher's howl of pain has subsided to a whimper, hope to compromise at three.

**Force the publisher to decide about reprinting.** Your termination clause should state that within a relatively short period of time, say sixty days from the date you notify your publisher in writing of your desire to see the book back in print, the publisher must inform you of its decision whether or not to comply. If the publisher decides it doesn't want to reprint, or fails to decide within sixty days, termination should be automatic.

**Require the publisher to reprint within a certain time.** If the publisher does agree to reprint your book, it should do so within an acceptable period of time. Traditionally this is six months from the date the publisher notifies you of its intention to reprint, and I see little reason to prolong that period. If after that six-month period (and barring circumstances beyond the publisher's control) the publisher has failed to reprint the book, termination should be automatic.

✍

Bear in mind that the publisher doesn't necessarily have to reprint the book to maintain its control. It can also license certain rights to other publishers. Suppose your Doubleday book is out of print and you serve notice that Doubleday must either print a new edition or revert the rights. Rather than opt for either alternative, Doubleday could sell paperback rights to Ballantine or Avon or some other reprint house, and would be within its rights to do so. Of course you might be glad to see your book back in print; you might also die a little every time you contemplate Doubleday taking its 50 percent share of that paperback reprint money.

Is there any way you can prove that your book is out of print? One simple but time-honored way is to get a friend, or a friendly bookstore, to order a copy of your book from the publisher (it's best to keep your name off the order). If the book is out of print, a clerk at the publishing company or warehouse will send back a written notice to that effect. You now have written evidence straight from the horse's mouth. However, the publisher might state not that the book is out of print but that it is out of stock, which is not quite the same as out of print. "Out of stock" means your publisher has exhausted its inventory, a state of affairs that may be temporary, for the stock can be replenished either by returns from bookstores or by new printings. A book can therefore be out of stock without being out of print. But frequently, "out of stock" is a prelude to a book's going out of print, so it can help your case to ascertain from your publisher that the book is out of stock.

Sometimes the only thing that prevents a publisher from declaring a book out of print is a large stock. You can therefore expedite a declaration of out of print by offering to buy back the remaining inventory.

Having determined that your book is no longer active, you should then serve notice on your publisher that you want your rights back. Even if your contract provides for automatic termination, it's a good idea for you to get the company to send you a letter declaring the contract terminated and reverting the rights to you, so that you will have written evidence that you are free to enter into a contract with another publisher.

The clock starts ticking from the date your publisher receives your request, and though your publisher may respond promptly, it's more likely that you won't hear for many months, if at all. The reason is that most reversion requests are accorded extremely low priority by publishing houses. Each publisher has a procedure for evaluating such requests, but because many factors go into making a determination, as we have seen, the decisions are by no means cut-and-dried. I find that getting action from most publishers on reversion requests is much harder than getting money from them, so we're talking *hard,* my friends. One publisher told me that its committee for reviewing reversion requests meets only twice a year. A degree of tenacity, then, is called for in following up reversion requests.

It is not always desirable to go by the strict letter of the contract, however, and a certain amount of common sense, compassion, or both, comes into play. There have been occasions when, after I pounced on a publisher with a request for reversion, I've received a call pleading for more time to evaluate the situation. "Look, we know the author's first book is out of print and you have us dead to rights. But if you could extend our deadline until his second book comes out, we'll do a new printing of the first to tie in with publication of the new one. And incidentally, may we remind you that *we* haven't canceled *his* contract even though his new book is three months late. So, could you cut us a little slack?"

In such circumstances (and even if the new book *isn't* late), I sometimes counsel my author to grant the publisher that extension, for in the overall picture such a course may be of greater advantage than recapturing rights that are of little value at the present time.

Certain provisions of your original contract may survive its termination, depending on how the termination clause is worded. If the publisher has an option on your next book, it may remain in effect even when the first book goes out of print. Your warranties to the publisher that the book is not obscene, libelous, defamatory, and so forth generally remain in effect after the contract is terminated; any still-active sublicenses contracted by your publisher also continue until they are terminated.

It is legitimate, too, for the publisher to require you to pay back any debts to the firm you may have incurred. For instance, if you bought fifty copies of your book from Random House and charged them against your anticipated royalties, but the book did not earn those royalties, Random House has the right to ask you for a check for those copies before giving you a reversion of rights. Some publishers try to require you to pay back the unearned portion of your advance in order to get your reversion, but that is totally unacceptable. Another legitimate "debt" you may incur is an overpayment of royalties to you, owing to your publisher's underestimate of a reserve against returns. Considering the outrageous reserves publishers are creating these days, I would consider an overpayment to be one of the least likely events in the spectrum of publishing possibilities.

Your termination clause should give your publisher the right to sell off the remaining stock of copies after termination, though of course not to print more. Authors should request the right of first refusal to purchase from the publisher all overstock or remainder copies at the best prevailing market price. You may want to buy some to stock your library or to resell at a profit.

Finally, upon termination of the contract you should be entitled to a final accounting from your publisher. As we'll see, there may be an undisclosed reserve against returns on your publisher's ledgers, and now is the time for it to be disclosed and for any balance in your favor to be settled up.

Putting all these elements together, we arrive at a rather formidable clause, but one well worth pushing for, however hard it is for you to envision that one day your book's life — at least its first life — will come to an end. Here it is:

> If after _____ years from date of publication the work is no longer on sale in any edition published or licensed by Publisher, and the Author makes written demand to reprint it, the Publisher shall, within sixty days after receipt of such demand, notify the Author in writing if it intends to comply. Within six months of notifying the Author of its intention to comply, Publisher shall reprint the work unless prevented from doing so by circumstances beyond its control. If Publisher fails to notify Author within sixty days that it intends to comply, or within six months after such notification the Publisher declines or neglects to reprint the work, then this agreement shall terminate and all rights granted hereunder except those deriving from the option and warranty provisions shall revert to the Author, subject to licenses previously granted, provided the Author is not indebted to Publisher for any sum owing to it under this agreement, with the exception of an unearned advance. After such reversion, the Publisher shall continue to participate to the extent set forth in this agreement in monies received from the sale of remaining stock or from any license previously granted by it. Author shall have the right of first refusal to purchase from Publisher all overstock or remainder

copies at the best prevailing market price. Upon termination of this agreement, Publisher shall provide Author with a final accounting detailing copies printed, copies shipped, copies sold, copies returned, and reserve against returns, and shall release said reserve to Author. Upon termination, Author shall have the right for thirty days thereafter to purchase the plates, if any, at one-fourth of their cost (including typesetting).

Like most other ambiguous provisions in publishing contracts, termination clauses can be made satisfactory through negotiation. Most publishers have committees or other systems for reviewing the in-print status of their books, and will give up their rights if it can be reasonably argued that those rights are no longer valuable to them or have no potential value in the near future. But the chances for a decision in your favor will be increased if you frame your contractual language carefully to begin with. The rest is a matter of persistence.

Many authors believe that there is a strong market for the recyclying of previously published books, but it just isn't so. Publishers are seldom interested in acquiring reverted books unless (1) the author has become a big name, and (2) the reverted books can ride on the coattails of new books by that author. In fact, though publishers might offer next to nothing for your reverted title, that same "retread" (as the industry sometimes deplorably refers to it) could fetch a handsome price when coupled with your new, unpublished work.

I have often referred to a backlist of reverted titles as money in the bank. It may be of modest value now, but it will appreciate as your career grows, and when you achieve stardom you can withdraw those books from your "bank" and cash them in for tons of money — unless, upon rereading your early work, you decide that a quiet burial is the more prudent course.

# 9 ✍

# Royalty Statements

Until his untimely demise, I represented a man who claimed to be a member of the underworld. "Joey, the Mafia Hit Man," as he called himself, wrote several successful books about his life in crime, and, for Joey, getting a fair shake from a publisher was easier than it is for most authors. He'd simply call the royalty manager and say, "If my royalty check ain't ready by noon tomorrow, I'm gonna marry you to a plate-glass window."

On January 20, 1982, Joey was slain by a shotgun blast outside a motel in San Mateo, California. I don't think a publisher did it. That's not how they kill authors.

Publishers kill authors by creative bookkeeping. By depriving authors of vital information about book sales, delaying disbursements interminably, obscuring the meaning of figures, manipulating collection dates of subsidiary income, and withholding excessive royalties as a cushion against returns, many publishers figuratively strangle writers and literally poison their good will.

Publishers have always cheated authors. One can imagine Ovid complaining that his publisher sold Phoenician rights to his *Metamorphoses* and kept the money, or Cicero discovering that his publisher had scribed an extra hundred scrolls of his Philippics and was pocketing the unreported revenue. "Barabbas," said the poet Thomas Campbell, "was a publisher."

I believe that some publishers may still be cheating authors. Many writers may find this statement hard to believe, for the publishing people they deal with, their editors, are often honest, congenial men and women, seemingly without a deceitful bone in their bodies. In due time, however, the dual personalities of publishing companies reveal themselves to most authors, and they discover that the pleasant faces mask corporate identities that are often ruthlessly indifferent to authors and think nothing of hiding or keeping their money or holding it improperly, possibly illegally, to boost profits. But whether it comes as a surprise or not, there is little question that many authors are being taken for a ride totaling millions of dollars.

Most trade publishers today are part of larger corporate complexes that demand of them the same annual growth rate they expect from subsidiaries that produce chemicals, vacuum cleaners, and industrial machinery, so the pressures placed on publishing executives to show high profits are therefore intense. And since that kind of growth is extremely difficult to maintain year after year in an industry so dependent on artistic creativity and luck, many companies turn to the treasure trove of authors' royalties to help make up the difference. The reason they are able to do so with impunity is that authors and their agents, in their ignorance, naiveté, complacency, inexperience, or timidity, all too often fail to require full disclosure of the vital information necessary to assess the financial activity involving their books. And those who do demand disclosure usually run up against a stone wall — or, perhaps a better metaphor, enter a labyrinth from which even the most intrepid certified public accountants have emerged babbling incoherently.

Almost all publishing contracts have provisions for reporting royalties to authors. By tradition, publishers issue statements semiannually, but some send only annual statements after sales activity has diminished. Though most publishers find it convenient to schedule the six-month reporting periods to correspond to the first and last six months of the calendar year, this is by no means universally true, and some firms conform their reporting periods to their fiscal years. It doesn't make much difference as far as authors are concerned, as long as the six-month reports are regular and timely.

Publishing contracts provide for the reporting and payment of royalties within a certain time following the close of the royalty period — in September, say, for the period ending June 30, and in March for the period ending December 31. The minimum seems to be three months, but many houses call for settlement four months or longer after the close of each six-month reporting period. One house, for example, now issues reports in February for the six-month period ending September 30, and in August for the period ending March 31. That's a minimum of four months, but in practice it can be as much as five. Indeed, in practice the waiting period often turns out to be more than five months, and you may be sure that lateness is by no means restricted to that publisher.

Why this stretching-out of settlement dates? It certainly can't be attributed to computerization of accounting departments. Some thirty years ago, when I went into publishing, royalty statements made out *by hand* were rendered in timely fashion no more than ninety days after the end of reporting periods. Why then should it take longer for statements done by lightning-fast computers?

Some observers charitably ascribe the delays to defective computers and incompetent programming. Most agents I know take a far, far dimmer view, pointing out that the lengthening of settlement dates jibes with the growing role of big business, with its emphasis on double-digit growth, in the affairs of publishing companies. Remember that an author's money appreciates every month it is held by a publisher. Figuring that at the end of a reporting period even modest-sized houses may be holding hundreds of thousands or millions of dollars, it's easy to see why publishers would rather give that money to bankers than to authors. So even before you receive your royalty statement, you may be the victim of a publisher's fiscal manipulations.

And when you finally do get your statement — ah, that's when the fun really begins.

What information goes into a royalty statement? There is no statute, uniform code, or tradition defining the form and content of royalty statements. Every company has its own idea of what and how information should appear, or not appear, on its statements. Until quite recently, few publishers adequately reported all that authors need to know, and the first edition of this book was highly critical of the publishing industry for obscuring vital data in royalty statements. I'm happy to say that I've observed a trend toward furnishing more, and more meaningful, information. Authors have become better informed about royalty accounting practices (I like to think the original version of this book had something to do with that) and now commonly ask questions that it never even occurred to them to ask ten or fifteen years ago. Nevertheless, many publishers still fail to provide everything you need to know to understand how your book is doing.

There are eight categories of information that together form a complete picture of a book's financial activity. Without any single one of these, you will be as much in the dark as you are when you try to calculate a baseball batting average without knowing the number of at-bats or hits. The components are as follows:

- Number of copies printed
- Number of copies shipped or distributed
- Number of copies sold
- Type of royalty: regular, special discount, Canadian, foreign export, etc.
- Royalty rate, in terms of a percentage and/or a dollars-and-cents amount
- Number of copies returned
- Reserve against returns, usually expressed in dollars
- Details of subsidiary sales and contracts and of subsidiary income

Let's look at these elements in detail.

**Number of copies printed.** Since this figure is critical to your comprehension of how your book is doing, you would expect it to be included in all royalty statements. Yet, astonishingly, practically *no* publisher states it. All too often, the only way you get an inkling of the size of your printing is when you read in an announcement or ad for your book that it's gone into its third printing, or that there are 50,000 copies in print. And all too often, those figures are inflated — sometimes wildly — for the trade or the press.

If you don't know how many copies of your book your publisher printed, or how many times the publisher went back to press for additional printings, you don't even know what ballpark you're playing in when you try to evaluate your royalty statement. If your publisher prints (or claims to print) so few copies as to make it impossible for you to recover your advance even if all copies sell out, you're in one ballpark. But if it prints so many, or goes back to press so often, that it is impossible for you *not* to earn back your advance, you're in quite another.

To keep authors in the dark about the sales activity of their books, then, most publishers do not report the number of printings, and the number of copies printed, when they issue royalty statements.

**Number of copies shipped or distributed.** Authors often confuse the number of copies printed with the number of copies shipped or distributed, but these figures are not always identical. Of a 50,000-copy printing, a publisher may ship only, say, 40,000, leaving 10,000 behind in the warehouse to cover further demand. Ultimately, then, your royalties will be based on what happens to copies shipped, and you must know that number to determine sales; for, aside from being lost, destroyed, stolen, or given away, only two things can happen to shipped books: Either they are sold, or they are returned. And because this *is* the critical number, you may be sure that publishers guard it jealously from the inquiring eyes of authors and agents.

Incidentally, I have seldom seen, on a routine royalty statement, any figures relating to copies furnished gratis for review, sample, or publicity and promotion, or copies lost, damaged, and so forth.

**Number of copies sold.** In most businesses, "sold" means that a product has been permanently transferred from seller to purchaser in exchange for money. The publishing business, however, is one of the few in which "sold" does not mean "sold." That's because books are merchandised on a fully returnable basis — that is, the bookseller may return them to the publisher for a refund, usually in the form of credit toward the purchase of other books.

So although your royalty statement may show 5000 copies sold — that is, paid for by booksellers or distributors — some of those copies may well show up unsold (returned) on a future statement, after booksellers or distributors have shipped back the stock they couldn't dispose of. Until it is clear to publishers that the copies they've shipped will not be returned, they hold some or all of your royalties. This fund of royalties is called a reserve. We'll be examining reserves in detail presently.

**Type of royalty.** As discussed in chapter 4, your contract has a schedule of royalty payments corresponding to various conditions of your book's sale. There is the "regular" royalty, or the basic percentage of your book's list (retail) price. There may be a Canadian or foreign export royalty, perhaps one-third or one-half of the regular royalty, reflecting the higher cost of selling a book outside national borders. There may be a reduced royalty covering the sale of your book at a larger-than-normal discount. These various types of royalty are listed on your royalty statement.

**Royalty rate.** Expressed either as a percentage or as dollars and cents, or sometimes both ways, this is the figure on which your royalties are based.

To help you visualize a typical royalty statement, here is a line from a recent one:

| Cover price | Copies sold | Percent of list price | Rate | Type of royalty | Amount |
|---|---|---|---|---|---|
| $4.95 | 35,863 | 8% | $0.396 | Regular | $14,201.75 |

In the above example, the publisher sold 35,863 copies of a book priced at $4.95. On each copy sold, the publisher paid the author 8 percent of the list price, which amounts to a royalty of $0.396 per copy. The number of copies sold multiplied by $0.396 comes to a royalty of $14,201.75.

**Number of copies returned.** This is the number of books returned to your publisher for credit, and appears as a negative number on your statement, either in parentheses, in red, or with the abbreviation "Cr." beside it, meaning "credit" — credited, that is, to your publisher. The number of copies returned, and the amount of returns in dollars, are subtracted from copies sold, and royalties earned, respectively. So after returns are calculated, the statement might look like this:

| Cover price | Copies sold | Percent of list price | Rate | Type of royalty | Amount |
|---|---|---|---|---|---|
| $4.95 | 35,863 | 8% | $0.396 | Regular | $14,201.75 |
| | (10,301) | 8% | $0.396 | Regular | -4,079.20 |
| | | | | | $10,122.55 |

Thus 10,301 copies were returned, which, multiplied by the $0.396 per copy royalty, comes to $4,079.20 deducted from the $14,201.75 you earned through sales, giving you a net royalty of $10,122.55.

Incidentally, hardcover books are returned to publishers whole, but in the paperback business only the covers are returned, and the books themselves (minus the covers) are destroyed. At least they are supposed to be. There is a thriving illicit business in so-called stripped books, books that are sold without covers for high discounts instead of being pulped. A group of paperback publishers instituted a suit in February 1982 against a number of firms allegedly jobbing stripped books.

**Reserves against returns.** Because books are sold on a returnable basis, publishers are entitled by contract to withhold a "reasonable" percentage of an author's royalties as a reserve against returns. This percentage is based on a publisher's past experience with sales of books of a similar nature. If a publisher knows that 50 percent of the copies of every novel in his romance line come back no matter how good the book, he will hold back at least 50 percent of the money he collects from bookstores and distributors, knowing he will eventually have to refund that much. Publishers frequently hold far in excess of the figure their experience tells them is normal and reasonable, however. For instance, for the above line of romances, the publisher may reserve 60 or 75 percent or more.

What is worse, many publishers do not even tell authors in their royalty statements that they are holding a reserve: They just hold it, period. Though they have been paid for the books sold, they keep the money, which earns interest, of course, until they see whether the books are going to come back. Some of them do — but some of them don't. After a while, publishers are supposed to release some of the reserve money as it becomes clear that many of the books out there are never going to come back. But publishers release the money in the most parsimonious fashion. And though ultimately, at the end of a book's life, the publisher is supposed to render a final accounting, and those held royalties are supposed to be released, as often as not the publisher "forgets" to release them, or perhaps decides to hold them another decade or two in case the books are still being returned in the year 2010.

This practice becomes all the more shocking when we realize that unless a book is a bestseller or a backlist classic, its sales fate will be sealed within a year of publication. In fact, as we've seen, the fate of many paperback books is often sealed within *weeks* of publication, for the shelf life of many paperbacks is only as long as it takes for the next month's releases to bump the previous month's to the back of the store, or out of it entirely. Yet publishers carry high reserves against returns on their ledgers for years, and, when the book goes out of print, quietly pocket the unclaimed royalties. Having no hard industrywide figures to go by, but estimating from my own and other agents' experiences, I would say that this is what happens to the *majority* of paperback books. Some authors and agents consider it to be fraud. I keep racking my brain for a gentler word, but so far I haven't come up with one.

In defense of publishers, I should point out that many of them do find themselves flooded with unexpectedly high returns from time to time: of unsuccessful books, for instance, that the stores have ordered in abundance in anticipation of a bestseller. Or when a paperback edition of a hardcover bestseller is released, the bookstores often ship back large quantities of the hardcover, whose price is now undercut by the paperback edition. Also, many distributors and stores are stretching out their settlement dates with publishers so that publishers have to wait longer to be paid. And some stores with cash-flow problems return to publishers books that might sell eventually but not immediately, and use the credit to buy books that will sell at once. So publishers themselves are to some extent being victimized by market conditions.

Nevertheless, my experience and that of other agents I speak to frequently is that reserves held by publishers are usually substantially higher than what they need to cushion themselves against returns. That excess rightfully belongs to you, the author, but it is kept by publishers until you discover it and fight for it, and during that time it earns interest for the publishers. As one agent said to me recently, "I no longer call them 'books sold,' I call them 'books admitted to being sold.' "

**Details of subsidiary sales and income.** As we've seen, the author grants his publisher control over certain subsidiary rights, and the contract provides a schedule of percentages defining how much of the subsidiary income the publisher keeps and how much is supposed to be credited to the author's royalty account.

Your royalty statement is supposed to indicate the sources of your subsidiary income, the amount collected, and the percentage of that amount that has been applied to your account. In reality, this information is often cryptically sketchy, inaccurate, or both. When a publisher handles subsidiary rights to an author's book, it becomes in effect the author's agent, and like any good agent it has a responsibility to collect the author's money, report to him, and remit payments due in a timely and accurate fashion.

Such is not often the case. Whereas agents generally pay their clients immediately after collecting money, publishers are not required to settle up until royalty statements are due. Since royalty accounting periods are six months long, and settlement dates of royalties due come three to five months after the close of the accounting period, a publisher could theoretically hold reprint, bookclub, or other subsidiary income for as long as nine, ten, or eleven months, or even longer if the publisher drags his heels rendering royalty statements.

For every one of those months, the publisher earns interest on the author's money. If you think this situation makes it tempting for publishers to manipulate collection of reprint and subsidiary income so that it arrives just after the close of one accounting period and the start of the next, you're right. This manipulation suits the subsidiary publishers, too, for if they are allowed to hold a payment for a month or two, they too collect interest.

In addition to such gimmicks, publisher's reporting of money collected from subsidiary publishers is often scandalously vague and inaccurate. Where is the author who has not opened a royalty statement and read something like "Other income: $175.98," with no explanation whatsoever? Unless authors or agents insist, publishers seldom furnish them with copies of contracts made with subsidiary publishers, nor do they furnish detailed statements describing money collected from other sources. That $175.98 may be correct — but it may also be $5000 off. How do you know without a detailed breakdown?

Nor do publishers often provide you with copies of invoices indicating money deducted from your royalty check. Such debits as books purchased by authors, authors' alterations on galleys, indexing charges, and the like should be accompanied by copies of bills; but rarely is this done. And those authors fortunate enough to have negotiated advertising and promotional guarantees seldom get to see a detailed accounting of money presumably spent.

"Publishing is starting to resemble the movie business," a colleague of mine recently commented. He was referring to the so-called star system, where the big names command millions and everybody else starves on minimum-wage scales. But he overlooked the most significant resemblance; namely, the way both businesses do their bookkeeping. Thanks to "creative accounting" in the movie industry, profit participants such as stars, directors, and producers rarely see any of their profits after the studio has buried or manipulated the figures. And similarly, despite growing author scrutiny, publishers still manage to hide royalties from *their* profit participants, the authors, through the many subterfuges I've described here.

The power of the publishing industry is enormous, and I can safely say that most writers reading this book are not among the privileged few who can boast that their publishers need them more than they need their publishers. What can each of you do to get a fair, or at least fairer, shake in regard to royalty statements?

There are a number of negotiating tactics available to you. Let's look at some that may prove effective:

**Combating delays.** As I stated earlier, despite computerization of accounting functions publishers have been stretching out the period between the end of their royalty-reporting periods and the settlement dates when the money is paid. A waiting period that used to be no more than three months is now an average of four or five months, *not counting late rendering of statements*. During this time the publisher earns interest on held royalties. There is no way that authors, working individually, can make publishers shorten their contractual settlement dates — collectively, yes; individually, no. But if a publisher's contract states that the publisher will render statements and royalties by a certain date, then a penalty should be exacted if the publisher renders them late. Some agents have suggested that publishers should pay interest on late royalties, but publishers usually reply that in that case authors should pay interest on their advance down payments when they deliver manuscripts late.

One solution is to make the contract terminable if royalty statements are rendered, say, fifteen days past their due dates. After all, publishing contracts invest publishers with the right to cancel on an author if that author delivers a manuscript late; the author should be invested with a similar right.

One approach many agents use in the case of hardcover books is to require the publisher to pay the author's share of paperback-reprint or book-club monies at the time the publisher collects them, or perhaps no later than thirty days afterward. This is known as a "pass-through" clause, and it works like this. Suppose you sell your book to a hardcover publisher for a $10,000 advance and, lucky you, your publisher sells paperback rights for $100,000, of which half is paid to the publisher on signing. Assuming your publisher takes the usual 50 percent of paperback money, your share of the $50,000 paperback down payment would be $25,000. Deducting the $10,000 your publisher has advanced you (and leaving hardcover royalties out of our calculations, for simplicity's sake), you'd be owed $15,000. With a pass-through clause, rather than wait until royalty-statement time to pay you that $15,000, your publisher would pay it to you on receipt, or within thirty days after receipt. A pass-through clause can be a most effective weapon for an author fighting payout delays, which can run up to one year if the hardcover publisher plays his cards shrewdly.

And incidentally, though pass-through clauses are generally used only in hardcover contracts, they could conceivably be important in paperback ones as well. If, say, you sold your paperback publisher world rights, including British and foreign translation, and your publisher sold foreign rights for a lot of money, you might well benefit from a clause directing your publisher to pass the excess foreign revenue along to you at the time it's collected.

**Requiring disclosure of vital information.** The key weapon publishers use to rip off authors is the withholding of information from royalty statements. As I have stressed, authors are helpless to understand their statements, and are at the mercy of their publishers, without such essential data as the number of copies printed, the number shipped, and the amount of money reserved against returns.

The "reasonable" reserve against returns is probably the biggest evil the publishing business perpetrates on authors. In paperback publishing particularly, the reserve is rarely explicitly stipulated on royalty statements, and because publishers refuse to narrow their definition of "reasonable," they can and do get away with murder (if I use a great deal of warfare imagery in this book, it's no accident). Although many publishers publicly rail against the archaic system that allows books to be returned for full credit, I suspect that most paperback publishers are actually opposed to shifting to a nonreturnable basis. The reason for this is that the system that permits them to reserve royalties against returns is, quite simply, a gold mine.

If the iniquitous reserve system is to be conquered, publishers must be required to provide enough information in royalty statements to enable authors and agents to see how much is being held in reserve, so that there is at least a basis for negotiating the reserves down to a truly reasonable level, and getting that money released when the book's life is over. I therefore propose that the following provision be inserted in publishing contracts in the place where publishers stipulate that they shall render semiannual royalty statements:

> Said statements shall specify the dates of first and subsequent printings and the number of copies printed in the first and subsequent printings; the total number of copies shipped as of the end of the reporting period; the number of copies sold, with details of type of sale, royalty rate, and discounts; the number of copies returned; and the number of copies or amount of royalties held in reserve against returns. Publisher further agrees to require similarly detailed statements of account from reprint publishers, book clubs, or other licensees of subsidiary rights to the Work, and to furnish same to Author with Publisher's statement of account and copies of pertinent contracts with said licensees. Publisher further agrees to furnish Author with a final statement of account, incorporating the information required in this provision, upon the termination of this agreement, and to pay Author any monies due under the terms of this agreement at that time.

To get publishers to accept such a stipulation is far easier said than done, for it calls for disclosure of everything publishers don't want disclosed. I know of few publishers who have agreed to this clause. Some offer side agreements — informal letters — stating that they will provide the information if requested.

Some agents send a form to publishers at royalty-statement time that says, in effect, "I'm sorry, but your statement is inadequate. Please send us the following supplementary information." The form has a list of items such as copies printed, copies shipped, and so forth that the publisher is asked to provide on the form. The effectiveness of this approach depends on the persistence of the agent, but it is no substitute for a contractual provision requiring full disclosure.

**Auditing publishers' accounts.** Few audits of publishers' financial records have been conducted by authors or their agents or accountants. With certified public accountants charging $100 an hour or more for an audit that might take weeks for just one book, the procedure is beyond the means of the average author — the person who needs it most. And since results of the few audits that *are* undertaken are usually kept confidential, the discovery of improprieties is rarely of use to other authors and agents.

It is significant, however, that when an author merely *threatens* to audit a publisher's books, the publisher often, most curiously, discovers bookkeeping errors in the author's favor, or decides to release some reserve money. In effect, the publisher offers a settlement that, when weighed against the cost of an audit, is usually enough to make the author call off the dogs.

The average writer can be doubly screwed — once when done out of royalties, and once when trying to conduct a prohibitively expensive audit. Here again radical action is called for, but meanwhile, in anticipation that you may one day want to audit your publisher's ledgers, you should insist on an auditing clause when you negotiate your contract. Otherwise your publisher may not even let you in the door, even though in other creative fields auditing has been determined to be an implicit right whether it's in a contract or not. Here's an auditing clause I try to insert in my clients' contracts:

> The Publisher shall keep and maintain at its offices accurate and complete records and books of accounts pertaining to the Work and all transactions conducted therewith and the Author shall have the right during normal business hours to examine, or cause to be examined by an authorized certified public accountant, such records. If a discrepancy of 10 percent or more shall be

found to exist in favor of the Author, the Publisher shall defray all costs in conjunction with the foregoing examination of accounts, and pay the Author any sums due within thirty days of determination of said discrepancy.

✍

The task of correcting the abuses I've described in this chapter is formidable. Even big-name authors find it difficult to wrest concessions from publishers in the area of prompt and detailed disclosure, for publishers fear creating a precedent for other authors to exploit. Unfortunately, though big-name authors have tremendous leverage with publishers, they often shy away from provoking the goose that lays the golden eggs. And less-known authors, individually, have little clout.

That leaves collective action. This can be a large-caliber weapon. It is my deep conviction that only by means of forceful collective action will the deceptive practices we've discussed be curtailed in any meaningful way. The machinery for such action exists in the form of writers' and agents' organizations. A number of these have the potential to take hard-hitting measures. There is the Authors Guild and well-organized writers' groups such as Science Fiction Writers of America, Romance Writers of America, Western Writers of America, and Mystery Writers of America. There is an agents' organization, the Association of Authors' Representatives. But although these groups do speak out on many of the issues we've been discussing, little has been done by way of aggressive action. Science Fiction Writers of America showed what a determined group can do when it challenged Ace Books' accounting practices a number of years ago and collected some $250,000 in royalties due many of its members. Other groups, perhaps working together, could do the same thing and more.

Because most publishing companies, like most public companies, are afraid of embarrassing revelations, it may not be necessary to undertake collective audits or class-action lawsuits to unearth hidden royalties or force publishers to disclose basic royalty information. The mere *threat* of such action might well yield the same results for a fraction of the cost. Even if publishers' settlements fell short of what is truly owed, these victories would make it harder for publishers to cheat in the future, and focus badly needed light on their high jinks.

Perhaps legislation will ultimately be necessary to make publishers disclose the information authors should have. Just as Truth in Lending and Truth in Advertising statutes have been passed by federal, state, and city governments, Truth in Reporting should be required of publishers by law. Perhaps it's time authors and agents began talking to their legislators.

Meanwhile, the first concrete step is to educate yourself, your fellow writers, your editors, and your agents. I am always amazed, when I talk to editors, that so many of them are ignorant about their companies' bookkeeping methods. Few publishing companies provide copies of royalty statements to their own editors to keep them informed about the status of their books or enable them to deal with puzzled or irate authors. Many editors don't know how to interpret royalty statements, and many of them don't feel they should have to do so. I don't believe this state of affairs is entirely coincidental, for this kind of ignorance, coupled with confusion as to whom one *is* supposed to talk to about one's royalty statements, is another tactic in publishers' game plans for making it as hard as possible for authors to penetrate to the truth.

Less forgivable is the ignorance and indifference of some agents. Many of my colleagues are as deeply concerned about these matters as I am. Others, however, don't study royalty statements as carefully as they should, or take a You Can't Beat City Hall attitude, or figure What the hell, as long as we earned *something* this period, why bother to discover if there's more the publisher hasn't told us about? By keeping pressure on your agents and editors to understand and act, you at least give yourself a fighting chance to get honest accountings.

What seems to be lacking at present is the courage to confront the industry in any significant sort of showdown. That courage will have to be found if authors are to receive the fair measure due them for their lonely dedication to their craft.

A last word about royalty statements. As I've said, they vary greatly in format from one publishing house to another. The only thing that is fairly consistent among statements is their general lack of pertinent information. The harsh glare of publicity has, however,

**Publishing Company,** *New York, New York*

---------------------- ROYALTY STATEMENT ----------------------

|  | For 6 months ending | 9/30/94 |
|---|---|---|
|  | List price | 19.95 |

Author: c/o Richard Curtis Associates Inc.
      New York, NY
Title:

**Earnings/Sale of Books:**

| Regular Sales | 197 @ 10% | List | 1.995 | 393.02 |
|---|---|---|---|---|
|  | 1,931    8 |  | 1.596 | 3,081.88 |
| Canadian Sales | 28    12 ½ | Net | 149.63 | 14.96 |
| Foreign Sales |  |  |  |  |
| Other |  |  |  |  |

          Total Royalty/Sale of Books    $     3,489.86

**Income/Sale of Rights:**

Book Clubs
Translation
Reprint           Paperback Company      10,000.00
Excerpt
Other

          Total Subsidiary Income     10,000.00
          Total Earnings       $   13,489.86

**Less Deductions:**

Advances                          15,000.00
Books Purchased
Author's Alterations
Index
Other                 Type MS        344.00
Unearned Balance Previous Period

          Total Deductions     15,344.00
          **Due to Author**     $(   1,854.14)

( ) Represents Unearned Balance

compelled a few major houses to incorporate reserved royalties in their reports, and they deserve commendation.

Since I've shown you a sample contract form, though, I should also show you a sample royalty statement, so I'm including one. It's about average in what it tells you. This chapter has been about what you should look for in a royalty statement. How many of the eight categories of information I listed earlier can you find in this one?

# 10

# Ancillary Rights

When I was hired by a large literary agency upon graduating from college, I was assigned the job of developing its embryonic foreign-rights department. College education had prepared me miserably for the publishing industry: I didn't even know what foreign rights were. Luckily, my supervisor didn't know much more. When I asked him where I was supposed to begin, he said, "You can begin by figuring out how to open those goddamned blue aerograms without tearing them in half!"

To this day I haven't mastered that skill, but I've learned a lot about foreign and other subsidiary rights, and in this chapter we'll be discussing what they are, who should reserve them and when, how valuable they are, and whether your publisher should be entitled to share in the revenue they generate.

As we have seen, when you sign a book contract you grant your publisher the exclusive right to publish and distribute an English-language edition in the United States, its territories and possessions, the Philippine Islands, and Canada. Traditionally excluded from your publisher's exclusive territory are the United Kingdom and members of the British Commonwealth of Nations, the rights to which are reserved by you to be sold eventually to a British publisher. You also grant your publisher the *non*-exclusive right to distribute his edition in the open market, which, as you may recall, I defined earlier as the area outside the territories reserved strictly for your American and British publishers, an area where both publishers are free to sell their editions of the same book simultaneously and competitively. Included in these open-market rights is the right to license other versions and editions in English in those territories:

book club, reprint, anthology, second serial, selections, and abridgments. These are called the primary subsidiary rights.

There is another set of subsidiary rights known as secondary rights, which, to avoid confusion, I'll refer to here as ancillary rights. These, which you may reserve or convey to your publisher when you make your original deal with him, include first-serial rights (magazine or newspaper publication before book publication), British Commonwealth rights, foreign-translation rights, and performance rights (dramatic adaptation for motion pictures, television, stage, radio, or related media). There is also the category of merchandising rights, which may not seem to have great commercial potential to the average writer but which can prove to be surprisingly lucrative if you create a character that turns out to be the next Snoopy or Darth Vader.

When you or your agent negotiates a contract, a host of questions arise as the discussion turns to ancillary rights. Should you grant some or all of them to your publisher? If you do, will your publisher know what to do with them? If you don't, will *you* know what to do with them? If your publisher does handle some or all, what percentage of the proceeds is he entitled to?

Generally speaking, if you have a literary agent, he or she will try to reserve all of the ancillary rights and to grant your publisher no participation whatsoever in the revenue from those rights. Agents usually are able to sell those rights on their own or through subagents in Hollywood and foreign countries. It also makes good business sense for your agent to reserve those rights, for two important reasons. First, your agent will generally take a lower commission than your publisher. Publishers often get, or at least their contracts call for, between 25 percent and 50 percent of the take on ancillary rights, whereas the range for agents is 10 percent to 20 percent for the same services. Second, publishers generally apply the author's share of ancillary-rights proceeds to the unearned advance; that is, to that part of your original advance that has not been earned back in royalties. What this means in plain English is that you may never see any of your ancillary money, a realization that has come to many a writer with devastating impact.

Let's see how it works. Suppose you've been paid a $7500 advance for your novel, and you granted foreign-translation rights to your publisher, who is entitled to 25 percent of any money he generates from foreign sales. Suppose further that your book earns back in royalties only $5000 of the $7500 advance, meaning an un-earned advance of $2500. Now: Your publisher makes a deal with a German publisher for, say, $2000. After deducting his 25 percent share of that money, or $500, your publisher applies the remaining $1500 toward the unearned $2500 balance of your advance. This re-duces your unearned advance to $1000; but of the German money you see nary a pfennig.

Does this mean you should never, under any circumstances, sell ancillary rights to your publisher? Not at all. Some publishing com-panies have first-rate subsidiary-rights departments, and on certain types of books they may be able to outsell your agent, and certainly outsell most unagented writers. For instance, if I sell a business or technical book to a publisher specializing in such books, I may de-cide to grant that publisher foreign rights if I can hold his percent-age down and get the author's share passed through. My thinking is that such publishers are usually more conversant than I with for-eign publishers of the same specialized kind of material, see them more frequently on business trips or at conventions, and study their catalogues more intently. So, though I hate to see the publisher taking a cut of that money, I figure that 75 percent of something is better than 100 percent of nothing. Bear in mind, though, that if you have an agent, he or she is going to take a commission on your share of any foreign money collected from your publisher, thus further reducing your net income. Suppose your publisher sells Swedish rights to your book for a $1000 advance and takes a 25 per-cent cut, and your agent then takes a 10 percent commission on your $750 share, reducing it to $675. You have in effect paid a 32.5 percent commission on the sale. As the sale is gravy, you may not care. But you should at least be aware of the numbers.

Ancillary rights shouldn't be given to your publisher free if you can help it. If your publisher offers you a $5000 advance for your book and says he wants world rights (the basic United States and Canadian territory, plus the British Commonwealth, plus the open market, plus foreign-translation rights), your answer should be, "No, for those additional territories you should pay something extra."

If your publisher is willing to raise his advance sufficiently to make it profitable for you to sell him British Commonwealth rights, and foreign, first-serial, and even performing rights, you may be tempted to grant them to him — again (and always) on the condition that he pass your share of the money through to you when he collects it, rather than apply it toward your unearned advance. You will then have to decide whether the additional money he is offering is more than you and/or your agent could earn selling those same rights. In weighing such an offer you have to evaluate a number of factors:

*What kind of book is it?* If it's science fiction or mystery, for which there are active foreign markets, you can probably do better on your own or through an agent and save on commissions as well (even with an agent, the percentage deducted will be less than what the publisher would deduct). But if it's a book about the pleasures of Arkansas cemeteries, for which there is a somewhat less than frenzied market in France and Denmark, you'd probably be foolish *not* to take your publisher's extra $1000.

*How good is the publisher's sub-rights department?* Some sub-rights specialists at certain houses probably *could* sell that Arkansas cemetery book to a French or Danish publisher. Perhaps your editor, despite an obviously vested interest, could assess the sub-rights capabilities of his company for you, or maybe you know other writers who've had experience at the same house. Naturally, if you have an agent, he or she will be able to provide you with the most accurate assessment of all.

*How well can you or your agent sell the rights on your own?* If you and/or your agent feel you can bring in more than $1000 net to you on that same book, then you should spurn your publisher's offer. You have a better chance of earning that money even if you work through an agent, for if the agent takes the usual 20 percent foreign commission, he only has to sell $1250 worth of foreign rights for you to make your $1000, as opposed to more than $1300 if your publisher sells them and takes 25 percent, and almost $1500 if your publisher takes 25 percent and your agent takes 10 percent of your share.

✍

The same sort of thinking applies to any request your publisher makes for control of first-serial or performing rights. But because few publishers have the capacity to sell movie or television rights, under no circumstances would I sell such rights to a publisher, or grant that publisher any participation in them, unless the author were in a disadvantageous bargaining position — if, for instance, the idea for the book originated with the publisher, and the publisher was therefore able to dictate terms to the author.

If you do sell reserved rights to your publisher, try to set a time limit within which your publisher must sell those rights, after which they revert to you. For instance, your publisher would have one year from publication date of your book to make deals for foreign rights to it. If at the end of that term your publisher had sold only, say, British, French, and Spanish rights, he would then have to revert the unsold foreign rights (German, Italian, Danish, Japanese, and the like), or at least revert them after the publishers now considering the book had made their decision.

It's extremely difficult for authors to handle their own subsidiary rights unless they study the magazine, film and television, and foreign markets the way bettors study racing forms. It can be done, however. There are directories of movie producers, magazine publishers, foreign publishers, and Hollywood and overseas agents, and you can garner tips from fellow authors about who handles or buys their work. But whether you, your agent, or your publisher handles the rights, a certain degree of patience, understanding, and common sense will make the task easier.

For instance, as most foreign publishers are unaccustomed to multiple submissions, they expect to be granted an exclusive option on all but hot properties. This is a free option of a few months' duration, for it takes that long for the book (along with all the other submissions under consideration) to be read by readers for whom English is usually a second language. (And that's scarcely longer than it takes many American editors, for whom English is a *first* language, to read a routine submission!) Add to this the time it takes for your book merely to reach its destination — airmail postage has become so prohibitive that most books are sent by sea, and take four, six, eight weeks or longer to arrive — and you can understand why patience is a necessary trait for anyone dealing in foreign rights. Similar delays occur in other subsidiary areas as well, so you must keep your cool.

Understanding and common sense help, too. Many books, or categories of books, are simply unsalable to magazines, movies and television, or foreign markets, or at least have lower commercial potential than others. Try and sell a routine western to the movies these days, or a detective mystery. The market for these used to resemble a vacuum cleaner, but today it's all but dead, and you shouldn't chastise your agent for failing to make a deal on such books. Nor should your expectations of a prepublication magazine sale be too high. The major magazines take very little in the way of condensed, excerpted, or serialized novels; nonfiction books may not always be in line with the tastes of the magazines' readerships; and the lead time — the time between your submission and the on-sale date of the magazine — may be too short.

The same goes for the foreign market. Japan, for instance, is high on science fiction and thrillers, but not particularly high on westerns or historical romances. Territories such as Italy, Spain, and South America, which have a strong traditional Catholic orientation, still tend to shy away from books that have graphic sexual content. Many American medical, diet, and health self-help books fare poorly overseas because foreign medical techniques, drug and vitamin formulas, dietary practices, and measurement systems are different from American ones. Many themes on which American readers dote, such as the Civil War, are of scant interest to foreign publishers. Even the length of books can be a critical factor: Many foreign publishers, because of high printing costs, won't look at a book that is longer than a certain number of pages, whereas here we consider such books to be nice juicy reads. In foreign markets, as in the American, it is becoming unprofitable to publish so-called midlist books, and more and more the demand is for bestsellers, bestsellers, bestsellers. So when it comes to foreign rights, do your best and hope for the best, and don't be shattered if your books are not among those chosen few billed as "published in fifteen major languages."

# 11

# Cyberbooks and Hyperauthors

In the spring of 1992, when it was brought to my attention that a new provision had been introduced into the boilerplate of a Berkley Publishing Group contract, I felt like an astronomer who had just detected an unidentified object in the heavens. The provision referred to something called "display rights," and there was some intriguing language in it.

The provision granted to Berkley the right

> to display the Work in any manner designed to be read and to license the display of the Work in any manner designed to be read, in whole or in part, by any means, method, device or process sequentially or nonsequentially ("Display Rights"), including without limitation mechanical visual recordings or reproductions (together with accompanying sounds), and all other forms of copying or recording of the Author's words and/or illustrations in any manner designed to be read, which are not either granted to the Publisher elsewhere in this agreement or reserved to the Author.

I pondered the clause. The first thing that occurred to me was, what kind of "method, device, or process" might Berkley have been thinking of when it cooked up this language? The key is in those references to "mechanical visual recordings or reproductions." A book is a device, but it is not a mechanical device. If we get the drift of Berkley's contractual provision, then, it would seem to envision a book published not on paper but on the memory circuits of a computer disk, cassette, cartridge, or smart card, and projected on a monitor or video screen. As sitting in front of a desktop computer monitor is not the most practical or comfortable way to read books, the device would be small enough to hold in one's hands like a book, and it would be portable, the visual equivalent of a Walkman. A Bookman? A Readman?

Is that what had stirred Berkley to install, long before any practicable and commercial application of this technology had been developed, a contractual provision designed to exploit it?

As a matter of fact, it was. It happens that a number of Putnam Group executives (Berkley is part of Putnam) were invited to a demonstration of a small computer in whose memory the entire Bible had been stored on one smart card the size of a credit card. The device was clunky, the resolution poor, and the problem of legibility in daylight had not been solved. "I wouldn't snuggle up in bed with that thing," one executive joked. "I wouldn't take it to the beach, either," added another. But when the laughing was over, the people of Putnam-Berkley had glimpsed the future. And they were stunned. For they knew that, given the daily strides being made in computer technology, it would only be a matter of time before miniaturization brought us within striking distance of a popularly priced tactical-sized palmheld Readman and a strategic intercontinental marketing campaign. After all, where were Walkman, Watchman, and Gameboy a scant decade earlier? Today we scroll Deuteronomy. Tomorrow, would it be Danielle Steele?

Another interesting phrase in Berkley's display rights provision was, "together with accompanying sounds." Except for book-and-tape packages or those kiddie books that play jingly tunes when you open them, books are not normally accompanied by sounds. But the wherewithal for sound enhancement of text was certainly on hand, as any kid who owned a video game knew, and Berkley's inclusion of sound in its display rights clause opened the door to all kinds of multimedia applications such as dramatized novels and animated talking books that read themselves to children at bedtime.

But the most provocative word in Berkley's display rights provision was "nonsequentially." Short of peeking at the ending of a mystery novel, is there any other way to read a book but sequentially?

In point of fact, there is. We know it as interactive fiction, of the "Choose Your Own Adventure" type, the kind of books in which readers elect to follow any of a number of alternative story lines and endings. Not only are most children familiar with them, but they have learned to travel with ease along the various pathways furnished by the books' authors, flipping from beginning to ending to middle to alternative middle to alternative ending with no concern whatsoever for the nonsequentialness of it all. And of course, today's children are completely at home in the responsive environment of Dungeons and Dragons and interactive video and computer games.

The process by which we "read" interactive books and games is called "navigation," and "navigation" may well become the byword for the way humans deal with information in the coming epoch. The applications and implications are almost beyond belief. The more questions I asked, the more curious I became about this new world. Were genuine alternatives to printed books a realistic possibility, or was the whole issue academic? I decided to do some homework.

I was in for a shock. For what I discovered was that I had just touched the sharp edge of a technological revolution whose profundity had scarcely been measured, even in the imaginations of our most prescient science fiction writers. Starting with the original language of Berkley's display rights provision, I found myself carried off on a wild journey that took me to the future of books and of humankind's relationship with information.

But let's keep our feet on the ground a bit longer before taking off for the farther reaches of technological development. Confronted by these new concepts in a conventional publishing contract, what practical action should a literary agent take? What advice should I be giving my clients?

At first glance, display rights would seem to fall under the category of information storage and retrieval, a phrase that has been hanging around publishing contracts for a long time, like an innocuous-looking time bomb with an exceptionally long fuse.

Information storage and retrieval is an extension of the publication rights that authors traditionally accord to publishers. At this point in time, the device of choice for displaying works designed to be read sequentially is called a book.

Publishers in our century, however, have seen many dramatic developments in the technology for displaying the printed word, and have glimpsed even more dramatic ones on the horizon. In particular, after gazing upon the screens of computer monitors, they knew a revolution was coming.

No one knew precisely what form computerized reading technology was going to take, but publishers felt inspired by the crude versions they saw. They also felt threatened by the possibility of losing control over this exciting and potentially profitable variety of the print medium. They concluded they must protect their exclusive franchise. Many expressed these proprietary feelings by according themselves, in their contracts, control over all versions of the printed word "now in existence or hereafter devised."

Berkley's provision may be seen as merely defining in greater detail the language extending a publisher's control over any and all variations on the conventional book. Thus, if your publisher were to produce your book by means other than folded and bound sheets of paper, it would pay you a royalty just as it (sometimes) does on each copy of your conventional book that it sells. By the same token, if your publisher licenses display rights to an outside firm, the proceeds would be split in much the same way that publishers share reprint or book-club revenue with authors.

I became seriously concerned about the implications of Berkley's display rights clause, and downright alarmed when similar language began to appear in other publishers' contracts. In a very short time the author and agent communities had awakened to the wonders of the new technology. They had also awakened to the possibility that they might not reap much — if any — of the profit generated by exploiting it.

On what grounds might authors object to the publishers' interpretation? Well, display rights, or electronic rights as they are more commonly known, could be thought of as falling under the definition of performance rights. These embrace such dramatic adaptations of the printed word as motion pictures, television broadcasts, and audio and video recordings. After all, when you think about it, a multimedia adaptation of a work of fiction is called — a movie! Such adaptations are by no means the uncontested province of publishers. Quite the opposite, they are a source of hot contention between authors and publishers.

The degree to which publishers will fight over them often depends on their capacity to produce those adaptations themselves.

For instance, most publishers do not have the ability to produce theatrical or television motion pictures and are not allied with firms that do. And even those that are part of a larger communications or entertainment complex cannot guarantee that your book will be acquired for pictures by their affiliated production companies. Publishers usually relinquish control over those rights in book contract negotiations if the authors or their agents put up any kind of fight for them. The same is true for other types of adaptations, such as video- or audiocassette tapes. If, then, electronic rights could be demonstrated to fall into the same category, authors would have a precedent for reserving them.

At a speech I gave at a conference in November 1992, introducing publishing people to computerized information technology, I made a number of predictions about the ways it would radically alter the roles of authors and publishers and such institutions as the bookstore and the library. At the conclusion of my speech, I predicted there would be war between authors and publishers.

Shortly afterwards the war erupted. Authors and agents, rushing to their contracts, awakened to the fact that they had given away the electronic rights, having agreed to that innocuous phrase granting publishers information storage and retrieval rights in *any* technology — including ones uninvented at the time the contracts were signed.

By early 1995 the battle had been joined by movie and television people, the legal profession, and the consumer electronics industry. The Authors Guild, the National Writers Union, the American Society of Journalists and Authors, and the Association of Authors' Representatives among others drafted position papers supporting the contention that electronic versions of the printed word constituted a separate medium that should be controlled by authors. Many publishers countered by dealing themselves, in their contract boilerplate, every electronic version of the printed word, including the right to enhance text with still pictures, video, animation, dialogue, and music; to combine one author's text with other texts in other media; and to communicate text online to users on computer networks.

As of this writing, a compromise seems to be evolving. Authors are acknowledging the publisher's right to electronically reproduce text verbatim, as long as authors are fairly compensated. Publishers on the other hand are keeping their minds open to the authors' contention that audiovisual enhancements of someone's text constitute a separate medium, and control of it is subject to negotiation.

An important question was raised by author and agent groups while these issues were being hotly contested: Do trade book publishers actually have the capability to produce electronic and multimedia versions of our texts? Although some business and professional publishers had begun converting their texts to computer-readable format, in the early 1990s most trade houses were still wandering around in (what now seems) the primitive world of electric typewriters, carbon paper, rolodexes, and three-by-five-inch file cards. Authors had a legitimate gripe: Why should we give publishers electronic rights to our books when they don't know the difference between a byte and a bit?

The publishers realized it, too, and launched a forced march toward the twenty-first century that Stonewall Jackson would have been proud of. Within two or three years, just about every significant trade book publisher had started an electronic rights division or department, or hired multimedia experts, or begun digitizing their texts for conversion to computer-readable format, or acquired or joint-ventured with game firms or other companies in the consumer electronics field. By 1995 a new wave of electronic miracles in the form of online services swept over us, raising the promise of more wonders — and more headaches.

Today the terrain of the publishing industry is almost unrecognizable from what it was at the dawn of the Multimedia Age. What will it mean for authors?

✍

Even as these words are being printed on that obsolescent medium called paper, bound into an old-fashioned artifact known as a book, and made available to readers by means of an archaic, nonelectronic distribution system (trucks!), you may visit your local consumer electronics store and buy a laptop computer. It sports a keyboard and color display screen and "plays" CDs.

CD-ROM stands for Compact Disk, Read-Only Memory, and because the information on CD-ROM is loaded by laser in digital format, their capacity makes the previous generation of memory storage devices look positively primordial. One standard-size CD,

4.72 inches in diameter, holds more than 250,000 typed (single-spaced) pages. That's the equivalent of about 1500 conventional double-sided floppy disks, or twenty 30-megabyte hard disks. And disks of many times that capacity have already been developed.

The astounding storage capabilities of CD-ROMs have created the potential for electronic books, works comprised not just of text but of audiovisual media like movies and music. Science fiction author Ben Bova dubbed them "Cyberbooks" in his 1989 novel of the same name. Because CD-ROM technology is interactive, these works behave like extensions of our senses, and so it is not hyperbolic to refer to them as living books. What is more, electronic "authoring systems" empower writers to create, not just in text but in all multivisual media, fulfilling a prediction made by another science fiction author, Greg Bear, that one day writers would be turning out movies on "visual typewriters."

But the advent of these miracles raises a host of questions, issues, and problems that will soon be the subject of intense debate: Will electronic books be accepted as universally as their traditional counterparts are today? How will they be standardized? How will the technology interface with conventional publishing techniques? What copyright issues will have to be settled? What will be the writer's place in a world in which the prevailing literature is electronic and multimedia? And — most important of all as far as I'm concerned — just how is an agent supposed to make a living, anyway?

In order for electronic books to replace paper ones, a consumer revolution will have to take place. It must be deep and permanent, something on the scale of the introduction of television after World War II. Such a revolution was predicted for desktop computers: the dream was that there would be one for every schoolchild. As dramatically as the cost of computers has dropped over the past decade, however, they are still not affordable for many families and school systems. What makes us think that electronic books will enjoy a better fate?

The answer is that a variety of high-powered handheld electronic devices is already available for a fraction of the price of desktop computers, and when the industry finally sorts out its systems and standards and begins mass-producing electronic books, prices may be expected to drop even further.

Skeptics are also dubious that children will ever emotionally relate to handheld cyberbooks the way they do to the board or paperbound variety. Their argument is that electronic hardware simply does not produce the same tactile responses as books.

This viewpoint may be more sentimental than realistic, and those holding it have probably never spent four hours in a car with an eight-year-old from whom the only peep during the trip is the muffled chime of his Gameboy. (I knew the Revolution had arrived when, instead of "Are we there yet?" my son exclaimed, "Are we there *already?*") It may take only one or two generations to condition children to the new technology.

The electronic book of tomorrow will probably take two forms. The first is a completely autonomous handheld device that plays entire encyclopedias stored on CD-ROM. The same tremendous memory capacity will enable tomorrow's users to store a small personal library between the "covers" of their portable reading machines, and to enjoy such peripheral benefits as music, animation, or spoken text.

The second form is a centralized archive. However phenomenal the capacity of the current generation of handheld electronic books may be, and even allowing for enormous strides in memory storage techniques in the future, it's hard to imagine a handheld computer that could contain whole libraries, including such support media as films. In order to open the doors of global knowledge to scholars, scientists, researchers, and other serious students, access to a central library or network of "information warehouses" is vital.

The idea of a systematic collection and synthesis of all human knowledge in one electronic database beggars my own imagination, so I am grateful that some great science fiction writers have paved the way for me to try to describe such a world.

The easiest way to depict it is to extrapolate the most powerful systems existing today into one computer of nearly unlimited memory capacity and computing power, a computer whose database is all human knowledge and one that is capable of drawing instantly upon every known medium. Its uses would range from such simple traditional tasks as reading a novel to highly complex works of research spanning dozens of scholarly disciplines. It would be completely interactive, enabling the user to design his own learning program and alter or augment it with his own input. It would be, in short, the only book you would ever need.

The user would access Knowledge Central by means either of a desktop PC or a handheld Readman that contacted the archives via wireless systems similar to cellular telephones.

"Knowledge Central" evokes a disturbing image of a monolithic automated society not unlike that described in Arthur C. Clarke's *Childhood's End*. Thanks to the fractious and untidy nature of human beings, such a world is not an immediate likelihood. But we do have the start of one in the Internet, a linked web of information sources that is navigable by anyone with a computer. Technological advances make this super-database accessible to a larger and larger populace, and access is getting easier every day.

The possibility of a central databank, not just for scholarly research but for pleasure reading as well, raises a pretty disturbing question: How will publishers make a profit if there no longer are books?

The answer is there if we try to think in twenty-first-century terms instead of eighteenth. For, if we continue in the direction in which we are heading, the economics of publishing will shift from the manufacture and sale of books to the creation and sale of electronically transmitted information. Instead of paying for paper books with paper money, we will exchange electronic credits for the services of data packagers. Copyright owners will receive a royalty for each use of their property by a subscriber.

Tomorrow's publishers will assemble these packages out of new or existing media content. Their profit will derive from the value they add to the individual components. The price of the movie-and-novel package that consumers retrieve from Knowledge Central will reflect the publisher's cost of acquiring the electronic rights to the book and the film, of integrating the two media into a package, and of transmitting or broadcasting it to your computer. Because the package will be unique, the publisher will be able to copyright and make a profit on it through time-lease or outright sale to users.

Nicholas A. Veliotes, writing in *Publishers Weekly*, asked readers to "imagine a future in which one copy of a reference work, probably stored on CD-ROM diskettes, resides in a computer to which the whole world has dial-up access." He cited an experimental system being developed by University Microfilms International that offers an integrated information system to the library, business, and professional communities. "Workstation hardware utilizes system software called BART (Billing And Royalty Tracking) which records the volume, issue and page being accessed and copied, producing complete records for compensating the copyright owner."

Where does that leave writers? That depends on who captures control over these electronic display rights. If publishers do, then the revolution will leave writers pretty much where they are right now. The literature they produce will be converted into data packages instead of books, and their publishers will retain electronic display rights, paying authors a royalty per use or sharing with them the proceeds from the sublicensing of their work — the way, say, book-club rights are sublicensed today.

If, however, authors fight to retain those rights, as they fight for movie rights today, they stand to reap a fair share of this lucrative industry. That is why the introduction of display rights language into book contracts, the event that launched this exegesis into its far-ranging orbit, is of infinitely greater importance than the innocuously worded little clauses would seem to suggest.

But if writers, too, will project themselves into the next century, they'll realize that their role will undergo an incredible metamorphosis when the axons of their minds are grafted, in effect, to the electronic brains being created today. Just as writers of the 1980s embraced word processing to extend the range, speed, and power of their creativity, those of the 1990s and beyond will embrace the navigational potential of the CD-ROM: they will not be writers so much as multimedia synthesizers. Futurist Grant Fjermedal speculated that, "In time the role of the author might change from that of the linear story teller to that of the creator of a world in which the reader will be able to roam at will, while sitting tall in the saddle of the built-in knowledge navigator."

And what about us agents? Don't worry, my friends, there'll be plenty of work for us. In addition to our traditional role as negotiators, we will earn our keep by helping writers assemble and license rights to the electronic packages they synthesize and making sure that these works are accorded copyright protection and proper crediting of royalties.

In fact, our hands will be more than full with copyright problems.

The current law gives copyright owners the exclusive right to "reproduce the work in copies." But the mere display of a work, such as on a computer monitor, does not qualify as copying under that definition. Although a special section was added to the Copyright Act in 1980 to accommodate the "copying" of a work that takes place when a computer program is generated, that isn't enough to protect the author. As Brian Kahin, writing in *Optical Insights*, pointed out, if a computer program is defined in the Copyright Act as "a set of statements or instructions to be used directly or indirectly in a computer in order to bring about a certain result," retrieved data would appear to be excluded from that interpretation.

Are display rights worth fighting over? The answer should be clear. The dawn of a thrilling new age has broken over the horizon, and traditional ways and means of reading, writing, and publishing will be profoundly altered as computer screens replace printed pages. By installing pertinent language in its book contracts, the publishers have demonstrated that it's not too early to anticipate this brave new world. It is incumbent on writers to rise to the challenge.

# 12

# Movie and Television Deals

No matter how long one has been an agent, it's still hard not to get excited when movie people express interest in a client's book. For me, there is something about the static crackle of a call from the West Coast that immediately quickens the pulse and stirs the imagination. Every experienced agent knows the odds against an interested party optioning a property; against an option-holder exercising his right to purchase; against a purchaser going into production; against a produced movie being released; against a released movie becoming a hit. But despite innumerable disappointments, frustrations, and betrayals; despite poignant wisdom borne of dealings with countless hustlers, fools, well-meaning but penniless producers, *ill*-meaning but penniless producers, powerless studio executives, obstructionist lawyers, dime-store agents, and other time-and-energy-and-money-wasters — despite all of it, there is no drug licit or illicit that can quite match the kick one gets from picking up the phone and hearing, "This is _____ Productions; we were wondering if movie and television rights to _____ by _____ are available."

So who am I to spoil it for you by telling you that such calls are utterly routine, that movie people express interest in anything and everything by anybody and everybody, and that the chances of anything significant materializing out of such inquiries are a little lower than those of converting plastic into platinum?

But as converting plastic into platinum is precisely what Hollywood is all about, I will now proceed to indulge your fantasies and help you figure out what to do if Hollywood actually calls and makes you an offer. Then the only things you'll need to set yourself up as a Hollywood agent are the Mercedes, the gold rings, watch, and chains, and twenty-five years of experience.

But first a word about Hollywood. Although many agents, producers, and other movie-and-television-related companies do have offices in Hollywood, Hollywood is far less a geographical location than it is an all-embracing term for the movie and television businesses and the success fantasies these engender. Movie studios and television production facilities and business offices are located everywhere in the greater Los Angeles area: Universal City, Burbank, Culver City, Beverly Hills, Anaheim, and elsewhere. They are also, of course, located in New York City.

By the same token, "movie deal" is a gross oversimplification for one of the most complex of business interactions. Agents may glibly boast that they "got a call from a Hollywood producer and made a deal," but hidden behind such casual remarks are hours of telephone discussion, weeks of preparation and examination of documents, months of back-and-forth haggling, and, not least, years of experience. The basic "deal points" of a movie negotiation are not, however, beyond the grasp of the average author, so at the risk of oversimplification I'll try to explicate them so that you can deal with inquiries and offers, or discuss them with your agent, without feeling like a complete simp.

Three elements are critical to the assembling of a movie: financing, production, and distribution. Financing is needed to acquire the property to be adapted (we'll be restricting ourselves to adaptations, not original screenplays), to develop it into a screenplay, to engage the necessary talent and technical personnel, and to produce the film. But then the film must be distributed to the theaters.

In some cases, all three elements come under one roof, so to speak, in the form of a studio that finances, makes, and distributes the movie; more often, however, the three elements are disparate and must be woven together by the producer or owner of the property. This is an incredibly complicated task, and all but the most powerful producers must, to put it vulgarly, hustle their tails off to get everything and everyone signed up. Someone like Steven Spielberg may be able to do it with a few phone calls, but most producers (or self-styled producers) find themselves in the position of being unable to acquire a property because they don't have the money; or being unable to get the money because they don't own the property; or being unable to make the film because they don't have a distributor; or being unable to find a distributor because they haven't signed up a big movie star; or being unable to sign a star because . . . well, the problems are endless. Even experienced insiders consider it no small miracle that anyone ever gets all the elements to stand still long enough to allow a picture to be made.

I am telling you all this because it's not, in all likelihood, going to be Steven Spielberg buying your book, but rather one of the vast number of men and women who beg, borrow, hustle, bully, plead, coax, and seduce their way into a "position," a point from which some influence can be exerted over a cruelly tough, cynical, and tight-fisted industry. It is therefore critical for you to understand the nature of this particular beast, to know what is going on in his mind so that you neither overreact nor underreact. Perhaps the first thing you should do, then, is ascertain the producer's recent credits, if you don't know them.

I'd guess that the majority of book writers don't read the film trade papers or notice or remember the producer's credits when they go to the movies. If a producer's credits are impressive, if you know his work, if you for instance learn that he's under contract to make two or three movies for Warner Brothers or Paramount or Twentieth Century-Fox, you'll deal with him on a more respectful basis than you will with one who's made two half-hour documentaries for the Moroccan government and has a brother-in-law whose kid goes to school with Robert Redford's.

Unless you've written a blockbuster bestseller that attracts the biggest name producers backed by heavy studio financing, it's unlikely that the person or firm that approaches you will want to purchase film rights to your book outright. Far more likely, they'll want to take an option on it for a period of time, during which they will try to line up the other necessary elements: engage a good screenwriter, get movie stars or their agents interested, woo studio executives or other backers, coax a commitment out of a distributor, and so on. If they are successful, they will "exercise" their option and pay you the previously agreed-upon purchase price.

A producer's acquisition of an option (and I'm using "producer" loosely to signify any purchaser) gives him exclusive control over the film, television, and related performing rights for a term usually ranging from six months to a year or eighteen months, in exchange for a consideration that is applicable to a purchase price. That consideration — the option price — can range from one dollar to hundreds of thousands. A routine option is somewhere in the neighborhood of five thousand to ten thousand dollars for one year. The option may also be renewable for a further consideration, and the extension payment may or may not be deductible from the ultimate purchase price — that's negotiable.

If there were no more to it than negotiating the price and term of an option, your life would be a breeze. Unfortunately, movie deals don't work that way. Why? Because both you and the producer need to know exactly where you stand if and when the option is exercised. You can't just say, "Okay, I'll grant you a one-year option for ten thousand dollars," because the producer will then say, "Ten thousand dollars against what? How much do I pay you if I decide to exercise my option?" You then negotiate a purchase price. But there's more — much more.

"What happens if, after I make the movie, I want to make a sequel?" asks your producer. "How much will you want for that? What if I sell the movie to television, how much will you want for that? What if someone likes the characters so much he wants to make a television series out of them?"

There are scores of such questions that have to be settled *now*, not left to negotiation at a later date when one of you may be in a position to take unfair advantage of the other. You will have many questions of your own: What happens if the movie never gets made — do you get the rights back? If it's a hit, will you be entitled to a share of the profits? If your character is made into a merchandising success on the order of a Miss Piggy, do you get anything for that?

In short, there are so many questions to be settled that *you must negotiate the entire contract at the time you negotiate the option!*

If you've ever seen a movie contract, you'll appreciate the magnitude of the task of negotiating one: You can pull a muscle just lifting the thing, and the fine print could give eyestrain to a Talmudic scholar. The usual practice is for the parties to sign a "deal memo" — a brief summary of the money terms, warranties, screen credits, and other key provisions — just to nail the deal down. But this short agreement is subject to the signing of a subsequent formal agreement.

Because of the complexity, value, and treacherous subtlety of movie deals, you are extremely well advised to bring in an experienced literary agent or movie agent or entertainment lawyer the moment the issue of terms is raised. To do it yourself or try saving a commission or legal fee at this point is to be penny wise and pound foolish. Not a few movie people will insist that you engage a professional to help you, because they know that if they take advantage of you today, you may sue them tomorrow when you realize how badly you were taken.

There's no reason, however, why you shouldn't understand the highlights of the negotiation — the deal points — so that you can discuss them intelligently either with the would-be buyer or with your representative. Let's pitch in at once.

**What rights are you granting?** A better question might be, What rights *aren't* you granting? The producer's license of movie rights to your work embraces every form of dramatization (except live stage, and even that is tightly restricted) in every medium known or possible, including multimedia and electronic games, in every language in every country in the world. It embraces sequels and remakes, entitles the producer to use your characters in other film and television works, permits him to alter the characters, story line, title, and all other elements of your book, and allows him to make, or license others to make, merchandise derived from the people or places or plot you created. *And* the term of this license is no less than forever.

The operative word in the above discussion of movie rights is *dramatization*. With one exception, all literary and publication rights are reserved by you or your publisher, the exception being your producer's right to publish up to 7500 (sometimes 10,000) words from your book for the purpose of promoting the film. Your reserved literary rights include readings of your book, as long as those readings aren't dramatized. This means you have to keep the "he saids" and "she saids" in when you do readings on radio, television, or before a live audience. Novelizations may or may not be included in the producer's license. Nonfiction books acquired by movie companies have occasionally been transmuted into novelizations of screenplays, but if it's a novel you've written, you obviously won't be granting your producer the right to create novelizations. (A memorable exception was a novel entitled *Red Alert*, which was made into a film so totally different from the novel that the producer engaged the author, Peter George, to novelize the screenplay, and the novelization was published under a pen name, by a different publisher from the one who'd published *Red Alert*! The name of the film? *Dr. Strangelove*.)

As for granting rights till the end of time, there is a small escape clause that exists in, or can be worked into, some movie contracts, providing you with a procedure for recovering your rights if the movie isn't made within a given period of time, say seven years. This is called a "turnaround" provision, and it gives you the right of first refusal to buy back the rights at the expiration of the specified period by repaying the producer everything he's expended (such as the cost of acquiring the rights from you, the cost of hiring a screenwriter, legal expenses, and so on and so forth), plus interest thereon. As it's unlikely you'll have that kind of money yourself, turnarounds are usually financed by some other person or company that wants to make your movie; in effect, the new producer pays you the money you need to pay the old producer his turnaround price.

Movie contracts give producers the right to exhibit the film on television, either before or after it is exhibited in movie theaters. Television-movie contracts give television producers the right to exhibit the film in movie theaters either before or after it is exhibited on television. Whether or not you are to receive extra money for such exploitation, and how much, is a matter to be negotiated.

Now: Just what are the rights worth? We'll break the answer into two parts: theatrical motion pictures and television motion pictures.

The price paid for theatrical movie rights ranges from a few thousand dollars to many hundreds of thousands, and occasionally runs over a million dollars. If you've written a blockbuster bestseller and you're negotiating with, to use a Hollywood expression, a heavy hitter, you're not unreasonable to expect a six-figure purchase price.

Most of the time, however, negotiations will be more modest. Heavy hitter or not, the interested party will want to spend as little money as possible, and will use a variety of techniques, arguments, and ruses. A big-name producer may use someone of more modest credentials to front for him, the way big real-estate developers use nobodies to acquire property cheaply, without alerting the world to their intentions. Or your prospective producer may plead poverty, reciting such a tale of abject hardship that you will be tearfully moved to bestow your movie rights upon him for the mere privilege of breathing the same air as he. Then there are the producers who assure you that the film they want to make will be a low-budget job, no stars, no expensive sets or locations, no union crews — virtually little more than an 8-millimeter home movie shot in the ol' back yard.

Some of these stories may turn out to be true. Movie lore is replete with tales of stars falling in love with the screenplay of some low-budget adaptation of an obscure novel, causing the budget, and the profits, of the film to soar into the stratosphere. Or a film for which the producers had modest expectations may become, to their shock, an Oscar nominee or a cult favorite. When such things happen, the author who sold his book for a song and a sob story howls with outrage, and not infrequently sues, as happened with the smash film *One Flew Over the Cuckoo's Nest*. But it may well be that the people who bought your book cheaply because they only envisioned a low-budget film and a marginal profit are just as surprised as you when millions of moviegoers begin lining up around corners in subfreezing temperatures.

Just as often, probably more often, the stories producers hand you are phony, and they know just what they're doing when they finesse you out of rights to a book they see as the next *Jaws* for $25,000 outright. Movie people are as tricky as any merchants in the world, the spiritual descendants of the sharps who bilked naive prospectors out of their stakes in the Gold Rush boom towns of an earlier California. Isn't there some way you can discern their motives and ascertain the true value they place on the rights to your book?

Well, engaging a knowledgeable agent or attorney will certainly help. But there is also a way of structuring the purchase price so that it's impossible for you to get burned too badly. And that is to *key the purchase price to the eventual budget of the film.*

When a producer begins developing a property for motion-picture production, he consults with his accountants, backers, and technical and business advisers, and out of their dialogue emerges a budget for the film. The budget is an educated estimate of the costs of acquiring the property and putting it in screenplay form (these are called "story costs"); engaging actors and actresses, directors, technical crews, special-effects teams, consultants, and others; building sets and arranging locations; paying overhead and interest costs; and paying for all the other fixed and contingent expenses, including the producer's own compensation. This budget is the hard, cold financial framework into which the movie must be fitted, and although we often read about budget overruns, sometimes horrendous ones, the budget is at least an attempt at a reliable declaration of cost.

If, then, you know that a movie of your book is budgeted at $1 million, it shouldn't take much calculation for you to realize that your asking price of $250,000 for book rights is way too high. Conversely, if the budget is to be $10 million, surely there must be enough loose change jingling around in the producer's pockets to enable him to spare you $200,000 or $300,000 for your book. A tried and true rule of thumb is that story costs should be about 5 percent of the budget. But don't forget that story costs include the cost of the screenplay.

But how do you know, when you are negotiating movie rights, what the budget is going to be? The answer is, you don't, nor do you have to. For if you can stipulate that the purchase price is to be a fixed percentage, say 5 percent, of the final budget, then you'll be fairly compensated whether the producer makes his movie on a shoestring or produces a no-expense-spared, cast-of-thousands major screen epic, starring the world's four most bankable stars (Hollywoodese for talent so important that its commitment to a movie project instantly opens a financier's bank vaults), supported by the next ten ranking stars in cameo roles.

Because neither you nor the producer knows what the budget will be when you begin negotiating, you'll work out a minimum and a maximum purchase price, or a "floor" and a "ceiling." You'll say, "All right, no matter how low the budget for your film is, I want a minimum of fifty thousand dollars for my book." Your producer will undoubtedly reply, "Fine, but no matter how high the budget of my film goes, I don't want to pay you more than one hundred fifty thousand dollars"; or "I want to exclude star salaries, say any over three million dollars, from the budget calculations." His wanting to put an upper limit on the purchase price, and to leave inflated star salaries out of the budget figures, is not necessarily unfair, because the higher his story costs, the harder it will be for him to sell the movie to financiers, distributors, studio executives, and others in control of the green light. Or he may want to spend some of his story money on a first-class screenwriter, for some screenwriters are bankable stars in their own right, and may well enable the producer to secure financing and other commitments by merely agreeing to do the script.

So now you know where you stand, and you have the outline of a deal: let's say a $5000 option for one year, applicable toward a $50,000 purchase price, which itself is applicable toward a sum equivalent to 5 percent of the final budget, up to a limit of $150,000. That $50,000 purchase price (less the $5000 option payment) is payable by or before the expiration date of the option. The balance, if any, should be payable to you no later than the day the producer begins principal photography of your movie. If the producer begins principal photography *before* the expiration of his one-year option, he must immediately pay you both your minimum purchase price ($50,000 less the $5000 option payment) and whatever extra, if anything, you have coming to you based on 5 percent of the budget.

Since the $50,000 purchase price in this example is equal to 5 percent of a $1 million budget, you'll be owed 5 percent of anything over a million-dollar budget. If the budget goes higher than $3 million, however, you'll be entitled to nothing further, because 5 percent of $3 million is $150,000, and you agreed that $150,000 was the maximum you could collect under this agreement.

**What other money can you make from the movie?** In addition to the basic purchase price, there may be escalator clauses, profit participation, and other contingency payments. As we've seen in our discussion of book deals, escalators raise the purchase price if certain things come to pass. Escalators have their place in movie deals, too. If, for instance, your book goes on the bestseller list for a period of time and/or reaches a certain high position on that list, you might collect a bonus from the producer, because headlines like "Forty Weeks on the Bestseller List!" or "America's Number 1

Bestseller!" are of inestimable promotional value to the producers of film adaptations of books.

There may be additional payments for television exhibition of the movie, or for adaptation of the movie or its characters into a weekly television series.

There are generally additional payments, ranging from one-third to one-half of the original purchase price, for remakes of, or sequels to, your film. A remake is a new adaptation of the original book or screenplay; a sequel extends the original characters and story, or introduces new characters and plot elements to the original adaptation.

And then there are profits. Ah, movie profits! You may search the world's legends in vain for a myth as enchanting as that of movie profits.

Yet we all set our snares for it in the form of extensively negotiated and elaborately worded profit definitions in movie contracts, for the lure of movie profits is so enduringly seductive that even the most jaded agents, who have yet to see a penny of those profits, would recoil in horror at the thought of not working such definitions into a deal.

The problem with movie profits is that they're so hard to define and so easy to conceal. A typical profit definition in a movie contract takes up pages of fine print, the bottom line of which is usually that the producer, studio, or distributor may write off everything that moves, or doesn't move, as part of the cost of making and marketing a movie. Therefore, the true profits a film makes are skimmed by these parties by means of inflated accountings of costs. "Producer's transportation" may well be the fellow's new Rolls-Royce Silver Spirit, and its cost comes right off the top as one of the expenses of making the film. "Overhead" charges may cover equipment that was paid for twenty years ago. This is why producers ride around in Rolls-Royce Silver Spirits with their names on the license plates, while authors drive creaky '75 Buick Skylarks whose mundane numerical license plates are held on with picture wire.

This may also explain why many producers are so obliging about profit clauses when they negotiate deals with authors. It's no skin off their backs to grant something they know will probably never come to pass. And yet — who knows? If the movie is a big enough success and the profits too stupendous to disguise behind accounting subterfuges, if your profit definition is sufficiently narrow and your agent and accountants utterly determined, you may well glimpse a profit.

So let's talk about profits.

For profit participants, which may include author, screenwriter, producer, director, actors and actresses, and others, the profit is a slice of a slice of pie. The pie itself is the gross box-office receipts, but, save a handful of stars of the greatest magnitude, nobody's profits are determined on the basis of the gross.

Rather, they are taken out of that part of the pie that's left after the theater owners have taken their cuts of the box-office take; after the distributor has deducted its distribution fee (approximately 35 percent); after the "negative" cost (the actual cost of making the movie) plus something like a 25 percent studio-overhead surcharge has been deducted; after interest on investment has been deducted; after the cost of prints and advertising has been deducted; after other distribution expenses, such as shipping costs and trailers and duties and taxes, have been deducted; after preferential profit deferments have been deducted — need I go on? Even if profit participants actually get a shot at realizing a piece of the action, studio accountants sometimes manage to apply profits from a successful movie to make up for losses from a flop — a gimmick called cross-collateralization, which book authors may recognize as joint accounting in movie-studio clothing. In short, if you have a choice between fighting city hall and trying to penetrate the profit calculations of a movie-studio accounting department, for God's sake go fight city hall!

But if you want even a snowball's chance in hell of realizing profits from your film, your profit definition should call for a percentage of 100 percent of the profits (5 percent of 100 percent is average). That means you're getting a slice of the same pie that the other profit participants (except preferential ones) are sharing. In other words, if you understand nothing else about calculating profits, you can at least request that the definition of *your* profits be identical to the definition of the profits to be earned by the guy who's buying the movie rights from you. Here's the way it might be worded:

If the Picture shall be produced based substantially upon the Work, the Owner [that's you] shall receive an amount equal to five percent (5%) of one hundred percent (100%) of the net profits derived from the Picture. "Net profits" shall be defined, and computed in the agreement between Purchaser and the financier-distributor of the Picture in regard to the financing and distribution of the Picture; provided that the definition of net profits with respect to Owner shall not include any deductions for "cross-collateralization" or "abandonment" of other projects and that Purchaser agrees to use Purchaser's best efforts to cause said definition not to include any deductions based upon "overbudget penalties" (as such terms are customarily used and understood in the motion-picture industry).

**What are your legal responsibilities and liabilities when you sell your book to the movies?** The warranties you make when you sell performing rights to your book are often spelled out in greater detail than those in your publishing contracts, but in substance they're pretty much the same: that you are indeed the sole owner of the rights you're conveying to the producer; that the work is original and doesn't violate any copyright or common-law right of any other party; that it isn't libelous or defamatory and doesn't invade anyone else's privacy; that the rights aren't encumbered by liens, claims, or pending litigation; and so forth. And your indemnification of the producers is the same as that which you give the publishers of your book: You hold them harmless (blameless) against any liability, cost, or expense arising out of your breach of those warranties.

One important difference, however, is that a movie producer has the right to alter your original material, add dialogue, create new characters, rearrange your story, and even alter the meaning of your message or change the ending of your book, without your approval or consultation. Authors seldom retain control over their stories once they sell them to the movies. So this raises the question, What if you're sued for something the producer (or screenwriter or director or actor) added to, removed from, or changed in your book?

That's a good question indeed, so you should add to the warranty and indemnification provisions language specifying that you are not liable for claims arising from such alterations.

**What about screen credits?** Every movie or television show acknowledges its contributors, naming the author and title of the book adapted (unless the work is based on an original screenplay or teleplay). The phrasing of your credit, the size of the type, and the amount of space accorded it depend on several factors. If a picture entitled *Portrait of a Lady* is based substantially upon the novel by Henry James, the credit might read, "Based on the novel by Henry James." If the title of the picture is different from that of the book, the credit would read, "Based on the novel *Portrait of a Lady* by Henry James."

Usually the author's credit appears by itself ("on a separate card") on the screen, in the same size and type as the credit accorded the screenwriter. But there are all sorts of variations, and exactly what the producer may or may not do as far as credits go (including credits in advertisements for the picture) is dictated by elaborate standards developed over the years by the Writers Guild of America (WGA) for its screenwriter members. If you want to do movie and TV scripts, you'll eventually have to, and want to, join the Guild, but even if you are not a member, you can try to stipulate in your movie agreement that certain definitions, such as screen credit, will be in accordance with the WGA Basic Agreement. (It is my fond, but I suspect vain, dream that one day, agents will be accorded credit in movies; to wit, "Deal negotiated by the John Doe Agency." Until that happy day, agents will have to be content to see their names in extremely fine print at the bottom of other people's contracts.)

**May you write the screenplay of your own book?** May you — or *can* you? Have you ever written a screenplay? Had one produced? Are you a member of the Writers Guild of America? Unless you have credentials, or unless your producer is an impoverished unknown who doesn't know whom else to turn to for a screenplay, it's unlikely that the purchaser of your book will ask you, or accede to your request, to write the screenplay. There's simply too much at stake for him to assign the job to someone who doesn't have the experience, skill, or track record of a professional screenwriter.

As we're in Hollywood, where all dreams come true, however, we can suppose for a moment that the producer says, "All right, the job is yours." What do you ask for?

The best-paid screenwriters receive hundreds of thousands of dollars for their scripts and not infrequently a piece of the profits.

Beginners, like beginners in all fields, get peanuts. The Writers Guild of America does, however, prescribe a scale of minimum scripting fees, and if, when your producer asks you what you want for your screenplay, you say, "Oh, Guild minimum will be fine," you won't do too badly. The Guild's scales cover the many stages, or "steps," of screenplay scripting, from treatment (outline) through drafting to final draft. The Guild minimum for a low-budget screenplay is, as of this writing, around $38,000, including treatment. At each step the writer may drop out or be removed from the project if certain conditions aren't fulfilled, and there are payment and screen-credit schedules for such contingencies as bringing in co-writers.

**What, if any, are the differences between television deals and regular movie deals?** Television-movie deals roughly follow the same basic option-against-purchase-price configurations as theatrical movie deals, but with several important differences. The most notable difference is that almost invariably, the people interested in buying a book must get the project approved by one of the major networks or cable companies *before* closing any deal.

As currently constituted, the world of American television is made up of four kingdoms — the ABC, CBS, NBC, and Fox networks — plus numerous petty baronies: independent local stations, smaller networks, and affiliates of the larger networks who have some discretion over what they accept from the parent network. I say "as currently constituted" because the explosive advent of cable television may well upset this long-stable system within a few years, destroying the networks' domination over the processes by which books get adapted for television. But for now, anyone who wants to make a television movie has to go to the networks initially for approval.

When a network gives the green light, it commits to the producer a sum of money known as the licensing fee. That fee follows a fairly rigid per-hour formula, which in turn is based on how much the network stands to make by selling to sponsors the time slot in which your movie will be shown.

Once your producer has a commitment from the network, he can then commit his own financing to the project. He may anticipate other sources of revenue from the exploitation of your television movie. For instance, after two showings on television (the première exhibition and one rerun) the network's license for the movie expires, and your producer may then syndicate the film to non-network stations, to cable networks, to foreign television companies, or to American or foreign theatrical companies for exhibition in theaters.

Without the primary commitment from a network, however, your producer will seldom be able to line up these secondary commitments or to raise the money necessary to make the film. Oh, the production company may have money of its own — it may be a Warner Brothers or Twentieth Century-Fox or MGM or Viacom — but under the rigid network system a firm would have to be very confident or very crazy to make a television movie on speculation. By the same token, a firm would have to be very confident or very crazy to buy television rights to your book not knowing whether the networks will feel it's right for TV.

Obviously there's a paradox here. The producer can't take your book to a network for approval unless he controls the rights through option or purchase; but neither can he option or purchase the rights from you unless he has network approval! And, just as obviously, there must be ways of short-circuiting this system, for television movies get bought and made all the time. How is it done?

Sometimes a producer shows the property to a network on the sly; sometimes he'll ask for your or your agent's permission to show it to a network without paying you an option; sometimes the network itself falls in love with a book and arranges for a favored producer to acquire it. There are countless ways to skin this particular cat. But again, from your viewpoint the important thing is that without network approval, your book will be dead as a doornail as far as television is concerned.

The other significant point about television is that the up-front money is generally much smaller, because the producer's budget is restricted by the rigid limits of the licensing fees he collects from the network. Profits are rarely as fabulous as they are from theatrical films; the producer's profits come from the difference between the cost of making the movie and the network's licensing fee, plus the proceeds from syndication, theatrical exhibition, and, occasionally, some other forms of exploitation, such as merchandising.

Therefore, television-movie deals are usually expressed as so many dollars for each hour the film appears on television in its first exhibition. You might make a deal for $50,000 for a movie of the week that has a minimum duration of two hours, plus an additional $25,000 per hour if the film is longer than two hours.

A miniseries is really just a long movie spread over several evenings within a relatively short period of time, but the principle of paying the author a given number of dollars per hour is still the same.

Contingency payments should be built into television deals, and here is where the profit potential can approach that of theatrical films if your TV movie is a hit. If the producer changes his mind and, instead of showing the movie first on television, shows it first in American motion-picture theaters, he should pay you a bonus — as much as 100 percent of the original purchase price — to compensate you for the additional revenue anticipated from such exhibition. Or if, *after* your movie has first been shown on television, the producer exhibits it in motion-picture theaters, he should pay you a bonus — as much as 50 percent of the original purchase price for exhibition in American theaters, and another 50 percent for exhibition in foreign theaters.

Television contracts also usually have payment schedules calling for additional payments to the author for a certain number of syndicated reruns and for adaptation of his movie into a regular series (such as *Seinfeld*) as opposed to a miniseries (such as the classic example, *Roots*). A typically structured clause providing for adaptation of a theatrical or television motion picture to series format looks like this:

If Purchaser shall produce a television series based substantially upon the Picture, then Purchaser agrees to pay to Owner [that's you] or cause Owner to be paid, and Owner agrees to accept as full and complete consideration therefor, the following: (i) One Thousand Dollars ($1000) for each half-hour episode produced; (ii) One Thousand Two Hundred and Fifty Dollars ($1250) for each episode produced in excess of one-half hour but not in excess of one hour; (iii) One Thousand Five Hundred Dollars ($1500) for each episode produced in excess of one hour; and (iv) an amount equal to twenty percent (20%) of the foregoing per-episode payments for each of the first five (5) "reruns" of any such episode, which payment shall be deemed full and complete consideration with respect to all subsequent reruns of such episode. All such payments shall be made within ninety (90) days of the applicable broadcast of each such episode.

In other words, in addition to, say, the $50,000 you got for your two-hour television movie, if that movie is then adapted into a regular series of half-hour programs, you'll get an extra $1000 when each episode is shown on TV the first time. Then you'll get $200 (20 percent) for each time the episode is rerun, up to five reruns. After that, you get nothing further.

And now, the $64,000 question: *How can I get my book into the hands of the producers?* The answer is, don't worry; by the time your book is published, the odds are very high that it's already been in the hands of the producers. Let me explain why.

Movie and television producers, studios, and networks are in a perpetual frenzy hunting for good adaptable properties. The competition is so keen that the company that waits until books are actually published will discover that the properties it's interested in have been sold months before. That's not always because the author or agent *showed* them earlier; often, perhaps most of the time, it's because the buyers, well, *captured* them earlier. The major studios, networks, and production companies have story departments and scouts in New York whose purpose is to keep in touch with publishers and agents, learn as early as possible what books are in the works, and get hold of outlines, manuscripts, galley proofs, or advance copies of those that sound important. The techniques they use would do honor to the CIA.

Despite intensive precautions ofttimes tantamount to the protection given classified state secrets, a manuscript, once it leaves an author's or agent's hands, may be subject to unauthorized replication by people interested in, or people in the service of people interested in, an early look. The interested parties aren't necessarily movie and television firms, but may also be magazines, paperback reprinters, and foreign publishers. Obviously, not every property is hungrily coveted, but these interested parties are constantly canvassing for someone who might be able to lay hands on a manuscript copy of anything potentially "hot." That might include clerks, secretaries, and even editors of publishing firms; book-club personnel; and the folks down at the photocopy shop.

This process is called sneaking, and, like sin, it seems to be something everybody does and nobody admits to. It's commonly known that money changes hands for certain sneaked manuscripts, and movie executives frequently refer to a shadow world of publishing-industry people who are on the unofficial "payrolls" of the studios. Yet I have never met a single soul who confesses to having paid or received such bribes.

Bribes aren't always the currency, however; favors are also exchanged. A magazine editor may trade a copy of the manuscript of a forthcoming blockbuster to a studio scout in exchange for the promise of an exclusive interview with one of the studio's stars; a copy of a manuscript being auctioned off by a hardcover house may be sneaked by a paperback editor to a movie company in exchange for an early look at the screenplay of a big film that has novelization possibilities.

Also, some publishing companies are subsidiaries of entertainment complexes that include movie and television companies, so it is not surprising that copies of manuscripts purchased by the book divisions of such conglomerates somehow find their way to the movie and television divisions.

As publishing is a gentleman's profession, no one in the business thinks of the Sneak as nasty or underhanded — at least, not until it's his own ox that's gored. Sneaking manuscripts is considered one of those things one must do to maintain an edge over, or even parity with, the competition. And of course, I myself have never done it.

What, never?

Well — hardly ever.

Everything I've said notwithstanding, not all properties get sneaked, or "covered," by movie people, and though many such properties are simply grossly unsuitable for adaptation, others may have hidden potential that requires a producer, director, agent, actor, or actress who is on the same wavelength as the author. Many a successful film has been made from a neglected book that finally found its way into the hands of somebody who "saw" the film the way Michelangelo "saw" David in the grain of a block of marble. A determined, enthusiastic producer, agent, director, actor, or actress may well be able to persuade others, such as studio executives, by making them see the film the same way, despite the fact that those same executives gave the property a "pass" — rejected it — earlier.

If you or your agent believes your book falls into this category, then you should select the movie people you think might share your vision, and submit your book to them. The odds are high against success, but at least it's better than sitting on your Barca-Lounger cursing your fate. Make a list of the producers, directors, actors, and actresses who have made films that you think reflect the sort of sensitivity that would respond well to your book. Then find out who their agents are. There are directories of members of the various movie guilds, such as the Screen Actors Guild, which list the agents of the persons you're interested in submitting to. Then send your book and a pitch letter, and pray.

There are also Hollywood agents who might agree to "shop" your book to movie and television people if you can kindle their enthusiasm with a strong pitch. Their names are known to your agent, or you can ask your author colleagues or your editors for recommendations.

Don't hold your breath waiting for Mary Tyler Moore, Robert De Niro, Steven Spielberg, or George Lucas to call. But then, who knows? This is Hollywood, remember? Listen! Your phone is ringing! Don't just stand there, pick it up! Who is it? It's . . . *who?*

# 13

# Miscellaneous Provisions

In addition to the fundamental contractual provisions we've covered, there are a number that don't fall into any easily defined category. That doesn't necessarily make them less important — just less classifiable. Bear in mind that either party can write anything into a contract it wishes if the other party is agreeable, or ignorant, or careless. One major hardcover publisher's contract calls for a medical examination of the author. Obviously, it's for insurance purposes and is designed to ensure that authors will not try to get out of their contracts by the sneaky tactic of dropping dead. Another contract extends the publisher's exclusive territory to the moon and the rest of the universe, so that when America colonizes the solar system and beyond, no English publisher will dare infringe on the American publisher's private turf. Authors can throw in some ringers, too. One stipulated that his publisher could use any kind of advertising for his book except cigarette ads, for the author hated smokers and would not allow his books to promote their nasty habit.

Not all of these miscellaneous provisions are laughing matters. In fact, some can have serious and costly consequences for authors if not modified. I've selected some of the most common problem areas.

**Copyright.** The responsibility for copyrighting the work is almost always that of the publisher. Usually there is a blank in the copyright clause of the contract for the name of the party whose work is to be copyrighted. Under normal circumstances, that's the author. If it's a work-for-hire contract, where the publisher is the creator of the literary property and farms the writing out to an author or authors, the work will be copyrighted in the name of the publisher. In other cases, particularly magazine publication, the publisher may take out a copyright in its own name and then assign it to the author upon request.

The copyright clause of your contract compels your publisher to print a notice of copyright in each copy of the published work, in accordance with the United States Copyright Law and the Universal Copyright Convention — that's the © symbol followed by the year of copyright and the name of the copyright owner. Author and publisher agree to compel licensees of the rights (reprinters, foreign publishers, and the like) to do the same in their editions. In the event of an infringement, it's the publisher who brings the action, at his own expense. The proceeds from a successful lawsuit are generally divided with the author 50–50 after the publisher has recovered his expenses.

As copyright law is vast and complex, it is impossible to explore its subtleties here, and any questions you have, beyond the very fundamental, should be taken up with your agent or attorney. But for practical purposes, as I said earlier, you need only know that under normal circumstances your work is protected when you produce it, when you sell it, and when you publish it.

And — oh yes — there's one other vital thing you must remember: It's "copyrighted," not "copywritten."

**Competing publication.** Many agreements prohibit authors from publishing books that compete with the one under contract. Obviously, you can't publish the same book with more than one publisher at the same time, but just how far you can go in publishing variations of your book at competing houses is not so easily sorted out. This applies particularly to nonfiction, where an author may expound a theory or program in one book, then elaborate on it in subsequent volumes published elsewhere. If your publisher has success with your *Thirty-Day Acorn Squash Diet*, and then you bring out a *Forty-Five-Day Acorn Squash Diet* with a competitive publisher, you can scarcely expect the first publisher not to squawk. Specialists such as dietitians, pharmacists, doctors, psychologists, and scientists do tend to repeat themselves from book to book by the very nature of their basic approach to their subjects. If you are in this category and are concerned that your book contract will seriously restrict you from elaborating your fundamental viewpoint from one book to the next, then you'd better try to rework the wording of the pertinent clause of your contract.

**Competing schedules.** Some contracts require that the book under contract be the only one you work on until you finish it. Such clauses are aimed at preventing you from taking on other book projects that might make you deliver your book late. If you are not a prolific author and are earning good money from your books, that restriction might not apply to you. If, however, you are hungry both for work and money, you may well feel hamstrung by such a provision. As long as you get your book in on time and it's acceptable, and as long as you honor your option clause, why shouldn't you be free to take on more work? Many writers can work on several books at the same time without detriment to any of them; indeed, many *must* work on more than one to keep from starving. Publishers who pay authors $4000 or $5000 to write a book in six months or a year — and remember, only a portion of that is paid on signing, and 10 percent or 15 percent of *that* often goes to an agent — have little right to be indignant if authors take on other contracts to supplement their income. In most cases, then, I try to eliminate that clause entirely.

A variation on the clause described above restricts the author from bringing out another book within a few months of the publication date of the book under contract. For example, a Pocket Books contract I have at hand states in part that the author "agrees that in no event will he publish or authorize publication of any other book-length work (excluding works contracted for prior to the date of this agreement) of which he is an author or co-author until three (3) months before or after publication" of the book under contract to Pocket Books. In other words, if your Pocket Books book is scheduled for June publication, you mustn't bring out a Bantam book in April or May or July of the same year.

Although it's not usually in an author's best interest to schedule books published by competing houses too close together, you should not be hobbled by your contract from bringing out your books whenever any of your publishers feels it's best. Besides, publishers often take months and even years to decide when they're going to schedule a book, and it's unfair to ask the author or his other publisher to sit tight until a scheduling decision has been reached. So I recommend you eliminate such provisions altogether, whenever possible.

**Deferred royalties.** Some contracts offer authors the option of deferring windfall earnings by spreading them out over a period of years in order to avoid heavy taxation of large sums in any particular year. Suppose your book hit the jackpot and your royalty account swelled to $200,000 in one accounting period. If you took the full $200,000 in one gulp, you'd lose much of it in taxes, for you'd be in the highest tax bracket. Had you agreed at the time you signed your contract (and you must agree then, not afterward) to let your publisher spread the money out in annual installments of no more than, say, $20,000, you would, assuming you had no other source of income, drop from a high tax bracket to a lower one, and thus in the long run collect more of that $200,000.

This gimmick made more sense when it was created than it does now. Then, tax brackets could go as high as 70 percent, and there were fewer ways for the average person to shelter his money legitimately. Now, it makes little sense to let your publisher hold your money, what with lower bracket ceilings, and the availability of government-sponsored and other shelters. One author, to her profound shock, woke up one day with some $600,000 in her royalty account, but she had filled in the blank space in her contract with such a modest annual figure that it would have taken her a lifetime to collect her money in such small increments — during which time the publisher would be earning interest on the principal. Naturally she changed her mind, but her publisher insisted she honor her contract — and so might you, with $60,000 or $100,000 of annual interest at stake. She had to sue to get her money released. So unless you love slow torture, cross out any clause that puts a ceiling on the annual revenue your publisher may pay you.

**Minimum royalties.** The above passage refers to ceilings. Now let's talk about floors. Most contracts say that if royalties drop below a certain minimum in any given accounting period, the publisher doesn't have to pay royalties to the author. The reasoning behind this stipulation is that tiny royalty checks aren't worth the cost of processing, so the publisher holds that money until the royalty account exceeds the minimum.

If we're talking about something like $10, I suppose one can grudgingly see the publisher's viewpoint and let him hold the money. But some contracts call for larger minimums, like $50, and that's where I say no. Fifty dollars may seem like petty cash to a publisher, but for an author it may mean a week's food for his family. Besides, if you multiply that $50 by the hundreds or thousands of authors whose royalty accounts have too little in them to be worth processing, you come up with a figure large enough to earn a publisher a tidy sum of interest. So I generally fight to put a $10 ceiling on the publisher's floor.

**Bankruptcy.** Almost all contracts provide that if the publisher goes bankrupt, agreements with authors are automatically terminated and each author recovers his rights without notice. A company in trouble may not necessarily go into bankruptcy, however; it can also file for reorganization, or take some other measure a step or two short of filing for bankruptcy. As far as authors are concerned, such measures amount to the same thing as bankruptcy if royalties are cut off or the publisher can no longer effectively conduct business.

You would think that the cure would be to write tougher language into the bankruptcy clause enabling you to recover your rights if your publisher takes advantage of any bankruptcy or insolvency statute. I have some bad news for you, borne of bitter experience witnessing the collapse of several publishing houses over the past few decades: Bankruptcy clauses offer no protection to authors whatsoever. Federal bankruptcy laws, which prevail over all others, consider book contracts to be in the same category of assets as the publisher's furniture. They may be liquidated or assigned to any creditor, meaning your book could end up being owned by your publisher's printer or landlord.

In practice, book contracts controlled by bankrupt publishers usually end up being acquired by or assigned to other publishers, who (generally speaking) have a better idea of what to do with them than real estate companies. But the process may take years, and though I pride myself in having a recommendation for just about any problem your contract may throw at you, I'm afraid I'm just about out of ideas this time. The only suggestions I can make are, (1) deal only with publishers that have a sound fiscal history, and (2) if it looks as if your publisher is in trouble, move like lightning and hound your editor for a reversion of rights before the company files for bankruptcy.

**Failure to publish.** Most contracts have clauses stipulating a date by which the publisher must bring out the author's book. Generally it ranges from twelve to twenty-four months give or take six months. The term may or may not be negotiable, but no contract should be without some sort of cutoff, otherwise you have no recourse if your publisher postpones publication of your book indefinitely.

The term commences from the date of acceptance of your manuscript, which is one good reason why you should ask for an acceptance letter from your editor. In the absence of such a letter, you can take the receipt date of the advance payment due on acceptance to signify the date of formal acceptance of your manuscript.

Although a publisher may schedule a book with a fairly short fuse, such as six or nine months, he may still wish to stipulate a long lead time in his contract in order to hedge against scheduling revisions, which are a common occurrence. I try to hold the maximum term to eighteen months. Delays due to *force majeure* — circumstances beyond the publisher's control, such as war, strikes, riots, or so-called acts of God such as earthquakes — stop the clock, as it were, so that if a publisher has eighteen months to publish your book but is prevented from doing so because of a six-month printers' strike, the term is automatically extended by six months.

If, however, the delay is due strictly to the publisher's choice or negligence, the author has the right to terminate the contract. Some contracts call for automatic termination, some require the author to serve written notice, and others give the publisher a grace period that allows publication within X months from the date the author gives notice that the term has expired. Naturally, I prefer termination to be automatic. Whatever provisions are made, upon termination all obligations author and publisher have to one another are nullified, and the author is, or should be, entitled to keep any advance paid to date. Any language entitling a publisher to recover his advance under these circumstances should be struck from your contract. Unfortunately, although an author may feel that his interests have been seriously harmed by the publisher's failure to publish, he is not entitled to damages, his only compensation being the advance already collected.

From time to time a publisher running late on production of a book will ask the author to grant him an extension. Whether the author grants it at all, or grants it without additional payment or renegotiation of other terms, depends on the circumstances.

**Assignment.** Publishing contracts generally permit the publisher to assign his agreements to another party, such as a corporation that acquires the publisher, or another publisher that merges with it. Sometimes contracts specify that such assignment can be made only with the author's approval, but usually that is not the case. The publisher also has the right to assign the contract to any subsidiary, affiliate, or parent company. Thus a Dell book could be assignable to Delacorte (a hardcover affiliate), Bantam or Doubleday (sister houses owned by the Bertelsmann Group), or to Bertelsmann itself, the parent company. Should your publisher assign your contract, be sure all obligations are transferred with it, so that the new publisher honors all the responsibilities undertaken by your original publisher.

Authors, too, may assign their contracts, but only with the consent of the publisher. After all, if the publisher hired John Doe to write a book, it doesn't want him assigning the writing to Joe Blow. Authors may, however, assign the money due them under the contract, and not necessarily with the publisher's approval. Thus if a bank advances you $5000 toward royalties you're expecting in a few months, you may assign your next $5000 in royalties (plus interest) to the bank. Such transfers don't affect your obligations under the contract, however.

Also, book contracts are binding upon, and inure to the benefit of, an author's heirs and successors. If you are receiving royalties on your book, they will go to your heirs when you die. On the other hand, if you die while writing a book, and neither your publisher nor your estate can arrange for it to be completed satisfactorily by someone else, then your estate may be liable for repayment of any monies advanced to you. Before you start hissing at your publishers for cruelty to widows and orphans, however, let me hasten to add that most publishers carry insurance against such contingencies, and seldom press estates for refunds.

**Jurisdiction of publishing contracts.** Publishing contracts are generally governed by the laws of the state where the publisher's headquarters are located, regardless of where the documents are actually executed. This stipulation can put out-of-town authors at a disadvantage if they wish to bring a lawsuit against their publishers, but as it's never been negotiable in my experience, you should seek your lawyer's advice about dealing with it if and when you have to bring an action against your publisher.

**Author's copies.** You are entitled by contract to a number of free copies of your published book, after which you may purchase additional copies at a discount of 40 percent or 50 percent. The number of free copies called for in most contracts is somewhere between six and twenty, but I try for as many as possible. It's amazing how many copies authors give away, despite their best efforts to hold on to them. Later, when you need more, they may not be in stock.

Aside from personal use, you have to anticipate copies necessary for subsidiary-rights exploitation. If you cover all of the major language areas plus the movies and television, and leave leeway for extra production copies needed by publishers or producers who buy rights to your book, you'll probably need between twenty-five and fifty copies. Fifty copies of a $25 hardcover book discounted by 40 percent comes to $750 plus taxes and shipping. So whatever you can secure gratis from your publisher will save you money.

You should try to charge copies purchased from your publisher, rather than pay cash for them. Your publisher will then add your purchase to the unearned advance, and deduct the sum from your royalties when your book earns back its advance. But since many advances don't earn out, and publishers have been left holding the bag for authors' copies charged to royalties, don't be surprised if your publisher requires you to pay cash for extra books you order.

# 14

# All About Agents

W ho is the most influential member of the editorial board of
your publishing company?

The answer is — your literary agent.

Wait a moment. Since when have literary agents been attending
publishers' meetings? Well, they don't actually attend in the physi-
cal sense. But so great is their power over publishers that it could
well be said they are an unseen presence at every publishing committee meeting. In fact, I would go so far as to say that many agents
cast the decisive votes at such meetings. Who will paint the cover of
your book? Who will be assigned to edit it? Where will it be advertised and how many cities will you tour with it? Such is the influence of some agents that a publisher would not dare make such decisions without taking into account their wishes.

How did agents come to have so much clout? How is it exerted?
And what other roles do agents serve beyond the stereotyped
image so many writers have of them?

I entered the publishing business in 1959, on the cusp of a revolution in the relationships among writers, agents, and publishers.
Until late in the nineteenth century, authors relied on their own
business acumen to deal with their publishers — which explains
why so many were horribly exploited, robbed of their copyrights,
cheated out of their money, and even hoodwinked out of their by-
lines. The introduction of authors' representatives afforded some
measure of protection to authors who engaged them. But such was
publishers' hostility to agents that many authors were afraid to hire
them for fear their publishers would drop agented authors in favor
of authors negotiating for themselves. And they were right.

Agents gained ground in the first half of this century, but even well into the 1960s publishers regarded them as necessary nuisances. Although the hostility, you will not be surprised to know, focused on the agents' demands for better pay and other contractual terms, there was more to it than just money. Editors felt intensely paternalistic or maternalistic toward their authors, and resented the formation of strong emotional bonds between those authors and literary agents.

All that was to change as the post–World War II paperback revolution took firm hold in the 1960s. Popularly priced mass market paperbacks boomed, and demand for "product" reached a point where we had an almost unprecedented situation — a seller's market. Whereas in the past writers would usually have to complete a book in order to merit a contract, during the buying spree of the 1960s, smart agents realized that they could make deals with publishers merely on the basis of a portion and an outline, an outline only, or even a one-page sketch.

The emerging breed of powerful dealmaker agents attracted many fine writers who felt that their publishers' professed appreciation of them did not extend to the size of their contracts. Like it or not, publishers began to depend more and more heavily on agents to furnish them with desirable, profitable writers. A major byproduct of this dependency was the elimination of the slush pile as a source of new writing talent, thus intensifying the updraft of reliance on agents by both writers and publishers.

The intense competition for writing talent drove many undercapitalized publishers into the arms of better-heeled companies, shrinking the number of important trade houses by, in my own estimation, 80 percent. Many editors were squeezed out of their jobs, while those who demonstrated skill at acquiring profitable authors were lured away from one house by another. Authors discovered that the stable, nurturing, affectionate relationships they had cultivated with their editors over the course of many books were shattered. My files are rife with horror stories of authors whose books were orphaned by the departure of their editors at a critical moment in the publishing process.

Agents abhor a vacuum, and few resisted the opportunity that these conditions created to tighten their control over both authors and publishers. Disillusioned authors, feeling abandoned by editors who had been stalwart friends for many years, transferred their feelings of affection and loyalty to their agents. The bonding was not without its price, however, for in order to satisfy their affection- and support-starved clients, agents had to learn or improve skills that they had been used to leaving to editors. In particular they had to become more active in the editorial process, criticizing their clients' work and even helping them develop ideas and projects from scratch.

The most important role an editor can play in an author's career is that of advocate in the publishing company. The editor sponsors your book through each phase of the publishing process, defending it from the countless dangers threatening to kill it before birth, ranging from bad luck to human error. But with the musical-chairs mentality that swept the editorial world in the 1970s and 1980s, authors lost these powerful allies. And when they realized that there was nobody at their publishing companies standing up for their books, they turned to their agents, and a cry was heard throughout the land: "*Do something!*"

What the agents did was step into the breach and start telling publishers what to do. Today there is almost no area of the publica- tion process that agents do not get involved with. I have reviewed page design and typography, criticized cover paintings, button- holed sales representatives, managed publicity campaigns, and of course brainstormed book ideas and edited manuscripts. I don't consider myself unique; I know of few of my fellow agents who have not taken a similar hand on behalf of their clients. Although we sometimes encounter resistance and resentment, more often agent input is thoughtfully considered and adopted, for it repre- sents a viewpoint that publishers don't always have the opportu- nity to consider. But if a publisher doesn't want to hear our two cents — well, that's too bad; they're going to hear it anyway. For many of us pack heavy armament in the form of important authors whose wishes and whims can make even the most powerful pub- lishing executive tremble with fear.

Luckily, most agents are not bullies. We realize that the publish- ing process is a three-way partnership and that the agent's most important task is to lubricate the sometimes abrasive interface be- tween publisher and author through patient diplomacy and gentle influence. I genuinely believe that if literary agents were to vanish overnight, publishers would miss them as keenly as would authors.

And believe me, we're not going to vanish overnight.

✍

To writers considering, or being considered for, representation by a literary agent, I can offer two precepts that will always serve them well. The first is, Always trust your agent. The second is, Never trust your agent.

Although the two are of course completely contradictory, both attitudes are indispensable to a healthy relationship with your agent. On the one hand, your agent is supposedly a professional with background and experience in evaluating and editing manuscripts, marketing them, negotiating contracts, collecting money, exploiting subsidiary rights, administering authors' business affairs, and guiding their careers. Because you are inexperienced in some or all of these areas, you want someone skillful to remove such concerns from your mind.

On the other hand, agents, like other professionals, are human. In fact, in terms of fallibility, they're considerably more human than other professionals such as doctors and lawyers, for, unlike them, literary agents do not have to go to any special school, pass any examination, or acquire a license. To become an agent, you need nothing more than one manuscript and enough change for a phone call. Thus there is a tremendous range in the ages, training, experience, and competence of the hundreds of literary agents listed in *Literary Market Place*.

So the solution to the paradox posed at the beginning of this chapter is, as you might expect, a double one. A good agent can help you achieve your career goals, relieve you of many business cares, and buffer you against the dangers and disappointments that menace the heart and mind of every writer. But there are also inexperienced and incompetent agents who can give you misleading market advice, tie you up with the wrong publisher, fail to exploit the full value of your work, and make negotiating errors that can lead to serious disputes with your publisher, or even lawsuits. And even great agents make mistakes from time to time.

Therefore, the wise author enters into an agent-client relationship with a mixture of trust and skepticism; and though you'll have to put a lot of faith into your agent's judgment, you owe it to yourself to study the contracts he secures for you and to be unafraid to ask questions.

At what point should an author approach an agent? My advice is, when the author has a track record and has written a book or has one in progress. Most agents I know look for some indication that the writer earns, or at least has the potential to earn, enough money from writing to make it worth the agent's while to accept him for representation; and that usually means books. A background consisting of publication of literary short stories or local newspaper articles doesn't impress the average agent, as these don't necessarily manifest earning capacity. The sale of short material to national publications on a regular basis is more impressive, but, as it's hard to make a living purely on journalism, an agent will still be skeptical about your earning power. So it usually comes down to books: A record of book sales to national publishers definitely arouses an agent's interest.

Even if you haven't had a book published, you shouldn't approach an agent until you have one to offer, generally speaking. Preferably it should be a finished one, particularly if it's a novel, for publishers are extremely skittish about giving authors contracts on partial novels, and so agents will generally tell you to finish yours before submitting it to them. An agent might, however, take on a portion and outline of a nonfiction book that looks strong, for it doesn't engender as much skepticism among publishers as to the author's ability to sustain the quality of a promising portion.

If the above describes your situation, then address a brief letter to the agent or agents you've selected, listing previous publications and stating the subject or plot of your book or book-in-progress. The summary should be concise and straightforward, without hype and without too much chat about your personal life.

A number of agents charge reading fees to cover the cost of evaluating submissions by unpublished authors. They justify the practice by pointing out that doctors and lawyers charge fees for consultation, so why shouldn't literary agents? The Association of Authors' Representatives takes the position that it is impossible to ensure responsible and ethical conduct on the part of fee-charging agents, and has therefore forbidden the practice among its members. That doesn't mean you can't get a perfectly valid analysis of your work for a reading fee, but you should be wary of any agent who promises to accept your work for representation for a fee. Investigate all fee-charging agents carefully, and ask them to give you a short list of recent sales. Some will waive their fees if you have a promising track record that suggests they can be compensated by commissions only.

How do you find and select the right agent? Perhaps you know a professional writer, or someone in the publishing business, an editor who's bought your work. They can give you some of the more prominent names. *Literary Market Place* has a section devoted to agents, and, as agents must demonstrate recent sales in order to qualify for listing there, you can depend on LMP for at least a minimum standard. You may also send an inquiry to the Association of Authors' Representatives, a trade association to which a great many agents belong. The AAR has stringent membership requirements, a code of ethics that all members must sign, and grievance procedures. Thus, while there is as much variance in conduct, commission structures, services, and business practices among AAR members as there is among agents who do not belong, membership in AAR does at least ensure that members have respectable sales track records and observe ethical standards. You may drop a line to the AAR at 10 Astor Place, Third Floor, New York, NY 10003, requesting a list of members, the organization's Canon of Ethics, and some other literature. There is a small postage and handling fee.

Another way to satisfy yourself about an agent's "legitimacy," or at least reputation, is to ask the clients or editors who've had dealings with that person. If possible, it's best to survey as many people as you can, for the testimony of one or two who have had terrific or ghastly experiences with an agent may not be representative of that agent's skill, judgment, standing in the industry, and the like.

Even after the testimony is in, different authors may assess it in very different ways. Authors' expectations are as varied as their writing styles, and the same character trait that alienates one potential client may endear the agent to someone else. There are authors who tell their agents, "Call me every once in a while, even if you have nothing to say," and others who tell them, "No need to call me unless there's real news." So authors' recommendations have to be considered in the context of their own value systems. The same goes for editors. An agent who is hated by an editor may have incurred that editor's wrath in the admirable pursuit of his client's best interests; and one who is popular among editors may simply turn out to be a pleasant luncheon companion.

When you have your list, write to three or four. Send original letters, not photocopies of a "Dear Agent" letter. Your letter, as I've said, will describe your sales background and the work you have to offer. Evaluate the responses (including the response *time*), then pick the reply that impressed you most. Look for enthusiasm, warmth, interesting agency brochures or other literature, fee versus free reading, and so forth, and submit your material there — and there only. If turned down, go to the next agent on your list. Your covering letter might ask whom the agent can recommend if the agent declines to take your material on. Often he will suggest a good young agent who may be hungrier for clients, or more tolerant of marginal track records, than the more established agents.

Let's say you've found an agent you feel comfortable with and who wants to represent you. What happens now? What happens now is that you and your agent discuss the terms and conditions of your association and enter into an agreement. I'll detail author-agent agreements presently, but for now suffice it to say that these agreements don't necessarily have to be written ones. There are several schools of thought about contracts between agents and authors, and they run the gamut from formal and elaborate fine-print documents to airy waves of the hand. The important thing is for you to question the agent closely about his or her commission structure and other policies, for you are about to enter into an arrangement that could bind you to that person for a long time, possibly a lifetime.

When I entered the publishing business in 1959, the role of agents was just emerging from the somewhat demure traditions of the "gentleman's profession." Agents were men and women cut from the same refined cloth as most editors, and negotiations were conducted in a far more subdued atmosphere than today's. Books were sold from completed manuscripts, seldom from outlines, or portions and outlines, or ten-word descriptions pitched over the phone or luncheon table. Multiple submissions were scandalous violations of industry ethics. Headline-making advances were exceptional, not commonplace as they are now, and indeed it was still considered slightly vulgar for writers to want to get rich.

Few agents departed from this restrained approach, and those who did were considered mavericks who gave the profession a black eye. Many publishers resisted dealing with agents — and so did many authors.

All of that changed drastically in the sixties, as the paperback revolution awakened publishers and writers alike to the fact that publishing was a business, and big business at that. Power vacuums were created, which in turn were filled by the agents, who adapted to the upheaval by assuming new roles and employing new tactics: multiple submissions and auctions, the concept of book packaging, multibook contracts initiated by a few pages of outline, sky-high advances calculated to nail publishers to heavy printing and promotional commitments, presold movie tie-ins, hard-soft deals, reverse paperback-to-hardcover sales. As one agent said at the time, "Hello, twentieth century, good-bye eighteenth!"

In the two decades since the paperback revolution, literary agents have become absolutely essential to the publishing process and all but indispensable to aspiring and successful writers alike. Though many agents are open to new clients, many more have become extremely selective, and take the attitude that authors need them more than they need authors.

There are signs that this situation is changing, however, and a smart agent will not become too complacent about his or her indispensability. Having observed how much money changes hands in the publishing business, many former editors and other book people have launched careers as agents, and in recent years the number of listed agents has soared. Competition for clients is intensifying. I remember a colleague saying, only a few years ago, "There are enough authors for all of us." I doubt if she would say that today. With a number of agents raising their basic commissions from 10 percent to 15 percent, authors are now giving much more thought to what they get for the commission they pay. And with the advent of recessionary trends in publishing, such as the precipitous decline of big reprint prices for midlist books, the amount of money to spread among agents is decreasing.

All these factors point to new attitudes, approaches, and business tactics for the literary agent of the future. Although agents' activities have never been codified, one agents' organization used to distribute among its members a brochure that they gave to prospective clients, describing the activities and conduct that authors could expect, or not expect, from their agents. Some of these functions we all take for granted, such as those listed under the heading "What the Agent Can Do for His Client." They include: "Negotiate sale or lease of certain rights in the work"; "Examine contracts and negotiate modifications whenever justified"; and "Collect monies due." Still, it might help you to visualize the processes if I describe them in detail.

When our agency accepts a manuscript, we determine whether it should be marketed to one publisher at a time or to several simultaneously. We weigh such factors as the book's quality, timeliness, and universality. If it's terrific and we know it'll appeal to just about any and all editors we show it to, or if it's on a hot topic and we want to get it out before someone beats us to it, we'll auction it. If it's of a more specialized nature, we market it to one publisher at a time, picking our best shots from the long list of editorial contacts we've developed over the years.

When we receive an offer, we negotiate the best terms possible, in consultation with the author, and then close the deal. We review the contract and "fine tune" it in further negotiation with the editor, then forward it to the author for signing. We then put in for the money due upon signing of the contract, a task easier said than done, for in these days of tight money, publishers do not part with checks readily. We then begin our exploitation of subsidiary rights to the material, offering magazine, translation, and movie and television rights to potential buyers. And when we get a bite, we negotiate and go through the collection process all over again.

In addition to these day-to-day or book-by-book procedures, there is the larger task of "building" the author. Every day, on the phone, at luncheons, in meetings, or at publishing functions, agents talk up their clients and try to enhance their value in the marketplace, so that with each success — a book-club selection, a good reprint deal, a foreign sale, a movie option — the author's reputation and price go up.

In the brochure issued by the literary agents' organization I mentioned, there were two other headings: "The Agent Cannot . . ." and "Standard Practice of the Agent." These list some functions that traditionally have fallen outside the obligations of agent to author. These days the new breed of agent is calling into question some of those proscribed functions, though, so let's take a look at a few and see whether they still apply to agent-author relationships.

**The agent cannot act as editor of a writer's work.** A great many agents I know edit their clients' work, not merely because they are compulsive editors but because the quality of editing in some areas of publishing has declined lamentably. Paperback publishers, for instance, have not hired topnotch copy editors to keep pace with the influx of topnotch authors writing originals for them. On a number of occasions I have gone over a writer's manuscript thoroughly, to improve its chances of acceptance, to help the author modify it for magazine serialization, or simply to make it the best book it can be; and I know that many of my colleagues would consider themselves remiss if they did not perform this service when circumstances warranted it.

**The agent cannot solve authors' personal problems or lend money.** As an author myself, and a friend or agent of many other writers, I can testify how tightly interconnected the personal, financial, and creative elements of an author's life are. Trouble in one area almost invariably indicates trouble in the others. The agent who turns his back on the author's personal problems may well be aggravating that author's earning power. So for reasons of self-interest if not compassion, an agent may find himself playing psychiatrist to a client, sticking his nose into an author's marital disputes or taking a depressed author to a baseball game. Naturally one must be able to draw the line, or risk being sucked into a client's plight beyond what might be deemed sensible, but I fail to see how an agent can walk away from it entirely. Because turbulent market conditions of the last few decades have caused so much job-hopping and what I call editorial musical chairs, the agent has replaced the editor as the only constant, reliable figure in most authors' professional relationships.

As for lending money, many agents commonly do, and, if it's done prudently, it's the sort of gesture that can forge firm bonds between author and agent. Those agents who do lend money to their authors generally do so only when revenue from a publisher or some other source is imminent, so that it is not so much a loan as an advance to tide the author over till the check arrives. Unfortunately, with publishers' checks arriving later and later in this time of glacial cash flow, agents are being asked more and more frequently to play banker. I personally would feel uncomfortable about charging interest on a loan to a client, but I'm not sure authors always appreciate that the agent who does lend them money lends it interest-free, or that the agent's total advances to clients at any given time may come to tens of thousands of dollars. Therefore most agents tell their clients, "Only if you desperately need it and can't raise it from another source."

**The agent cannot be available outside office hours except by appointment.** Many business and personal crises arise for authors at times that do not correspond to regular business hours. Book negotiations can carry over into the evening, for instance, and the time differential puts Hollywood three hours behind New York, and New York at least five hours behind Europe. Thus an agent's day may not always be the same as a civil servant's, and the phone rings at all hours. Many of my clients have my home phone number, and I only ask them to use it sparingly.

**The agent cannot perform the functions of a press agent, social secretary, or travel agent.** A lot of agents I know take on these functions to supplement the author's or publisher's efforts. Literary agenting is a service business, and anything an agent can do to free a client from care should not automatically be considered out of bounds. For instance, I have become particularly sensitive about the failure of publishers to publicize authors and their books, and, to remedy that failure, I once engaged a public-relations firm to boost client visibility and publicize clients' lives and work. In an age where hype seems to give authors an edge, publicity is becoming a sine qua non for struggling authors, and helps the successful ones stay in the forefront. If publishers cannot or will not provide it, and authors cannot afford it, perhaps the agent will have to become more aggressive in that area.

As for the functions of social secretary and travel agent, rare is the agent who has not driven clients to the airport or booked them into hotels, arranged business or social appointments, or helped them secure tickets to that hot Broadway show. I have cashed their checks, babysat for their kids, visited them in the hospital, painted their walls, and even, in the case of a client writing about the underworld, bailed them out of jail.

In fact, the rapidly changing nature of the publishing business has once again created numerous vacuums, and for agents the challenge of the coming era will be to find ways to fill them. Perhaps, then, the most important question you can ask yourself, when deciding among literary agents, is how creatively the candidates meet that challenge.

## Agent-Author Agreements

The relationship between author and agent is one of the least codified and worst defined of professional relationships. There are no standards, statutes, or rules governing the way they enter into their association, conduct it, or sever it. Agents who are exquisitely precise about the language of book contracts negotiated for clients may, at the same time, have nothing more than a handshake or a flimsy and amateurish scrap of paper to signify the terms of their relationship with their clients, a relationship that in many ways is as important and complex as that between authors and publishers. Even agents who do have contracts with their clients often make so many exceptions as to render those contracts all but meaningless.

A written, detailed contract has the virtue of specifically spelling out terms and mutual obligations, but it also binds a lot tighter than a verbal agreement. My colleagues and I can report experiences of splendid agent-author relationships that lasted decades on the strength of a verbal understanding, and on the other hand of highly elaborate contracts between agents and authors that were gotten around or out of by the determined efforts of an aggrieved party. Both types of experience illustrate that it's not so much a matter of what's in your agreement as of how much good faith is behind it. If agent and author have to hire attorneys to negotiate an agreement between themselves, the relationship is already starting off on an adversarial footing. But if good faith exists, the relationship will be a secure one, and any differences that arise will inevitably be ironed out.

Let's focus on some of the terms of the understanding, written or otherwise, that are created when you and an agent agree to work together.

**Exclusivity.** You engage your agent on an exclusive basis; that is, he or she is the only person authorized to represent you in the marketing and licensing of your material, in the collection of money generated by the sale of that material, and in the exploitation of reserved rights to that material. That means that even if you meet a publisher at a cocktail party and somehow, *mirabile dictu,* get him to make you an offer right then and there, you must nevertheless turn the matter over to your appointed agent.

Most literary agents have their own network of subagents in Hollywood and overseas, and so when you engage an agent you engage those subagents automatically. Occasionally an author will tell an agent, "Marty X has always handled my movie deals, and Hans Y has sold everything I ever wrote in the German market, so won't you use those subagents instead of your own?" Different agents have different policies about such things, but it's worth exploring if it's important to you.

Some authors require, or feel they require, an attorney to supplement or at least review an agent's contractual work. Many agents are, or at least feel they are, experienced enough to work out the wording of ordinary publishing agreements, or even movie agreements, as well as any attorney. In fact, many an agent groans inwardly when he hears that his client is showing a contract to an attorney. The reason is that unless a lawyer is quite familiar with publishing traditions and conventions, he will (so agents and other publishing people believe) exasperatingly raise questions about contingencies that seldom occur ("Does delay of publication by killer smog come under the definition of act of God?"). Nevertheless, any competent attorney looking after his client's best interests can only help an agent and strengthen a contract. But the author and agent should reach an agreement as to who pays the attorney's fee.

**Type of material.** Generally speaking, authors appoint agents to handle all of their output. But exceptions are many, and must be hammered out at the time agreement is struck. For instance, if you earn your living as a newspaper correspondent or salaried reporter, it's likely that your newspaper articles and the income from them would be exempted from your arrangement. Some authors have agents to handle screenplays, and those dealings are kept separate from the dealings of their literary agents. But strict separation is not always possible, as is the case when there is a movie deal on an author's book and the author is hired to do the screenplay. Then the literary and movie agents have to sort out their individual contributions — and commissions.

Many literary agents, as I have said, will not handle short stories for their book-writing clients because of the low profitability of the short format. Some authors accept and even welcome this exception, and contentedly continue their direct relations with magazine editors. But others are disappointed, having looked forward to relief from the ofttimes onerous chore of marketing short stories and articles and chasing magazines for their money. Are such authors justified in retaining an agent (if one exists) who'll be glad to take on such material while the first agent handles the book deals? A deeper quandary for an author arises when an agent rejects his book or idea for a book. What if the author can't accept that the material is unsalable? Is he justified in asking another agent to handle it while his regular agent handles everything else? There are no guidelines, but there's plenty of potential for mischief unless author and agent establish some ground rules promptly.

**Fiduciary responsibility.** The client authorizes his agent to collect money payable to him. Although agents aren't licensed the way banks are, they have a fiduciary responsibility to their clients that is as solemn as that of a bank. The Internal Revenue Service, for instance, regards money collected by an agent to be in effect collected by the author. Short of taking a client's money and running to Brazil with it, however, literary agents operate within a wide latitude when it comes to disbursement of money they collect for their clients. Except in the case of large amounts, where a check paid to and deposited by a client before the agent's deposit has had time to clear might bounce, most agents I know try to adhere to payout policies ranging from same-day disbursement to payout within a week of collection of revenue on behalf of an author. The policy should be explicitly declared by your agent when you enter into your agreement with him.

Whatever the form of your contract with your agent, the fiduciary relationship is also spelled out in every contract you sign with a publisher or other buyer. I'm referring to the agency clause that appears on such contracts, or that agents insert in them. Such clauses typically read something like this:

All statements and payments due under the terms of this agreement shall be rendered to the X Agency, whose receipt shall be considered full settlement of the Publisher's obligations, and who

is authorized to act exclusively in the Author's behalf in all matters arising out of this agreement.

The above clause makes X Agency the "agent of record" and entitles it to an irrevocable financial interest in revenues generated by
that contract. Some agents have detailed agency clauses that they
splice into every publishing, movie, and other contract, spelling out
commissions and other considerations, and those clauses supplement or take the place of a separate contract between author and
agent.

**Commissions.** The question of commissions is a complex one,
and the only point I wish to stress here is that you should make sure
what commissions your agent charges you, and what services and
expenses are included in those commissions. At present the range
for sale of American book and serial rights is approximately 10 percent to 15 percent; for sale of film and television rights, 10 percent to
20 percent; and for sale of foreign rights, 10 percent to 25 percent.
But agents perform a broad variety of functions in exchange for
those commissions, and they differ from agent to agent. For instance, some agents who are also lawyers, or retain lawyers, offer
legal counsel (except for litigation) and tax advice as part of their
regular service. Some may offer to conduct, at their own expense,
audits of publishers' financial statements. Some undertake editing
of clients' manuscripts as part of their bargains with authors. Some
undertake a limited amount of promotional and publicity work on
behalf of their clients. You should ask your agent exactly which
of these services, if any, he'll perform for you.

Then there is the question of so-called extraordinary expenses.
These are expenses that many agents feel to be above and beyond
the normal costs of doing business, and charge to the client in addition to commissions. Among the most common are long-distance
phone calls; telegrams, cables, and fax messages; the cost of pho-
tocopying manuscripts or lengthy documents; the cost of special
messengers for pickup or delivery of urgently needed manuscripts,
contracts, or checks; the cost of copies of authors' books bought by
the agent for the exploitation of subsidiary rights; and the cost of
air-mailing those copies to overseas publishers and agents, as opposed to the cheaper but slower method of shipping them by sea at
the agent's expense. Not all agents agree on what is an ordinary ex-

pense and what is extraordinary, so you'd do well to ask your agent how he feels about these.

**Term.** Professional writers with track records in book sales generally enter into an author-agent relationship with the attitude that the relationship will be a long-term one. Authors who have just produced their first books, however, tend to feel anxious about a long-term commitment until the agent has proven he can do the job, and it's not uncommon for them to set a time limit within which results must be demonstrated. Depending on the time period and the nature of the property, this request isn't entirely unreasonable.

Such trial marriages aside, it's understood that an agent-author relationship should last as long as the two are mutually happy and making a profit together. Nonetheless, written author-agent contracts often stipulate a term — a year, two years — renewable automatically unless one party notifies the other of a desire to terminate. From the author's viewpoint, the shorter the term the better. An author who is miserable with an agent he regards as incompetent shouldn't have to be tied to that agent because their contract has another six or twelve or fifteen months to go. From the agent's viewpoint, the term of a contract with an author isn't intended to be punitive, but is rather an expression of serious commitment. Many agents tell how, after they've broken their backs to get an author into print, that author has jumped to another agent or made a direct deal with his publisher for a second book, cutting the agent out.

Such horror stories notwithstanding, if an agent-author contract is backed by good faith, the term of the relationship can and should be worked out as reasonably as all other aspects of the author-agent agreement. It's when things break down that the good faith between agent and author is most critically tested. We must now speak of the unspeakable, and discuss what happens when the bond is severed.

## Breaking Up with Your Agent

Like any other divorce, the termination of the author-agent relationship is seldom characterized by the same spirit of good will with which it started. On the author's part there are inevitably grievances concerning the agent's incompetence, or lack of aggressiveness, or inaccessibility, or other real or perceived shortcomings. The agent, too, may have complaints about his client's demanding nature or unreasonableness. At any rate, one or both parties feel the arrangement has become unprofitable. The time has come for a parting of the ways. What do they do now?

As with so many other aspects of publishing, the obligations of author and literary agent to one another have never been thoroughly codified or tested by a fully litigated court action. Unless a written agreement between them exists, there is little but common law and common sense to guide them in sorting out precisely what rights and other interests an author may withdraw from his or her agent when the relationship ends. Of all the provisions of an agent-author agreement, then, the one dictating the terms for the dissolution of the relationship may be the most important. For when things are going well, agent and author can work problems out in an atmosphere of good faith, but when they're going poorly, those problems are steeped in suspicion and resentment.

Thus, though no one likes to think about providing for the death of the author-agent relationship, any more than one likes to think about real death when one writes a will, it is essential that author and agent provide for that eventuality in writing when they draw up their agreement. Or, if they have no formal agreement, such provisions can be made on a contract-by-contract basis in the agent's clause of the publishing contract.

Perhaps the easiest way to sort things out is to divide your properties into three categories: (1) works not yet placed by your present agent; (2) sold rights to published books; and (3) unsold rights to published books. These are the bargaining chips in your negotiations with your former (or soon to be former) agent, and as you prepare to play them, ask yourself three questions: How amiable is your departure from your old agent going to be? How valuable are the properties under discussion? And what is your new agent's attitude toward those properties?

**1. Works not yet placed by your present agent.** Any manuscripts currently on submission by your agent should be returned to you as soon as they come back from their present market, or within a reasonable deadline, say thirty days. Or, if you wish, they may be withdrawn from the market at once and returned to you.

Your agent should provide a list of all markets to which the work has been submitted, and include in that list the names of the editors involved.

What if the editor currently considering your manuscript makes an offer? That is a matter to be decided between you and your present agent, and perhaps your future agent as well. Although it seems only fair for you to honor the first agent's role in placing the book, I know of instances where authors have turned deals negotiated by one agent over to new agents, who then became the agents of record, cutting the first agent out. Ethics aside, the success of such a maneuver may be determined only by how loudly the first agent howls, "I'm gonna sue!"

**2. Sold rights to published books.** Suppose your first agent sold your first novel to Random House, then sold German, British, and Italian rights. Can you cut that agent out of those contracts and cut your new agent in? Highly unlikely. Your former agent will remain the agent of record on those editions, and rarely will you be able to remove him once contracts have been signed. If those editions go out of print and the rights revert to you, however, you are free to arrange new editions through your present agent, with no further obligation to the old one.

**3. Unsold rights to published books.** The biggest source of contention between author and former agent is unsold rights to books that agent has placed with an American publisher. For instance, say your agent sells your book to Simon & Schuster, reserving first-serial, movie, television, British, and foreign-translation rights for you. Before those rights can be sold, however, you break up with that agent. Who gets to handle the rights, your old agent or your new one?

If your former agent specified in a written agreement with you that he or she was to handle them, then that's that. But if there is no such provision, a dispute will probably arise. Your ex-agent may feel that because he was responsible for the birth of your book, he should participate in all subsidiary benefits that accrue thereafter. Depending on how much good will you feel toward him when you part company, you may agree. You may, however, feel (as many authors do) that the very reason you left him is that he didn't successfully exploit subsidiary rights to your other work, and want your new agent (whom you presumably feel has skills in that area that your former agent did not) to have a crack at them.

Your former agent may dig in his heels at the prospect of having this anticipated income taken away. Threats and counterthreats may ensue, but it probably won't do either of you much good to go to the statute books, for, to my knowledge, the matter has never been settled satisfactorily in a court battle. So, as in the case of numerous lawsuits, a formal dispute may come down to a question of who is prepared to spend the most money to prosecute or defend; and, as with so many lawsuits, the big winners will be the lawyers. Is there any way to reach a satisfactory agreement short of this expensive and exhausting procedure?

Yes, though it may mean compromise on the part of one, two, and perhaps all three members of the cast of this triangle: the author, the old agent, and the new agent. One solution that seems eminently fair is for the author to give his old agent a period of time in which to sell subsidiary rights currently on submission, at the end of which these rights revert to the author. Sixty days seems quite ample for agent to wrap up pending sales or request decisions from markets considering properties for sub-rights purchases.

Or the author may have to offer an extra commission to the former agent, even if that agent doesn't do anything to earn it, as compensation for turning the rights over to the new agent. For instance, if your former agent was looking forward to a 10 percent commission on foreign sales, he might accept 5 percent for relinquishing them to a new agent. Though that's only half of what he would have gotten had he agented the property himself, he will have done no work, spent no time, and incurred no overhead to earn it.

If you're a particularly persuasive bargainer, you may even be able to persuade your *new* agent to relinquish 5 percent, on the grounds that he didn't do anything to sell the book originally to an American publisher, so his participation in future proceeds should be less than ordinary. You are, after all, placing a gift of sorts in his hands.

In other words, by getting your new and old agents to split the usual commission, you create a compromise that doesn't take anything out of your own pocket. Many agents are friendly with each other and may in fact help you fashion this settlement. But even if it costs you a few extra percentage points, you may feel it's worth it to save peace of mind and to avert a much more costly legal fight. And if your former agent refuses to part with those rights and you have to leave them with him, you can be fairly sure that his profit motive will make him market and sell them as if you were still a client in good standing. Rare is the agent so vindictive as to kill sales because an author has left him.

How, exactly, do you leave an agent with whom you're unhappy? The first step is to find a new one, which is usually done through referrals by editors and other authors. Because some agents have compunctions about taking on clients belonging to colleagues with whom they're friendly, you should make it clear to prospective agents that you have determined to leave your present agent.

After interviewing prospects and coming to an agreement with the one you have selected, it's time to inform your former agent. Some authors prefer to deliver the painful news face to face. They may have been associated with an agent for many years, and built up a loving friendship that deserves more than a cold letter serving notice of severance. Other authors, for that very reason, find it unbearably discomfiting to look into the face of the person with whom they've shared so many joys and struggles, and choose to do the deed by mail. For the author or agent for whom the relationship has declined (and it's clear to both parties that it's all over), a letter is a much simpler proposition. Some authors feel compelled to explain why they are leaving, but you aren't required to do so beyond saying that for various reasons you've decided to seek other representation, and that this decision is based on business, not personal, reasons.

Even if you perform this unpleasant task face to face, a follow-up letter is still desirable, stipulating what properties and rights you wish to take with you; for on reflection your former agent may, however cordially he's treated you in the past, feel betrayed and angry, and dispute your right to turn certain rights or materials over to another agent. Therefore, a letter is best, and it should request confirmation from the former agent that he won't stand in the way of your turning those rights and properties over to a new agent. If you've agreed to compensate him with an extra commission, it should be stated in this letter. You may also want to give your former agent a period of time, such as thirty or sixty days, in which to sell properties he is now marketing, or subsidiary rights he is trying to sell in various territories.

Leaving an agent is one of life's less agreeable tasks, but if it's done gracefully and graciously you'll have one less piece of heavy baggage to carry into the next phase of your career.

# 15

# To Publication Date

The previous chapter should have made it clear that an agent's usefulness isn't restricted solely to matters concerning the book contract. One very important function of the agent — especially the agent of a writer just breaking into publishing — is to educate the client in the often arcane ways of the publishing world. What follows, then, is a primer to give you an idea of what to expect *after* you've negotiated yourself a good deal.

The time it takes for a book to be published has often been likened to the gestation period of a human baby. This is a poor simile. It is closer to the gestation period of a baby elephant. Although publishers can and still do bring books out in approximately nine months, they are more comfortable with twelve. But fifteen, eighteen, and more is by no means uncommon. That is particularly true today, for the number of books published annually has shrunk somewhat over the high-water mark of the 1980s, and inventories of unpublished works are building at many houses as editors hold them out for the best possible positions on their future lists.

Besides, for humans the gestation process starts with nothing (or very little, at any rate) and gradually develops into a fully formed creature, whereas the publication process *starts* with a completed book. So from the author's viewpoint the analogy is closer to the parent who has to wait a year or longer to take a newborn baby home from the hospital.

Professional writers learn to fill this period with a variety of tasks (not the least of which, of course, is writing another book) and have conditioned themselves to bear the wait with a degree of resignation. But I doubt if any of them accepts it happily. And for the new writer, the agony is nothing short of exquisite. No matter how thoroughly their agents or editors depict for them the many tasks that must be rendered in order for their books to come into the world, and the high complexity of the undertaking known as publishing, first authors find it nearly impossible to understand how they can be expected to endure this torment gracefully. It is scant consolation for them to be told how amazing it is that the process doesn't take even longer.

To begin with, you'd do well to remember that yours isn't the only book your editor is working on. Even a modest-sized publisher releases a couple of books every month, and the bigger ones publish a dozen or more monthly. Because of the many procedures involved in getting a book ready for the printer, publishers create work schedules with lead times of a year or more. Printers often work for more than one publishing company, so publishers have to reserve time on the printer's schedule. The book must be announced in the publisher's semiannual catalogue, and the company's salespeople must be introduced to the product. Advertising and promotional campaigns, if any, must be organized, and time or space in advertising media must be booked. Oh, it's easy to eat up nine months getting a book out!

The first procedure to look forward to, after your manuscript (or revised manuscript) has been accepted by your editor, is copy editing. An editorial specialist, not necessarily the same person who acquired your book in the first place, now scrutinizes the manuscript with several ends in mind. First, he marks it in such a way as to make the printer's job as easy as possible. Because printers charge sky-high hourly rates for their skilled labor, goofs that require resetting of type can cost a publisher or author dearly. A good copy editor's instructions to the printer are therefore worth their weight in gold. The copy editor also brings the manuscript into conformity with the stylistic preferences of the publishing company. Most companies adhere to the stylistic rules set forth in *The Chicago Manual of Style*, but there may be individual variations from company to company. For instance, does your publisher prefer to print "$1,400,000" or "$1.4 million"? Does it spell out "three hundred" or print it as "300"?

A copy editor also does a close reading of the manuscript, seeking out inconsistencies in plotting and characterization, errors of fact, undocumented assertions, potentially actionable statements, and the like. Authors often get their manuscripts back from their copy editors with "flags" — colored strips of paper containing editorial questions and comments — attached to problem pages. "Carla's hair is red in this chapter but blond in chapter 2," a typical flag might read; or "That would make Churchill only 15 years old on D-day, please check dates," another might say.

Most publishing contracts give the publisher the right to edit, make corrections in grammar, punctuation, and spelling, and adapt the manuscript to the company's style. Any contractual language that gives a publisher the right to alter title or text should be struck, or at least modified to say that the author must give written approval of such alterations.

Although the practice of showing copy-edited manuscripts to authors is more common in hardcover publishing than in paperback, where timetables are tighter, it's a good idea for all authors to request a look at their copy-edited manuscripts before these go to the printer. You may want to make last-minute changes in your book, and it's cheaper to do them on the manuscript than to insert them at the printed-proof stage. You may also want to see your copy-edited manuscript in order to check on your copy editor's work. Copy editors are highly professional people and very, very good at what they do, but they may nevertheless occasionally misconstrue an author's meaning or take liberties with the text.

While the manuscript is being copy edited, copies are distributed to other members of the publishing staff, such as the art director, who'll develop a cover concept and send the manuscript to an artist or a design studio; production specialists and designers, who'll measure the book for pagination, design the layout, figure out paper and other production costs, and establish production schedules; sales and marketing directors; advertising, publicity, and promotion specialists; blurb copywriters; subsidiary-rights specialists; and others. In a small house, or with a routine book, these tasks may be telescoped and handled by one or two people. In the case of a big book, however, copies of the manuscript may go to many staff members, to generate that all-important collective frame of mind known as in-house enthusiasm. If the book is shaping up to be a blockbuster, the publisher may try to sell subsidiary rights on the basis of the manuscript, rather than waiting until the work is in proof or finished form.

While this editorial beehive is beginning to buzz, the copy-edited manuscript goes to the compositor, where it's set into type. The type is set on long, unpaginated sheets called galley proofs, or in page proofs, which have been paginated at the compositor's before the publisher sees any proofs. Today, most manuscripts go directly into page proofs, skipping the galley stage altogether. Galleys are used, for the most part, for books that contain illustrations or are likely to have extensive revisions at the proof stage. Several sets of proof are run off for review by author, proofreader, book designer, and copy editor, and for the production department to check to make sure design and type specifications have been followed.

The uncorrected proofs of most trade hardcover books and some special paperbacks are cut into book-sized pages and bound with stiff paper covers. These bound, uncorrected proofs (commonly known as "bound galleys") are submitted to book clubs, reprinters, reviewers, and well-known people who may be willing to write plugs for the book. (Author and agent often get a number of sets, too, in order to begin exploitation of reserved rights.)

In the meantime, the author and a proofreader do close readings of the loose galleys or page proofs and mark their corrections on them. The quality of the setting job may vary from typesetter to typesetter, publisher to publisher, book to book. It's never perfect, and can range from a sprinkling of errors to horrifying botches of dropped paragraphs, transposed sentences, and garbled and mangled words. The cost of correcting printer's errors is the printer's; but the cost of typesetting new material, at this stage known as author's alterations ("AA's"), is borne by the author after the cost of the author's changes has reached 5 percent or 10 percent of the total cost of composition — a percentage dictated by the publishing contract. Therefore, you're advised to keep such changes to a minimum and try to lock up the text of your book in the manuscript stage, where additions don't cost anybody anything.

The task of reading galleys or page proofs is a little less exciting than watching one's fingernails grow, and nothing is better calculated to disenchant an author about the virtues of his book than a word-by-word reading of it in proofs. Yet this is one of the most essential of all publishing processes, for every error that escapes detection turns up in print as a glaring, indelible testimony of somebody's carelessness. Typographic, spelling, and editing errors in books are embarrassing to author and publisher, and distracting to readers at the very least, as when an actor fluffs a line during an otherwise flawless performance.

I am appalled at how many errors I come across in books published even by distinguished houses. Perhaps I'm blinded by nostalgia, but I don't recall the problem having existed twenty or thirty years ago, and it appears that proofreading is succumbing to the same decline of pride that has affected so many other skilled crafts. Nevertheless, though the job of correcting galleys is, technically, your publisher's, the *responsibility* for clean copy is ultimately yours.

Proofreading is nothing like reading for pleasure. Your eyes must stop on every word, indeed on every syllable of multisyllabic words where errors are beautifully camouflaged from the hasty reader. When you are through, give the proofs to your spouse or someone else who can be counted on to read the copy with precision. Personally, I would rather lend someone money than read his proofs, so intensely boring do I find the task. But it's a job that must be done, and done not merely well but perfectly; so after the appropriate groans, mutters, oaths, and procrastinations, give the task the fullest measure of your concentration.

When you turn in your corrected proofs, your copy editor will transfer your changes and corrections to the proofreader's corrected set. The master set of proofs is then returned to the printer.

While this is going on, the rest of your publishing company has not exactly been idle. At the same time, the book's cover art, the blurb, and the biographical information are being completed, to ready the covers (if the book is a paperback) or the dust jacket (if the book is a hardcover) for printing. Marketing, sales, publicity, advertising, and promotional strategies are being devised or made final. The semiannual catalogue, which contains announcements of the upcoming season's books (including yours) plus backlist information, is ready for printing and mailing to booksellers and others in the publishing trade.

✍

With the exception of the occasional superquickie release (the kind of paperback that is blasted through the system in weeks, such as those released shortly after the death of Jacqueline Kennedy Onassis or the murders of Nicole Brown Simpson and Ronald Goldman), all books require some sort of formal announcement to the book trade. The purpose is to prepare the sales representatives, the distributors, the bookstore buyers, and others along the supply and demand chain for publication or release of the book. If buyers or sellers are unfamiliar with the product and its sales features, it simply cannot be sold. It's as simple as that. Catalogues are sell pieces. Or, as one editor reared in the textile business said to me, "Catalogues are our swatch books."

Although there are many significant differences between hardcover and paperback catalogues, the fundamental format is the same for both types of publication. It usually starts with a black and white photo of the book's cover (art book catalogues may use color photos), accompanied by a description of the contents. There is a paragraph about the author, and some promotional highlights. In small print are details of the book's length, price, ISBN number, publication date, type (hardcover, trade paperback, mass market paperback), and number of photographs or other illustrations, if any. At the end of the catalogue are order forms (or at least order information), and sometimes there is a rights list. The latter tells interested parties, such as movie producers or foreign publishers, who controls the subsidiary rights to the books in the catalogue. In some cases that may be the publisher, in others the author, and in still others the author's agent or sub-agents. If the publisher controls foreign rights, it may list the names and addresses of its overseas agents for the benefit of interested foreign publishers.

The featured books for the season (or, if it's a mass market catalogue, for the month) are usually given a full page, or even a double-page spread. Books of lesser import may get a half-page, a third, or a quarter, or may simply be listed with a minimum of description. Although it's usually well understood by everybody on the publisher's staff which books are going to get which treatment, editors nevertheless often jockey for better positions or more prominent display for the books they are sponsoring. "Sometimes the infighting gets pretty bloody," one editor told me. A good catalogue, whether it be trade or mass market, gives the impression of sound balance between the featured titles and the secondary ones.

Many catalogues contain backlist information; that is, lists of previously published books that are still in print and available, or at least are supposed to be. As most of the books sold in this country annually are backlist titles, you would think that publishers might make more of their backlist catalogues than they do. But as backlist is not as sexy as new books, one seldom sees more than a page or two in most catalogues listing a selection of recently published books plus a price list. Crown Publishers, to its credit, issues a separate backlist catalogue.

Owing to the fact that trade book publishing is seasonal, and mass market paperback publishing monthly, the approaches to catalogues differ widely between the two types of product. Trade hardcover publishers publish catalogues for spring and fall seasons, and sometimes winter, as well. The style and format of trade publishers' catalogues convey the sense of majestic stability and dependable rhythm that one associates with hardcover publishing. They are vital components of the semiannual sales conferences. They resemble small, elegant magazines, printed on glossy stock and boasting four-color covers, and they invite browsing. Although they have visual appeal, they rely heavily on evocative text for their impact. They are written to be read.

Mass market catalogues are commonly referred to as author information kits (AIs for short) and have greater variety of format, depend more on pictorial appeal, and, as they are issued on a monthly basis, reflect the more frenetic rhythm of the paperback industry. As it is obviously impractical to hold a sales conference every month, there is less emphasis on AIs as formal instruments for presentation of the company's list to the accounts. Instead, they are issued along with cover proofs to the publisher's sales reps, to chain store buyers, and to major paperback wholesalers, independent distributors, and rack jobbers.

There is wide variety in the monthly material sent out by paperback publishers. Some AIs superficially follow the format of hardcover catalogues but are printed on pulpier stock. Others have beautiful, glossy, four-color, elaborately die-cut or pop-up promotional pieces for the lead books accompanying their conventional lists and order forms. Included in the sales kit may be posters, bookmarks, and other gimmicks. The Berkley Group's monthly package is a particularly stunning array of handsomely packaged promo items for the lead titles for each company in the Group:

Berkley, Jove, Ace, and Diamond. Whatever else may go out from paperback publishers, the focus of most monthly AIs is the cover. "The biggest difference between hardcover and paperback catalogues is that the former depend on words, but the latter depend on pictures — on the covers," says John Douglas, senior editor at Avon Books.

At some publishers the catalogue copy is written by the sponsoring editor for each book. At others, it is prepared by specialists in the publisher's promotion department, and at still others it is farmed out to freelancers. Promotional and cover copy call for very special writing skills, as any author quickly realizes when asked in his publicity questionnaire to summarize his book. As authors we are taught to use adjectives and adverbs sparingly, but promotional copywriters revel in them.

I recently showed some catalogues to the buyer for a major bookstore chain and asked him for his impressions. "I think of catalogues as publishers' personal emissaries," he said. They accompany the sales reps as they make their rounds pitching their lists to the buyers, and after they leave, the catalogue remains behind to help the buyers make their selections and place their orders. The buyer I spoke to said he likes his catalogues to be attractive, concise, and meaningful. He is wary of those that promote midlist books as enthusiastically as blockbusters. He looks for signs that certain books are going to be pushed, such as news of author tours, advertising and promotional commitments, and anticipated printings. Unfortunately, much of that information is unavailable at the time catalogues go to press, and the buyers look to the sales reps to furnish that type of supplementary information. Nevertheless, some of it may be garnered from catalogues, and that helps the store buyer to set his purchasing strategy.

The closing date for a hardcover catalogue usually occurs about nine months before the publication season. In other words, the copy, cover art, and other information must be in hand by, say, February for the fall list, August for the spring list. In paperback, the period is shorter. Whatever the lead time may be, once the catalogue goes to the printer, the list is locked. Any book for which the catalogue entry arrives after closing must be postponed until the next available season, or, in paperback, the next available month.

Writers usually call their agents or editors when they expect to deliver their books late and ask precisely how late is too late. The answer should now be apparent. Except for books with inflexible deadlines — say, movie tie-ins — there is usually a grace period of a few weeks, or perhaps a month or a bit more, before it becomes appropriate to alert the publisher that a book is not going to be delivered on time. After that, several inexorable deadlines begin to impinge on the editor's consciousness, and one of these is the catalogue closing date. It's worth finding out what that is, for while there may be leeway with your publisher in some respects, there is none once the catalogue is closed: Your book will be pulled from the schedule.

✍

Now that your book is locked into the catalogue, a final decision must be reached about how many copies to print. Of all the mysteries surrounding publishing, none seems so deep to authors as how a publisher determines the number of copies of a book to be printed. Authors seem to feel that this figure is arrived at strictly on the strength of the publisher's enthusiasm for the book, so that if the company really loves a book it'll do a 50,000-copy first hardcover printing, but if it's indifferent the print run will be only 5000. True, enthusiasm does play a part in such decisions, but they depend on far more than that.

Every six months, publishers conduct sales conferences, where the editorial staff introduces the next season's books to the salespeople. These affairs range from strictly businesslike meetings conducted on the publishing company's premises, to junkets to resort hotels, where business is mingled with golf, tennis, swimming, dancing, and partying. Editors describe their books to the sales staff in verbal presentations, and distribute copies of the proofs, synopses, and/or sample chapters, plus samples of cover art, advertisements, promotional schemes, biographical sketches of the authors, news of movie or television deals or book-club or reprint sales, plugs from big-name authors and other celebrities — anything, in other words, that will make their books stand out and that will fortify the salespeople's pitches when they sally forth to bookstores and distribution headquarters. And by the time the sales conference is over, decisions will have been made concerning the amount and kind of advertising and promotion to be given each book.

Occasionally authors are invited to sales conferences, but not very often. I've always thought this a shame, for although not all authors make good impressions, many are articulate, animated people whose enthusiasm can prove infectious and who often have nifty ideas for promoting and marketing their books, ideas that may not otherwise filter down to the salespeople.

Fired up, one would hope, with enthusiasm, the salespeople now make the rounds of the buyers in their territories, highlighting each book with the sales material and information furnished at sales conference. On the strength (or weakness) of a sales pitch, the store or chain buyer will order a number of copies. If the book is another big one by an author who's had two or three previous best-sellers, obviously the buyer will order a great many more than he will of a first novel that sounds like too many other first novels (despite the salesperson's attempt to make it sound like the greatest book since *Moby-Dick*).

The salespeople then file their orders with the head of the sales department of the publishing company, and the orders are tabulated. Orders for the new novel by the big-name author may total 50,000 copies; for the first novel, perhaps 3500. These totals are called the "advance sale," or sometimes just the "advance," a term not to be confused with advances against royalties. Thus you'll hear publishers saying that this or that book "advanced ten thousand copies," which means that that's how many copies were ordered before publication. The publisher might then do a first printing of 12,500 copies, to accommodate the 10,000-copy advance plus a reserve for the warehouse. The printing presses will be poised for another run if demand surges, but publishers are very wary of overprinting, for, remember, books are usually returnable for full refund, and warehouse storage of books is expensive. Despite the finality of the word *sale* in the term *advance sale*, an advance of 10,000 copies doesn't mean that those 10,000 will never come back. Some of them may, and if a publisher is too quick on the trigger with printings, or overestimates demand with large printings, he may end up "eating" a lot of copies — a diet that has given many a publisher excruciating ulcers. At any rate, you can see that the number of copies printed is a function of demand more than it is of the publisher's enthusiasm.

For many authors and agents, the phrase "Sales doesn't like it" is like an irrevocable decree of execution. If Sales believes a title doesn't fly, a package doesn't work, a book is too long, too short, too tame, too dirty, too trivial, too ponderous, an author defies the decree at his peril.

Exactly who are the people generically described as "Sales," and how are they able to influence so forcefully the way our books are published?

Like salespersons in every field, book sales representatives possess the gift of presenting their product to potential buyers in a colorful and enthusiastic fashion, making it seem irresistibly desirable if not indispensable. Although literateness is not imperative — salespeople like to feel they can sell anything — the intellectual nature of the book sales rep's stock-in-trade makes a touch of the poet a definite asset. "When it comes to books, you're selling ideas as much as anything else," one rep told me.

Most book sales reps receive salaries plus commissions. Bonuses and other incentives are offered for achieving quotas or other sales goals. A company car or a car allowance is usual.

Many sales reps work for more than one publisher, particularly if the houses are small and cannot afford to retain a staff of full-time salespeople.

Sales reps try to educate themselves about their product by conferring with publishers and reviewing the books on the coming list in the form of proofs, excerpts, or synopses. Their reading is supplemented by catalogue information, highlights of authors' track records, news of prepublication action such as movie or book-club deals, promotional plans, and even gossip: anything, in short, that individuates books and gives the reps a handle, however slim. Presentation of the list may take place by means of a briefing in the modest offices of a small publisher, or an elaborate dog-and-pony show at a sales conference conducted in an exotic resort hotel.

Most sales reps cover a specific territory — Northeast, Midwest, South, Southwest, West Coast, and sometimes an even more narrowly defined area. The big national chains have buying offices in central locations, where orders are taken for stores nation- or regionwide. Reps make appointments to see the buyer and arrive bearing proofs, sample covers, catalogues, promo pieces, and gimmicks such as bookmarks, posters, displays, and novelties. They also carry vital information about their publisher's discount, returns, settlement, and other business policies and practices.

The conditions under which the rep operates are seldom conducive to serene and leisurely presentation. Buyers, particularly owners of independent bookstores, are frequently distracted by the exigencies of running a business, and the rep's well-rehearsed pitch is interrupted by phone calls or curtailed by the pressure of stacked-up appointments on the buyer's crowded calendar. Under these trying circumstances, reps find themselves with an average of thirty seconds to describe each book. They are therefore highly adept at extracting the very essence from the material at hand. As you might imagine, however, they don't give all of their wares equal time. Nor would the buyer have them do so. The impatient men and women on the other side of the table are prepared to take certain things for granted, such as the virtues of a routine mystery, romance, or cookbook. On the other hand, they want the rep to dwell on the books to which the publisher has made a strong commitment. "Tell me what you're enthusiastic about" is a remark that sales reps frequently heard from Spencer Gale, former merchandise manager for Doubleday Book Shops. Chainstore buyers eagerly elicit news of the publisher's advertising and promotion plans, special discounts, impressive printings, and other indications that the publisher is getting behind a particular book.

Often, seller and buyer discuss aspects of the book that may furnish the publisher with valuable feedback, and because most books have not been locked up at this stage, there is time for the publisher to remedy problems and make mid-course corrections if the consensus is that such actions will improve sales potential.

Some reps visit bookstores only a few times a year. Others drop in every week to check on inventory or display, or just to keep their fingers on the pulse of business. Some are well read, even erudite, and quite savvy about the competition.

The rep wraps up the presentation. He or she departs. Presently the buyer will evaluate the data, fill out and return to the rep order forms stipulating the number of copies to be supplied to the store or chain. The orders are tallied by the publisher's sales manager, and, in the case of most books, the printing is then fixed. If a book is a major one, the printing may have been set before the sales reps went out into the field, but it may be adjusted downward or upward depending on responses by buyers as reported by the sales reps. When a publisher sets large printings in advance, the reps are given sales quotas to meet, and some hard pushing may take place at the stores and at chain buying offices. Sometimes the buyers resent being pushed, but if the author — and the incentives — are right, they enthusiastically rise to the challenge.

The sales manager is the publishing executive responsible for the gathering of orders and interpreting them as well as weighing the less tangible feedback from the field. He must then articulate his conclusions to editors, marketing executives, and other members of the firm, such as the art director. The sales manager is often a former sales rep and sits on the publisher's editorial board, tempering the hopes, hunches, speculations, and wishful thinking of editors with sober practical experience and brutally hard statistics.

There are three stages of a book's life in which the sales manager will be involved: acquisition, production, and sale. In the acquisition stage, book salespeople seldom have much say. They are not present when acquisition meetings are held, and their opinion is not usually invited. This can be a source of resentment among some sales reps, who complain they are handed a list of books two or three times a year and told, "Here, sell these." But their sales manager *is* on hand when acquisition decisions are debated, and his or her opinion is actively solicited, welcomed, and respected; in a great many cases, it is decisive.

Good sales reps try to keep up with news of acquisitions so that their initial reaction to their publisher's list is not one of total surprise. But their first important exposure to upcoming books comes when they receive a copy of their publisher's catalogue or attend sales conference. By that time, books on the new list have moved to the second stage of their life: production. Rarely is production at such an advanced point that it is too late to be affected by criticism from the reps, and because they mingle freely with the editorial staff at sales conference, they seize the opportunity to take a direct hand in shaping the final product. Sometimes they express their own opinions and sometimes they pass along the reactions of buyers.

The reps' input draws on hard experience dealing with local, regional, and national accounts. They may know that in their territory dark covers are death for romances but great for murder mysteries, that glitzy women's fiction works better in the spring and serious nonfiction in the fall, or that the stores don't want another visit from an author who toured unsuccessfully on his last book. They may not always be able to explain the behavior of the buyers or articulate their own feelings, and sometimes their views may border on the superstitious: One-word titles sell better than three-word titles, photographic covers sell better than painted ones, yellow attracts more buyers than blue, and so forth.

Some of this must be taken with a grain of salt. After all, if you show a cover to fifty people you will get fifty varying opinions, and a sales rep's may not be more valid than yours or mine just because he or she is a sales rep. Here is where the sales manager's role is critical. "We evaluate those grains of salt," the director of sales of one paperback company told me. "If a rep says 'Change the cover,' that's one thing, but if he says 'Change the cover because the buyer will increase his order,' that's quite another."

The interaction between sales reps and editors is of paramount importance to a book's fate. "We have often repositioned books as a result of open discussions at sales conference," a Doubleday editor told me. Another editor described an internecine conflict that arose when her company's editors presented the sales reps with a book about a famous rock star. The reps had been geared up to sell a photo book with sparse text; the book they got was heavily weighted with biographical information. The dialogue between Sales and Editorial became stormy, but after both viewpoints were aired, a compromise was reached that was satisfactory to all hands. "You have to understand that outside sales reps are conduits," one sales executive explains. "They're not expressing just their own opinion, but what their accounts are telling them. If they're negative about something, it's not because they hate it; it's because they can't sell it."

Authors have a responsibility to communicate with Sales by providing their publishers with information about themselves and their achievements. Attention to publicity questionnaires is a good way to start. By providing biographical, sales, and other details to your publishers you will be giving them those all-important handles to emphasize when they make their pitch to buyers. By updating your publisher about your travel plans, upcoming events that may tie in with themes in your books, useful media contacts you have made, you may be aiding your sales reps immeasurably. Above all, try to think like a sales rep. Put yourself in a rep's place and imagine what he or she needs to know in order to impress a buyer during the scant time allotted to the presentation of your book. Then, the next time you're told that "Sales doesn't like it," you'll feel more compassion for the folks who are out there busting their humps to sell your book.

# 16

# Is There Life After Pub Date?

If you believe your book will be launched by a lavish party hosted by your publisher, you're probably living in the past. Though publication parties still take place, they are usually thrown for books that have already cost their publisher a million dollars or more, and what difference is another $50,000 going to make, anyway? If you feel your book deserves a publication party, buy some soft drinks and pretzels and have a ball. Don't be surprised if the press doesn't show up. Don't be surprised if your editor doesn't show up.

Your editor may have better things to do, like thinking up ways to promote your book with the modest budget allotted to it, or with no budget at all. If you've done your homework, you may be able to furnish your editor with lots of creative ideas about how that can be done.

Naturally, the obvious one is advertising and promotion. To most authors it makes eminently good sense that the only way to tell the public you have a good product is to advertise it. This makes eminently good sense to publishers, too, but they have a bottom line to wrestle with, and advertising costs money — lots of it. A modest-sized one-time ad in one newspaper or national magazine costs thousands of dollars, which is more than the profit anticipated from many midlist books! Many publishers agree that for an ad campaign to have a chance of succeeding, it must cost a minimum of $100,000. Few books can earn that kind of profit.

Yes, you say, but maybe they *would* earn that kind of profit if publishers advertised them! More good sense, but not necessarily accurate. For every book that's skyrocketed because of advertising, publishers can point to two that have flopped despite it, and indeed they can point to three that have hit the bestseller lists completely unabetted by advertising.

In book advertising, as in any other kind of consumer advertising, we know that 50 percent of all ads are effective — but we don't know *which* 50 percent. Despite a great deal of marketing research, book advertising is as far from becoming a science as ever. This is another case, then, where a publisher's enthusiasm for a book isn't enough to make him whip out his checkbook and invest in a big advertising campaign. But if the auguries of book-club and reprint deals, movie and magazine and foreign sales, reviews and endorsements, and in-house enthusiasm and word-of-mouth bode well — if, in short, the merchandise is moving — a publisher may feel that advertising will *keep* it moving. Because such a book will clearly be making a profit, the publisher will now have the money to spend on ads. At this point a self-sustaining cycle comes into operation: The bestseller's sales produce the advertising fuel, and the advertising fuel energizes more sales.

The same may be said of sending authors on promotional tours. To book a proper tour to, say, twenty key urban markets costs thousands if not tens of thousands of dollars in air fares, hotel accommodations, and per diem expenses, plus the publisher's own overhead in developing and coordinating the campaign, producing and mailing promotional material, and so forth. Unless the publisher feels that such a tour is cost-effective, he is not going to send the author on one, it's as simple as that. Besides, not all authors are promotable, well spoken, or have books that lend themselves to promotion. First novels and midlist fiction, much genre fiction, juveniles, and some nonfiction simply cannot be promoted effectively, no matter how much money and effort authors and publishers put into it.

Some months before the actual publication date — "pub date," as publishers call it — your book will get its first reviews. These will appear in *Publishers Weekly*, *The Kirkus Reviews*, *Library Journal*, and a few other review media aimed at the publishing trade and libraries. In some cases these reviews have little effect on the publisher's attitude toward, and plans for, your book; in others they may well presage and affect your book's fate, encouraging your publisher to get behind it or making him cancel plans for advertising, big printings, and the like. In due time after publication, reviews will turn up in newspapers and magazines across the country. Your publisher usually subscribes to a service that looks for and clips any reviews and references to the books and authors on his list, and from time to time these will be forwarded to you. If they are favorable or unusually enthusiastic, your publisher may be heartened to spend some money on advertising, or on making a second round of sales pitches to the stores and chains in an effort to persuade them to order more copies, display the book a little more prominently, recommend it to consumers a little more vociferously. If the publisher hasn't yet sold reprint rights to your book, he may now inundate reprinters with copies of good reviews, and pressure them to make bids.

What can you do to help your publisher help your book? I recommend a number of tactics.

**Visit your publisher.** Although I don't think it's a good idea for you to visit until your book has been accepted and your contract signed, there is some benefit to be derived from a visit afterward. Some of that benefit is intangible. Publishers, like business people the world over, become better motivated after meeting the face behind the voice on the phone. Indeed, authors may become better motivated as well, as they and their editors begin to feel more comfortable with each other. Other benefits are more concrete, because a great deal of business can be accomplished in an hour or two of face-to-face discussion that cannot be carried out by phone or mail.

If you live near your publisher's office, call your editor and ask if you might drop by just to shake hands and chat for a few minutes. If you can maneuver a lunch or drink invitation, so much the better, but because many editors are on tight expense accounts you might get further by offering to buy: As such offers occur infrequently, it's not a kindness your editor is likely to forget. You needn't necessarily discuss heavy business; you just want to say hello and thank-you and offer your cooperation in whatever way your editor requires. Your editor may have some business, though, and might want to discuss some changes in your manuscript, or solicit your ideas about marketing the book, or just tell you what procedures you may now look forward to as your book wends its way toward pub date. He or she may wish to introduce you to a few colleagues, such as your copy editor, the head of sales, or the publicity director. Unless you've actually managed to schedule meetings with them, though, just shake hands and ask them what you can do to help, or tell them you'll be in touch with some suggestions that might help them do a better job on your book.

Even if you don't live in the vicinity of your publisher, it might well be worth your while to make the trip. Obviously it would be best if you could tie this in with a vacation or some other business you have in the same city, for unless yours is a big book you can't expect to spend days and days in deep conference with your publisher; we're talking about an hour or two, maybe less.

The best time for a visit might be about six months before publication, when plans for your book are just beginning to congeal. Ask your editor to set up brief appointments with people in the sales and publicity departments, and maybe subsidiary rights; and ask if while you're there you could perhaps shake hands with the editor-in-chief or publisher.

**Offer written suggestions.** Before you make your trip, or perhaps immediately after, type up some ideas you can give to staff members, proposing ways they can do a better job on your book. Few publishers are so arrogant as to reject suggestions from authors. Indeed, most of them solicit help and are grateful for it, as long as authors don't pester them or overwhelm them with tasks beyond the limits of their time, energy, and budget. A list of authors, reviewers, and/or celebrities you personally know and who might give your book nice endorsements is extremely useful to your publicity department. And the sales staff will be glad to get a summary of unique features that raise your book above the common herd: "This is the first book to tell you . . ."; "This is the only book that . . ."; "My book differs from all others on the subject in the following ways . . ."; "No other book on the subject has illustrations . . . easy-to-follow charts . . . a program for improvement in just one week . . . the endorsement of the American Medical Association . . ."; "It's been sold to Paramount Pictures . . . ABC for a miniseries . . . Jane Fonda . . ."

Send copies of these suggestions to the other key people at your publishing company, including the editor-in-chief or publisher, whether you've met them or not. The more staff members you can expose to your book, the better your chances that some of your points will stick in the minds of those who stand to do your book some good.

**Be prepared to spend your own money.** By now it should be abundantly clear that your publisher's resources are limited and must be husbanded for the major books on his list. If you feel that the only thing holding your book back from success is expenditure of a little money, and you can't persuade your publisher to spend it, then spend it yourself.

On what?

Assuming you have a limited budget, perhaps the best thing you can spend money on is a tour of bookstores. Start with those in the cities closest to your home, and then you can either radiate outward or hop around to proven book-buying cities such as New York, Chicago, Boston, and Los Angeles. Bring copies of your book with you. Introduce yourself to the manager of each store, tell him about your book, give him a copy if he's not familiar with it, describe its special features and sales points to him, and persuade him to order some copies from your publisher's sales representative or distributor. This may not always be as easy as it sounds. In the case of bookstore chains, for example, the buying for individual stores is done on a regional or national basis, and it's unlikely you'll be allowed to make your pitch to the buyers in central headquarters. Nevertheless, approaching bookstore people can often be effective, and I have seen authors charm store managers into ordering copies, displaying books more prominently, stacking copies in store windows, or even throwing impromptu book-signing parties.

Another thing money can buy is advertising. Ads can prove a complete waste of money if the books aren't available, and that's why I put priority on getting books into the stores. Once they're there, ads may move them into the hands of the consumers. I suggest you talk to the advertising director about what you can do to integrate your advertising budget and ideas for your book with those of your publisher.

Though it's nice to buy a string of ads in the Sunday *New York Times Book Review* for $10,000 or $15,000 apiece, this may not necessarily be the most effective use of your ad budget, even if you have that kind of capital. Try to ascertain what newspapers or magazines are read by the people who might read your book, and place your ads there. You may discover that $1000 spent in a small specialty magazine will stretch a lot further and attract more buyers than the same amount invested in a general, national magazine. Not too long ago, my agency handled a novel about a ballet dancer, and the publisher discovered that advertising it in dance magazines was far more effective and cheaper than advertising it in the book sections of major papers.

Then there's promotion. As with advertising, promotional tours must be coordinated to ensure the accessibility of books in the stores, otherwise you might as well toss your money off a mountaintop. This, too, is a job best handled by professionals. There are a number of companies that specialize in booking author tours, at prices ranging from a few thousand dollars to the-sky's-the-limit. These companies will coach you in such matters as dress, diction, and presentation of your subject. They may also help with publicity, disseminating press releases, gossip-column items, and feature stories that tie in with your work tour. The person or agency hired should of course work in coordination with the publisher's publicity department, which should be consulted about all of your plans for promoting the book. An important event in the promotion of your book is the ABA, the American Booksellers Association convention. You hear much about the ABA, if for no other reason than that it's impossible to get anyone important at your publisher's offices during the week or two preceding it. What is the ABA? Should you attend? Will your publisher invite you? Will your presence make a difference?

For most writers genuine satisfaction comes so seldom that when it does happen they may be forgiven for gloating. Gloating is essentially an antisocial activity that promotes one's own accomplishments while denigrating those of one's colleagues. That's what makes it so delicious. What is the point of achieving success if you can't make your friends feel like failures?

Authors contesting to show each other up usually measure their excellence in terms of big advances, large printings, full-page ads, bookstore signings, distinguished awards, and, of course, high positions on the bestseller list. These are all well and good. But there is one boast that consistently trumps all others: "My publisher is bringing me to the ABA." Mention that one in your writers' circle;

watch your friends' eyes widen with envy and listen to the awed hush that blankets the room.

ABA is a trade fair, no different in purpose from those conducted by shoe, cosmetics, electronics, and home appliance manufacturers. The idea is for sellers to display their wares to buyers and interest them in placing orders for the coming season. In this case the wares are books; the sellers, publishers; and the buyers, booksellers. ABA is held annually on or around the Memorial Day weekend. Until recently it was hosted by a different city every year. In recent years Washington, Anaheim, Las Vegas, and New York have been the sites. It is now permanently located in Chicago. The fair is open to the public to introduce the ultimate buyer, the consumer, to exhibitors and to allow the consumer to see and sample the products that are (or are soon to be) available in the literary marketplace.

Trade fairs are an honorable tradition dating back to medieval times, and many great European and Asian cities rose out of the sites where these bazaars were held. Although the ultimate goal is to move merchandise, they serve a number of other significant purposes as well. Fairs are wonderful places to make or renew the acquaintance of those with whom you have conducted business only from afar, particularly foreign publishers. For, despite wondrous modes of communication that were never available to our medieval forebears, there is still no substitute for meeting your counterpart face to face. Also, although ABA was never known as a "rights fair" until recently, there has been a marked increase of late in on-the-spot dealmaking among agents, publishers, and movie producers.

The ABA also offers an important forum for ideas that are of concern to the publishing community. Book-and-author breakfasts, luncheons, and seminars air such significant issues as literacy, censorship, and technological advances, as well as more esoteric subjects such as distribution, discounts, and incentives. Among the topics for such events at a recent convention were "Stopping the Shoplifter," "Off-Beat Promotions," "Bargain Books in Bad Times," and "Positioning African-American Books in Our Marketplace."

Those functions notwithstanding, the most important reason for holding the ABA is public relations. Younger and smaller publishers vie to make their presence known, while the larger and more established ones mount grand, gorgeous displays aimed at impressing their superiority upon visitors. If this behavior reminds you of mating rituals conducted in the wild, you will find many analogies to support the metaphor.

Dominance is manifested in a variety of ways. One, obviously, is the size of the exhibit. Publishers that take up vast areas of floor space appear in the eyes of many beholders to be superior to those that occupy booths smaller than the frankfurter concession. Another is the location of booths. Competition for central space or space near the main entrance of the building is intense, and exhibitors accorded a location in the remotest regions of the hall are keenly aware of how low on the pecking order they are.

Another criterion for judging exhibitors is the beauty of their exhibits. The design and decoration of their booths is a year-round occupation for larger publishers, and it shows. At a convention held in New York City's cavernous Jacob Javits Center, for example, the industrial carpet that was good enough for most exhibitors was covered by a deep and fleecy white one at the HarperCollins booth. Alfred Knopf, promoting a picture book about the Vatican's Sistine Chapel, designed a stunning mini-Sistine Chapel under which to display its fall list. It was the first thing visitors saw upon entering the main hall, by the way. Zebra's booth, as might be expected, was decorated in black and white stripes and was as striking as a float in the Rose Bowl parade.

Yet another way for publishers to distinguish themselves is with giveaways. Experienced ABA-goers know to bring shopping bags to haul away the books, bound proofs, catalogues, buttons, banners, posters, and gimmicks that are given away to promote publishers and their products. And if you forget to bring a shopping bag, that's all right — publishers hand those out, too. There are also clowns, conjurers, and other entertainers, such as the master paper-folder whose origami demonstration promoted several books on the subject for a publisher of Orientalia.

And then there's the free food. Publishers pushing a cookbook on their list may whip up a batch of the author's specialty. One year Bantam Doubleday Dell served pizza slices, for instance, and a smaller house concocted some fish balls to tie in with a Caribbean cookbook.

By far the biggest giveaways at ABA are the parties. Thorstein Veblen's theory that conspicuous consumption elevates a tribe's status in the eyes of its peers has seldom been better demonstrated than in the profligate bashes hosted by the major publishing houses on ABA weekend. I cannot personally report on all of them, as many are for booksellers only and agents are not invited. Perhaps that is just as well, for anyone struggling to maintain a semblance of sound diet and weight control will be resoundingly defeated at these potlatches. Any bookseller unimpressed by such Lucullan spreads must have a stone heart and a cast iron stomach.

Yet the centerpiece of these feasts is not the food but the authors. A recent bash thrown by Putnam featured twenty-nine of its most illustrious stars. Sporting elaborate blue ribbons, such mega-bestsellers as Tom Clancy, Bill Cosby, George Burns, Amy Tan, Dale Brown, Dick Francis, Piers Anthony, Linda Ellerbee, and LaVyrle Spencer were exhibited on the restaurant's mezzanine, where hordes of journalists and photographers recorded their every word and gesture, and hordes more of onlookers strained for a glimpse of these idols. Mind you, these were not World Series or Super Bowl champions, or the President and First Lady of the United States, or the reigning screen kings and queens of Hollywood, or the stars of the hottest rock group in the country.

These were authors.

If you were to survey the world's professional writers you would find few who felt that this kind of lionization was the pinnacle to which they aspired. They would tell you that for them the payoff is the satisfaction of perfectly expressing on paper the complex or beautiful vision that is in their mind's eye; or the thrill of holding a bound copy of their first published book; or the pleasure of reading an intelligent and complimentary review in an important journal; or the glow of pride when their work is nominated for a literary prize by an eminent jury of their peers.

Far be it from me to denigrate such noble sentiments. But no writer who utters them has ever stood in the glare of spotlights at an ABA party hosted by a major publisher, crowded by frenzied media people and adulating fans. Whether we approve or not, events such as this have become the ne plus ultra of authorly ambition, the ultimate fantasy trip.

Of course, any writer can *attend* ABA. All you need is the airfare, the hotel tariff, and a guest pass. And any author can *appear* at his publisher's booth. Just show up and introduce yourself to the staff members in attendance. They'll be glad to say howdy if they're not too busy taking orders from booksellers. Many authors do visit the fair for an instructive look at what is published and by whom. But this is not the same as being flown in, transported in a limo, booked into a swank hotel, squired all over town, and vigorously promoted at the convention, all at your publisher's expense.

I know there are authors somewhere who don't secretly desire all this. I also know there are unicorns, trolls, and fairies. If I haven't found them, it's undoubtedly because I haven't looked hard enough.

Dazzled as we are by all the hype and hucksterism, we've almost forgotten to ask the most important question of all: Does the ABA sell books?

We know that books get sold: Every booth has a table where sales reps can sit down with booksellers and write up orders. But do they get sold in numbers significant enough to justify a publisher's investment of time and money in mounting a display at ABA?

Interestingly, the smaller presses may have the edge over the leviathans on that score. Most big publishers acknowledge the largely public relations function of the fair and consider books sold to be a bonus, but not one that makes much of a dent on the balance sheets. The little houses, however, rely on the convention to attract buyers and do real business. With their lower overhead, these companies stand to fare handsomely if orders of any appreciable size are written.

One major player who decided the game was not worth the candle is Thomas McCormack, the head of St. Martin's Press. Looking at a cost of some $300,000 in direct expenses and incidental overhead (like staff time lost), McCormack defied the opinion of his peers and declined to exhibit at ABA starting with the 1991 convention. Interestingly, he did it in a year when the event was in his back yard, for St. Martin's is headquartered in New York City. But the cost of accommodating out-of-town sales representatives in Manhattan is actually higher than the cost of transporting the New York staff to another city.

McCormack made good on his promise to invest the savings by hiring new sales reps, particularly for the growing paperback division of his company. Although the pullout did not materially affect the balance sheet of the convention, McCormack's daring move provoked a great deal of thought and attention in the publishing community. If even a few other big publishers take a page out of his book, the ABA may never again be the same.

✍

A month or two after publication, the destinies of most trade books have been sealed — but not all of them. A steady stream of good reviews, recommendations by word of mouth, unexpected news coverage, or other events may unexpectedly boost a book into orbit long after publication date. Say a producer options your novel and manages to put together a movie or television deal. Twelve or eighteen months later — maybe even two or three years after publication — it's released in theaters or exhibited on television, and it's a hit. Now a lot of people want to read this book that few wanted to read when it was first published. Did I say two or three years later? Why, we can all cite instances of movies made decades after publication of the book on which they're based. Or your first or second novel may achieve little recognition and sales until your third or fourth or eighth book has come out and you've built up an audience that will read everything of yours, past, present, and future.

So you mustn't be discouraged if your first book or books don't take off into the wild blue yonder. Few famous authors burst into prominence with their first books, but rather achieve success through sustained effort over the course of many books. Although we live, unquestionably, in a publishing world governed by the blockbuster mentality, few blockbusters are first books. Rather, they are the culmination of years of dedication to craft, and a number of flops or indifferent successes. The bestseller list must be restocked by fresh talent. Until that magical moment when you are exalted into membership in that exclusive club (assuming you want to belong; not everybody does), my advice to you is, get published, get published, get published. Do what you can to make your book succeed, but after you've done all you can, go back to your typewriter and write another, and another after that, and yet another after that. Keep your spirits up and think about what you're going to say when you accept the Nobel Prize.

# 17

# Beyond the Bestseller List

The year 1995 marked the hundredth anniversary of the concept of bestseller lists. But the controversies ignited by Harry Thurston Peck, then editor of *The Bookman*, rage as acrimoniously today as they did almost a century ago when he devised his listing of "New Books in the Order of Demand." In the fall of 1990, for instance, the press reported yet another allegation of attempts to influence the Sunday *New York Times* bestseller list, generally held to be the standard by which most people in or out of the publishing industry judge the commercial success of books. It seems that executives of the Gannett Foundation, a nonprofit organization, were asked to purchase copies of *Confessions of an S.O.B.* by the organization's founder, Allen H. Neuharth, at specific bookstores in their areas. The foundation would then reimburse them and donate the copies to journalism schools. *The Washington Post* reported that these purchases were aimed at affecting the *New York Times* list as well as that of *Publishers Weekly*, the trade magazine of the publishing industry. The author rebutted the assertion, saying, "I wish I knew how to control the *New York Times* bestseller list, because if I did, my book would still be on it."

Are bestseller lists an honest and objective form of market analysis? Or are they, to use the word employed by Jerry Lazar in *More* magazine, a sham contrived by publishers and booksellers to push their featured merchandise?

From all that I have been able to gather through research and discussions with publishing people, I've concluded that the answer to both questions is — yes. While information-gathering procedures used by many publications are admirably impartial, few list-makers claim that their surveys are, or can ever be, scientific: "haphazard at worst, imprecise at best," in Lazar's words. They characterize the bestseller list as a rough analogue of selective realities, an *impression* of what a certain segment of the reading population is buying from a cross section of the bookselling trade. Others are not nearly as charitable, cynically describing the bestseller list as nothing more than a subtly — and sometimes not so subtly — disguised form of paid advertising.

Bestseller lists are the results of surveys of bookstores, bookstore chains, and distributors, and certain flaws are built into the data gathering and processing procedures that make precision impossible.

One problem is time lag. Although computerization of data reporting and analysis has shortened the time between the tallying of book sales and the reporting of results to the public, many factors prevent rapid digestion of the information, and the result is often a picture of a situation that existed a few weeks ago or longer. Because the lag makes it hard for publishers to plan printings, advertisements, and promotional activities, editors and agents are constantly scrambling to get their hands on advance copies of key publications. Every Thursday a certain phone number at the *New York Times* is jammed because that is the day the newspaper releases the list of bestsellers that will appear in its book review section two Sundays thence. Many publications that list bestsellers are monthly, and, like the light from a distant star, they report information about a very different world from the one of the moment.

One proposed solution to the time-lag problem is to base bestseller lists on orders rather than sales. Book wholesaler Baker & Taylor does it that way. Such a system poses a different set of problems, however. For example, as a result of huge orders, Jean Auel's *The Plains of Passage* was ranked seventeenth on Baker & Taylor's bestseller list *five months before publication date!* Had that fact been disseminated outside the book trade, Auel fans might have rioted when they discovered they would have to wait so long before the book became available in stores.

An even larger problem is selection criteria. Decisions about which stores to survey, or which types of books to report on, are biased by definition, for they are weighted by such factors as locale or subject matter. The vaunted *New York Times* list is designed to embrace the entire national scene, and therefore may not reflect a book that is selling ten times better in Los Angeles than in any other place. And because the *Times* list is general in nature, it does not necessarily report certain types of books, such as cookbooks or religious works. There is nothing wrong with this method as long as the publication's selection criteria are not deceptively presented to its readers. The monthly bestseller list printed in *Locus*, a science fiction trade publication, is drawn largely from bookstores specializing in fantasy and science fiction because the magazine's audience may safely be presumed to be more interested in those genres than in romances, mysteries, and westerns.

Serious controversies may arise, however, when a publication fails to make manifest to its readers the basis for posting or not posting certain books on its bestseller list, or for posting them lower than publishers or authors believe is fair. *More*'s Jerry Lazar reports that as far back as 1949, Harcourt, Brace (as it was then called) took a full-page ad in the *Times* demonstrating that its *The Seven Storey Mountain* by Thomas Merton deserved to be the number one nonfiction bestseller, rather than eleventh as the newspaper's list had it. This incident triggered a furious debate culminating in an investigative piece in the *Saturday Review of Literature* entitled "Bogus Best Sellers." Lazar also cited a storm that arose in 1975 when the *Times* failed to list Billy Graham's *Angels* despite the sale of 800,000 copies, "more copies than any other three 1975 hardcover books combined." A Waldenbooks buyer raised a great hue and cry with the *Times* editor in charge of the newspaper's bestseller list, and subsequently *Angels* showed up on the list.

One author, William Peter Blatty of *The Exorcist* fame, felt so aggrieved over inequities in the *Times*'s bestseller selection process that he brought a $6 million lawsuit against the newspaper in August 1983. His complaint alleged that his subsequent novel *Legion* sold enough copies to merit appearance on the *Times* bestseller list. Accordingly, he claimed negligent and intentional interference with a prospective business advantage, negligence in maintaining the list, and trade libel. With some 105,000 copies in print and 84,000 shipped, the book went on the bestseller lists of the *Los Ange-*

*les Times,* the *Chicago Tribune, Time* magazine, and *Publishers Weekly.* "It drove me nuts that I hadn't gotten on the *New York Times* form," Blatty said. The case went all the way up to the U.S. Supreme Court, which refused to consider it and let stand a lower court ruling that Blatty had no grounds for a lawsuit.

The *Times* successfully stood on its First Amendment right not to disclose the way it produces its bestseller list, claiming that if it "must reveal the identities of the booksellers it surveys, ensuing manipulation of sales at selected places by publishers and authors will render the list meaningless." The controversy did focus attention on how the *Times* and other publications devise their lists, however, and some observers felt that these lists had already been rendered meaningless by the manipulations of publishers and authors.

One questionable area has been the curious way that ads boasting that a book is a bestseller are run in a newspaper on the day that the book first goes on the list. This "coincidence" may be attributable to the time lag I described, which gives an advertiser information about bestsellers ten days or more before the list is published. But John Leonard, who edited the *New York Times Book Review* between 1970 and 1975, suggested there were "under-the-table deals between someone in the *Times* ad department and a publisher who wants to find out in advance when the issue goes to bed, what's on the list. I suspect even bribery — not to move it up or down the list, but to get the information they want."

A more flagrant source of influence is the practice of sending employees, family, and friends to bookstores to buy large numbers of copies. Publishers and authors try to guess which stores will be surveyed by bestseller list-makers, then descend *en masse* to purchase enough copies to register significantly on the bestseller tally. Although this is an expensive technique, it may pay off if the book appears on bestseller lists and begins a self-sustaining chain reaction of big sales.

I can document at least one instance of this technique for, in my wild and foolish youth, I agreed to go around to bookstores with a wad of cash provided by a publisher and buy a bunch of copies of a novel he was trying to put on the bestseller list. Most assertions of such hanky-panky are harder to prove, however, such as the

Neuharth book or the best-selling novel *Love Story* by Erich Segal, sales of which were widely believed to have been "supplemented" by purchases by the studio that made the movie.

Another charge of subsidized sales was reported in various trade publications in the summer of 1995. Addison-Wesley published *The Discipline of Market Leaders* by Fred Wiersema, a senior vice president at a firm called CSC Index, and Michael Treacy, an independent consultant with links to CSC. Despite mixed reviews, the book went on the *New York Times* bestseller list, reaching as high as number 5.

According to *Business Week*, however, the authors spent about $250,000 to reimburse third parties who bought 10,000 copies of their book in small bookshops around the United States. Bulk purchases by corporate clients, once again at small bookshops, apparently accounted for another 30,000 to 40,000 copies. Since those clients probably could have bought large quantities of the book at a discount directly from the publisher, you have to wonder why they would pay full price at a retail store. The obvious answer is that the bestseller list reflects sales at those stores they bought from.

We know that it is common practice to sell display and shelf space, particularly in wholesale outlets. In fact, bestseller lists posted in supermarkets and similar stores outside of bookshops are often nothing more than shopper recommendations created by the stores or by the book distributors that supply them, and publishers pay incentives to induce such bestseller listings.

The realm of bestseller listings is well guarded, and many able investigative journalists have blunted their spears attempting to penetrate its secrets. Michael Kagay, editor of news surveys for the *New York Times*, described the paper's bestseller list as a national projection of weekly sales compiled from surveys of three thousand independent bookstores, as well as wholesalers representing twenty-eight thousand other retail outlets around the country, including chain stores. The list of designated stores and the formulas employed to weight the tallies are confidential, and to shake interested parties off the trail, the newspaper's surveyors change many of the stores annually. "We also have a standard procedure to detect and query sales activities that are out of the usual pattern for a typical store," Kagay says. "If a store sold seventy copies where it would normally sell five, or if a stranger came in and paid cash for sixty copies, that would ring warning bells and we would adjust our computer model to take account of it."

Given all that we know, we may be forgiven for greeting this statement with a touch of skepticism. There's a good reason why "B.S." is the abbreviation for the term "Bestseller."

# 18

# Consenting Adults

Everybody needs approval, but nobody needs it more than authors: approval of editorial alterations of manuscripts; approval of cover art and copy; approval over reprint, book-club, and foreign licenses; approval of titles, ad texts, and more.

New authors quickly discover that they have very little leverage when it comes to controlling the fate of their books. As their work grows in demand, however, they develop the clout to demand the right to approve many procedures. In fact, a concise biography of a successful author might read something like this:

> His first contract gave his publisher total control of everything.
>
> When he achieved modest popularity, his publisher gave him consultation rights.
>
> After he became very popular, he secured "approval not to be unreasonably withheld."
>
> At length he became a star, and his publisher gave him total control of everything.

Which processes are subject to author consultation or consent? And what kinds of concessions may an author expect from his publisher as he rises to the top of his profession? Are there limits to those concessions? Are there some issues so hot that a publisher would risk losing a superstar before yielding the right of approval?

The foundation stone of the author-publisher relationship is the text. Today we take it pretty much for granted that book publishers will make no substantive changes in the text of a book without the author's express consent. This state of mind is of relatively recent vintage, however. Well into this century, a widely held attitude was that the editor was the best judge of what an author intended to say and how well he said it. And, though that assumption still prevails at the copy editing level in such areas as grammar and house style, when it comes to the overall text, today's editors prefer to reason with authors than coerce them. Even new authors consider it their natural right to review copy-edited manuscripts and galley proofs of their books. In hardcover publishing, where the production process moves at a courtly pace, it is easy to grant this right to authors. In the frenetic world of paperbacks, however, authors are not always granted such courtesy, and books may be rushed into print without review by the author. Few publishers retain, in the boiler-plate of their contracts, the right to alter an author's text without his approval, but in practice it is commonplace, at least on the paper-back level.

Approval over textual changes is about as far as the tyro author can expect to go when it comes to control over publication of his work. Although some publishers may informally consult with new authors about such matters as cover art, it's considered out of line for them to demand a voice in the selection of the cover artist, or be allowed input in such matters as cover art and blurbs, book design, style, or typeface, or negotiations over subsidiary rights. For a new author, the life of his first book is full of surprises, not all of them pleasant by any means. He sees his cover and cover copy for the first time only after the book is printed, learns about reprint and other subsidiary rights deals only after they have been closed (if then; sometimes he learns about them through inexplicable entries on royalty statements), or first sees the text of an ad for his book at the same time that the public does. If there are embarrassing typo-graphical errors, if the cover is a horrible misrepresentation of the author's vision, if the subsidiary rights deal is disappointing, if the book ad is dumb — well, tough luck, kid.

Actually, most publishers are not callous about authors' rights in these areas. They simply feel that authors are not necessarily wise when it comes to making those decisions, and I have to say there is some merit in this judgment. Many authors do not hold a strong suit in grammar, have decidedly bizarre notions about what should go on their covers, are poorly informed about appropriate terms for book-club, reprint, and foreign deals, or have little feel for advertising, publicity, and promotion.

Such shortcomings do not prevent them, however, from demanding a say in those activities, and as they achieve success and build comfortable relationships with their publishers, some contractual prohibitions will inevitably be relaxed. Veteran authors are assumed to have acquired a degree of professionalism, restraint, and respect for the problems of publishers, and can be expected not to insist that David Hockney be commissioned to paint an original cover, or that the publisher take out half a million dollars in television advertising.

This growing tolerance for author input is reflected in the language of contracts by use of the term "consultation." Consultation is of course one of those vague words that carries as much meaning and good faith as a publisher wishes to instill in it, so it is not much skin off a publisher's nose to grant it to an author. It must be understood, though, that while "consultation" might well mean, "If you don't care for what we've done, we'll try our level best to improve the situation," it can also mean, "I called you and you weren't home, so consider yourself consulted."

Publishers' policies are frequently resistant to the formal granting of consultation rights to authors, but they might agree to what is called a side letter, an informal statement of good intentions. Although such letters are not binding, they are better than nothing, and are particularly useful if there is a change of personnel and an author wants to show his new editor that his former editor wished to accommodate him.

The closer to stardom that an author moves, the more accommodating his publisher is willing to become, and this attitude is manifested in contractual language giving the author explicit approval over certain aspects of the publishing process. For the first time there may be some real teeth in the author's right to say yes or no to subsidiary licenses, cover art and copy, and ad campaigns. Nevertheless, publishers will fight against conceding absolute power to an author, even an important author, and will hedge their contractual language by granting approval only on the condition that such approval is not to be withheld unreasonably. The adverb "unreasonably" restores a degree of ambiguity to the author's right of consent, giving the publisher a fighting chance if a dispute turns nasty and ends up in court. By demonstrating that an author withheld his consent spitefully, whimsically, or in some other fashion that injured the publisher's opportunities to maximize a book's literary or commercial value, a publisher can negate the power conveyed to the author with the term "approval." (On reflection, I realize that over the many years I have been in the publishing business, I have never seen the phrase "consent not to be unreasonably withheld" litigated or even invoked by a publisher. I'm not sure why, but I would like to think it speaks well of the reasonableness and responsibility of authors.)

Of course, the hardest victory to achieve is absolute and unhindered approval by an author in the areas we have been discussing, and its stipulation in a contract invariably bespeaks a star author, a tough agent, or an agreeable publisher — probably all three. I should stress that such control is not of necessity the goal of all authors. Some are indifferent to what goes on the covers of their books, or to the design and style, or to the size of ads. Others entrust such matters to their publishers and try not to second-guess or criticize them. They take the attitude, "I write the best books I can, and if everybody else does his or her job as conscientiously as I do mine, I can't ask for more than that."

A growing number of authors and agents is not content to cast their destinies to such capricious winds. As one writer expressed it to me recently, "With the midlist emerging as the trash heap of the publishing business, ambitious authors are obligated to involve themselves in every aspect of their publishers' activities, from titles to typography, to help give their books a big feel and image."

If you feel compelled to get involved in those activities, and to bid for a measure of control over them, there are a number of concrete measures you can take.

The first is to educate yourself about your publisher's tasks. By studying catalogues, examining the design, typography, and covers of books, scrutinizing ads and ad campaigns, and above all by talking to your editors and other staff professionals, you learn what is possible, reasonable, and economical. You do not want to come on to your publisher as ignorant about such matters as the cost of an ad campaign or the technical difficulties of producing die-cut covers. If you can speak knowledgeably about such matters, your pub-

230 How to Be Your Own Literary Agent

lisher will feel a little more comfortable about soliciting your input or giving you a measure of control over certain decisions.

The second thing to do is learn how to deal with your publisher in a nonconfrontational way. Find opportunities to spend some time with your editor and with the various specialists at your publisher, such as the art director, sales manager, and the head of publicity and promotion. If you can't meet the top man or woman, an assistant will do, as long as you have the ear of someone who might serve to sponsor your wishes at the company. You can accomplish this by having your editor introduce you to these people when you visit your publisher's offices or attend such publishing functions as parties, conferences, sales meetings, and conventions. It is important to be a good listener, and to couch your wishes as unthreateningly as possible.

Publishing people being among the busier breeds in the corporate kingdom, one-on-one discussions may not always be possible. You may be able to communicate some of your ideas in writing. Publishers' publicity questionnaires are an underutilized source of persuasion, I've observed. These questionnaires, usually sent out with contracts, invite authors to furnish their publishers with suggestions about approaches to exploit the promotional value of their books. By taking time to answer the form's questions in detail, you give yourself a perfect opportunity to contact the appropriate staff members with offers to implement your ideas. Letters rather than phone calls, at least at the outset, will give your publisher an opportunity to think about your ideas and circulate them among the movers and shakers at the company. Be polite, helpful, knowledgeable, and reasonable, and you may find yourself acquiring de facto control over many publishing decisions that have not been granted to you contractually.

A time may come, however, when all of your graciousness, diplomacy, and reason are incapable of winning your publisher over on an important issue, and you are forced to take a stand. It might be hoped that by now you have an agent who can go to bat for you. That's fine, but your agent might have reservations about taking a hard stand on your behalf. Talk it over with him and listen carefully. Talk to friends and professional colleagues, gathering as much information as you can in order to make as informed and effective a decision as possible.

It is important that you prioritize the items over which you seek approval. Which are borderline, which serious, and which will you martyr yourself for? Be prepared to trade those of lesser weight in exchange for the dealbreakers. Exhaust all avenues of persuasion before taking the hard stand, but if push comes to shove you must state, as clearly and firmly as you know how, that you cannot sign the contract, cannot permit your book to be published, will not countenance a title change, will not suffer this cover or that advertisement. For most authors, and even for agents, taking a tough stand can be anxiety-making, but once you have made up your mind and prepared to gamble everything to win your point, there must be no backing down. Publishers who discover that your bottom line is not chiseled in granite will quickly find you out, exploit your ambivalence, and never again take "no" for an answer from you.

Though you risk losing a deal, and maybe a lot more than that, by taking a hard stand, you may be surprised to learn that as often as not it is your publishers who back down. *Their* bottom line may be more flexible than they led you to believe. Or they may not want to risk losing money that they have already paid to you or invested in your work. You never know until you try. If you win, you will push your relationship with your publishers to a higher plateau. And if you lose, you at least walk away with your pride, dignity, and integrity. And nothing is more important than that, right?

Right?

Why are you looking at me that way?

# 19

# Collaborations

One of the liabilities of being a professional writer is that you attract people who want to collaborate with you. What author has not been collared at a party by a drunk who wants him to write his life story or has this fantastic idea for a novel?

Few such propositions have any commercial value. But from time to time you may meet someone whose story *is* compelling enough to entice you into collaboration with him. Or your agent may offer you an opportunity to team up with a famous movie or sports star, doctor or astronaut, beauty expert or political figure. If that happens, do you know how collaborations work? How the proceeds are to be divided? Whose byline goes on the cover of the book? Who pays the expenses of flying to Washington or Los Angeles or Hawaii to interview this person or to do research? Whose name goes on the copyright?

As a writer who has collaborated on seven or eight works of fiction and nonfiction and as an agent who has welded together scores of collaborations for clients, I can testify that teaming up with someone on a book can be richly rewarding, elevating, and great fun. It can also turn out to be a nightmare if the parties are ill matched, have unrealistic expectations of each other's contributions, or fail to spell out their contractual arrangements before getting down to work. Collaborations are complex undertakings because the authors have to please themselves, each other, and their publishers at one and the same time, the literary equivalent of three-dimensional chess. In this chapter, perhaps I can show you how to enter into a collaboration with your eyes wide open.

For openers one might ask, Why collaborate at all? Collaborations often sound like twice the headaches for half the money, and sometimes that turns out to be the case. But the opposite may also be true: You can end up making more money than you can writing solo, doing less work and turning out a better book. Collaborations can broaden experience, create new areas of expertise, and open up markets for a writer's work. They are also refreshing changes of pace from the isolated, solitary nature of freelance writing. Indeed, some writers thrive on the stimulus of another mind and a second pair of hands, preferring collaborations to writing alone. In my collaborations on a number of novels, I found that my co-authors' contributions made for much more rounded characters and plots than I could ever have produced on my own.

What kinds of book projects and co-authors lend themselves best to collaborations? The most obvious is the autobiography of a celebrity, the movie or sports star, television personality or famous politician, who feels (or is persuaded by a publisher or agent) that his or her story would make compelling reading for a large audience. There are other well-known people — business leaders, scientists, and psychologists, for example — who want to expound on a subject they know well — to comment on the decline of American business initiative, the dangers of nuclear armament, the threat of Latin American insurgency, the fragmentation of family life.

Then there is the person suddenly vaulted into the limelight, in whom the public becomes interested overnight: a released political hostage, a captured notorious criminal, a dedicated crusader whose cause is at last taken up by the majority. There are also the obscure people who have a great tale to tell if only someone could help them publicize it with a book: the valet-housekeeper-butler-nanny-secretary of some great household who is prepared to reveal the intimacies of the master or mistress; the victim of some affliction whose bravery in the face of acute suffering will inspire those in similar circumstances; the dedicated crusader whose cause has *not* yet been taken up by the majority.

Finally, there is the common case of two writers whose strengths and weaknesses complement each other: One is good at plotting, the other at narrative; he writes better male characters, she better female ones; one hates research but loves to interview people, the other can sit in a library all day but won't hold a microphone in someone's face and ask a lot of personal questions.

These people have one thing in common: a story to tell but insufficient time, talent, or energy to tell it without help. That's where the collaborator comes in. But collaborations, like any other genre, are an art form, and not all writers are constituted to handle them well. Their personalities, views, and working habits must blend with the subject-author's, and considerable tolerance on both sides is therefore necessary. The subject-author may be difficult, demanding, extremely busy, and excessively vain. He may be so close to his own story that he insists on stressing the dullest aspects of it and glossing over the most intriguing and exciting. He may respond with dismay and even horror to the picture his collaborator has created, even though every word of the book has been taken verbatim from tape recordings. Collaborations are often mirrors that reflect what one doesn't want to see.

Co-authors, too, may be poorly matched to the people they've been hired to write books with. They can be headstrong, insensitive, and impatient, unused to working with and deferring to another person. The subject-author may feel that his collaborator is "writing his own book," subordinating the essential material to the collaborator's own vision, content, or style.

Bad collaborations, then, are like houses built by warring contractors: The seams are poorly joined, the materials don't match, the style confused and uninspired. If you have misgivings about your writing partner, drop the collaboration before it goes too far.

How are collaborations put together? Do they start with the principal? The writer? The publisher? The agent? Sometimes it's one of these, sometimes another. Often it depends on how well known the subject-author is.

For instance, if he is a celebrity, the chances are that he will be pursued by a publisher. Once he has committed himself to doing a book, finding a collaborator is relatively easy. Sometimes the celebrity initiates the search for a publisher, perhaps because he has decided to go public with his life story or because he wishes to promote his career or practice or views. Here again, it's relatively easy to assemble a collaborative deal, for the publisher is virtually sold on the book and doesn't require convincing. The publisher can make a commitment with little prompting, assess the book's value and sales potential, and work the collaborator's fees into the project budget. Unless the celebrity already has a co-author, the publisher will usually contact literary agents and negotiate with them for their clients' services as collaborators — assuming the subject-author and the collaborator hit it off together.

If the subject-author is not a celebrity, however, it is much harder to find a collaborator, for a great deal of development must be done to interest publishers and make them feel the story is worth investing in. A writer must be found who is willing to sit down with the principal, interview him, and write an outline for prospective publishers. That in itself is no easy feat, for professional writers like to be paid for their time, and because in this case there is no guaranteed publication deal, the writer must do all this preparatory work on speculation. Of course, if the subject-author has money, he can be asked to pay for his collaborator's time during the development period, usually on the condition that the first monies collected from a publishing deal go to reimburse the subject-author. But if the principal cannot pay, the project could die right then and there unless the writer is so wildly enthusiastic about the book's potential that he considers his time a good investment.

There is another way, and that's for the subject-author to interest a big-name writer in collaborating with him. For the big-name writer is a celebrity himself; presumably he has a following that will buy and read any book he sets his hand to. If this writer is enthusiastic about a story, however obscure, that's often good enough for his publisher and a deal will be struck requiring relatively little presentation. But — famous writers are approached every day of the week by people who feel their story will make best-selling reading if only some big-name author will work with them on it.

In short, if it's not one helluva story, it had better be one helluva celebrity, or one helluva writer, writing it. (Or, I might add, one helluva literary agent selling it.)

What are the contractual arrangements in a collaboration? Well, when you talk about contracts, bear in mind that there are two kinds in a collaboration. One is the publishing contract; the other is the collaboration agreement. Depending on the nature of the project, sometimes the former comes first, sometimes the latter. If the book is already sold — a celebrity autobiography, say — the first contract drawn up would be the one with the publisher. Thereafter, when a co-author is found, a collaboration agreement would be drafted. But if the book requires the celebrity and the writer to spend several weeks together to work up a presentation for publishers, then the collaboration agreement would be the first document drawn up, the publishing agreement coming later, when the book is sold. Sometimes the terms of the collaboration can be worked into the publishing agreement, but I recommend a separate collaboration agreement because things often need to be worked out between collaborators that aren't covered in publishing agreements. Publishing agreements define the collaborators' joint obligation to their publisher, but they don't define their obligations to each other.

Let's examine a collaboration agreement and discuss the principal terms.

The first thing is how the money is to be divided when the book is sold. There are countless ways to do this, depending on the project, the amount of money involved, the relative importance of the celebrity and co-author, and many other factors. Let me outline a few scenarios.

- A famous actress is offered a lot of money by a publisher to write her memoirs. Though her story, like any other, requires a certain degree of skill to tell, she and her publisher agree that just about any competent writer will get the job done. They go to a young journalist eager to get his name on a book and offer him a flat fee of $10,000, which to him is a lot of money. They also offer him a "with" or "and" byline on the book, but no participation in royalties, magazine rights, or foreign translation or any other subsidiary rights. He accepts the offer because it's a good opportunity to break into books, earn some money, and bask in the presence of a legend of stage and screen.
- A young dairymaid is walking through the woods, minding her own business, when there is a tremendous roar and a blinding flash, and next thing she knows she's in a spaceship being interrogated by little green aliens. They take her to their world for a year, then return her to earth and drop her off in the woods where they picked her up. She immediately runs to a literary agent's office babbling about what happened to her. Persuaded that her tale is true (agents are suckers for a good story) but realizing she's going to

have a tough time making anybody else believe her, he convinces her to team up with his client the Pulitzer Prize–winning journalist, whose identification with the project will legitimize it in the eyes of his publisher and his public. For that privilege, however, the journalist wants 75 percent of all revenues earned by the book. He also wants the first $25,000 of the publisher's advance; if his agent is unable to line up a deal for an advance greater than $25,000, the dairymaid will receive nothing until the book earns more. The principle here is that professional writers depend entirely on their writing for a living, whereas their collaborators usually earn a living from some other source (acting, running a business, playing ball, milking cows). Thus the writer's financial needs must be served first. In no position to argue, the dairymaid agrees to these terms.

• A tycoon who built Fingfang Enterprises from scratch into a multibillion-dollar multinational octopus decides his life would make fascinating reading and goes to an agent, asking him to package his life story. Since the agent is by no means as sure as the industrialist that publishers will fall all over themselves to bid for such a book, he tells the man he'll have to pay a writer $5000 to spend a month interviewing him, examining news clippings and other documents, and writing an outline. The man will recover his $5000 if and when the book is sold, but if the book isn't sold he loses his investment. After recouping his $5000, he and the writer will split all income 50–50. The man balks at 50–50: After all, it was *his* life, and all this writer is doing is putting down what he tells him, right? Wrong, says the agent; there is far more involved in collaborating on a book than merely taking dictation. The man still balks. After all, once the book is out the writer's contribution ends, but *he's* got to go on all those talk shows the publisher is going to send him to. Seeing his point, and realizing that this is the kind of man who isn't happy unless he thinks he's gotten a better deal than the other guy, the agent suggests that after the book earns $100,000, the split will go from 50–50 to 75–25 in the mogul's favor. "Done," says the man, switching his cigar to his left hand so he can shake the agent's hand with his right.

As you can see, there is no one way to slice the pie, but there is a kind of guiding principle. In theory, all collaborations should be

50–50 propositions because the subject can't get his book written without the writer, and the writer doesn't have a story without the subject. But on many occasions one member of the team turns out to be more important than the other, or feels he's more important, and an accommodation must be negotiated. When that happens, some tradeoffs may be made on the other terms of the collaboration.

After the question of dividing the proceeds, the thing that concerns writers most is the byline: Will their name appear on the cover of the book, and if so, in what form? With a "with"? With an "and"? In the same-size typeface or smaller? For many writers, the byline is almost as important as the money; for some, it is more so. For that reason, the byline is the commodity most frequently used as barter in negotiating with the subject-author: "I'll keep my name off the book if I can have one-third of the proceeds instead of the one-quarter you've offered me."

The byline may be worked out in all sorts of ways. Prominent figures often feel that the appearance of a co-author's name on their books implies that they are not entirely literate. That may be a reasonable assumption for, say, some athletic stars or ex-convicts (though I can think of exceptions), but if it's the chairman of a conglomerate's board or a former President of the United States, the appearance of a co-writer on the byline of his book may cause potential buyers to question just how candid or interesting the book will be. Therefore, the subject-author may insist that the book be done as a straight ghost job, and recognition of the writer's contribution restricted to an acknowledgment inside the book. Even here the writer might be able to negotiate a separate acknowledgment on its own page, as opposed to citation in a long list of contributors to the preparation of the manuscript, which reduces the writer's involvement to the same level as that of the copy editor, typist, and secretary.

For other principals, the issue of the byline is a matter of complete indifference, and indeed, they can be most gracious in according credit to their partners. In still other cases, the co-author's byline is the more recognizable of the two, almost the *raison d'être* for the book, and the publisher insists that it appear prominently on the cover and in all advertising.

Related to the byline is the question of whose name the copyright will be taken out in, and this should be stipulated in the collaboration agreement. But generally speaking, if both the subject-author and the collaborator are signatories to the publishing contract, then the book will be copyrighted in both their names, for both are defined as "Author" in that contract even if the co-author's name does not go on the cover of the book.

Liability is the next matter to be considered. If someone brings a lawsuit against the publisher and authors claiming libel, invasion of privacy, defamation of character, infringement of copyrighted material, or some other grounds, which of the authors is liable? It's easy to imagine the responsibility going either way. On the one hand, the subject-author might tell his collaborator a story whose veracity the collaborator cannot check and that subsequently triggers a lawsuit. Is the collaborator to blame? On the other hand, suppose the co-author embellishes on something the subject-author told him, or goes to the library and plagiarizes a quotation, or is lazy about checking the accuracy of the principal's assertions, and a lawsuit ensues. Is the subject-author to blame?

If both of them signed the publishing contract, the publisher is not going to try to sort out who is responsible, or more responsible, for the actionable material in the book. Both agreed to the warranty and indemnity clauses in the contract, and both are therefore equally liable for any breaches of those clauses. If, however, the two made some provision in their collaboration agreement about who was responsible for what in the book, then one may be able to recover his legal expenses or damages from the other. If, say, the subject-author guaranteed that he would be liable for the truth of any anecdotes, assertions, or opinions and the co-author guaranteed that he'd be liable for the veracity of his research and of his interviews, there's a chance that the blame for a lawsuit could be clearly assigned to one or the other of the authors. This procedure is known as cross-indemnification: I indemnify you, you indemnify me.

In actuality, it's extremely difficult to keep sharp the dividing line between the authors' responsibilities. The co-author is responsible for checking the things the subject-author tells him; the subject-author is responsible for reviewing the research and writing of his collaborator. For safety's sake, the manuscript should be reviewed by both the authors' lawyers and the publisher's.

Another important matter is expenses: How are they defined, and who pays for them?

Among the more common expenses in a collaboration are research assistance, the transcription of tape-recorded interviews, picture permissions, legal expenses, and typing. If the collaborators don't live in the same place, there may be expenses for travel and accommodations and for long-distance phone calls.

The collaborators should agree at the very outset which expenses are legitimate and perhaps fix a ceiling on them. It might, for example, be inappropriate for the co-author to charge for the cost of paper, cassettes, or public transportation to the library for research, as these are usually part of a writer's costs of doing business. It can work the other way, too. Suppose a famous Hollywood movie director is collaborating with a New York writer and has to come to New York on business. While in New York, he intends to sit down with his collaborator and work on the book, but that's not the sole purpose of his visit. It would be patently unfair for him to charge his first-class airfare and one week's lodging at the Sherry-Netherland Hotel to the collaboration.

The expenses are usually laid out by the party incurring them, who then recovers them from the publisher's advance on acceptance of the manuscript. The burden of expenses is usually divided in proportion to each collaborator's participation in the proceeds from the book. Thus, if the collaborators are splitting all revenue from the book 50–50, they should split the expenses 50–50, too; if 75–25 in favor of the subject-author, then he should pick up 75 percent of the costs while the co-author assumes 25 percent.

Like the expenses, the duties of the collaborators should be spelled out, though they are usually harder to quantify. The subject-author should agree to make himself available for interviews by the collaborator; to furnish newspaper clippings, diaries and journals, and other written material; and to cooperate with the co-author in arranging interviews with his friends, family, and business colleagues. The co-author pledges to supplement the principal's interviews with his own research, which includes checking the veracity of statements and assertions made by the subject-author. The co-author may also stipulate delivery dates of the manuscript to the subject-author; he may also have to clear permissions for quotations or pictures and to deliver signed permissions or other releases to the subject-author. Other duties and obligations may be specified here: The co-author might have to promise to phone the subject-author every two weeks with a progress report or send him each chapter of the book as it is finished.

It is very important to stipulate approval of the manuscript when you prepare a collaboration agreement. In most cases, the subject-author is granted sole approval, or sole approval subject to the editorial judgment of the publisher. This seems only fair, for after all it's his or her book, not the collaborator's. Yet the collaborator may have some strong objections to the subject-author's inclusion or exclusion of certain material. So there is sometimes built into the agreement machinery for settling disputes, with the agent or editor or a lawyer being appointed arbiter.

If an agent is involved, there should be language in the collaboration agreement mutually authorizing that agent to act on behalf of both parties in the submission of the manuscript, the negotiation of the book contract, the collection and disbursement of proceeds, and in the exploitation of subsidiary rights, including serial, British and foreign translation, and movie and television. The agent's commission schedule must be detailed, along with any special provisions concerning him: authorization for him to deduct certain expenses, a time limit on his handling of the project or of subsidiary rights, appointment of him as final arbiter of disputes between collaborators, etc. If there are two agents, as sometimes happens when the principal is represented by one firm and the collaborator by another, the questions of which one will handle the marketing of the manuscript, negotiation, collection of proceeds, and the exploitation of subsidiary rights must be answered.

Finally, there ought to be some provision for the termination of the collaboration in the event of the death or disability of one of the parties, because of failure to perform contractual obligations, or because the collaborators simply don't get along. If the collaboration does collapse, both authors may owe the publisher a refund or one member of the team may owe the other some money advanced toward the development of the project. Precisely how the accounts are to be settled should be made clear in the agreement between the writing partners.

No document can blend two conflicting personalities, which is why I repeat my advice that if you and your collaborator don't hit it off, break off the relationship before it mires the project in grief if not in a lawsuit. But if the two parties enter the relationship in a spirit of good faith, a well-constructed collaboration agreement will go far toward insuring the success both of the friendship and the book.

# 20 ✍

# Book Packagers

What are book packagers? Are they nothing more than glorified literary agents or are they closer to publishers? Are they saintly benefactors of indigent writers? Or greedy exploiters who use authors the way plantation owners used indentured slaves? Since I have heard book packagers — sometimes one and the same person — described in this wide variety of terms, it might be worthwhile to examine what they do and how they do it.

Book packagers, like their products, come in many editions, ranging from the recently fired book editor trying to hustle a series idea out of his studio apartment, to the head of a beautifully organized multimillion-dollar writing factory, boasting scores of authors on its roster. Regardless, the concept is pretty much the same: Buy a literary property cheaply and sell it dearly. The fact that a packager buys the property from an author distinguishes him from a literary agent, who of course does not acquire material from his clients but accepts it on consignment, as it were, and is compensated by a commission. On the other hand, the fact that a packager sells the property distinguishes him from a publisher, who retains the rights to works he secures.

Some book packagers prefer to call themselves book producers, likening their functions to those of their namesakes in the film business. To the extent that packagers develop someone else's raw material into a valuable literary property, I suppose they can lay claim to *producer*. But since their function is often strictly mercantile, perhaps the right term for them might be *broker*.

Perhaps the best way for me to illustrate the role of the book packager is to show how you might become one yourself.

Suppose you have a terrific idea for a book, but you can't or don't want to write the book yourself. You do, however, know some writers and editors, and you have a little money. You have lunch with the editors and tell them your idea; they say it does indeed sound terrific, could they see a manuscript or an outline? You tell them you could have something for them in a few weeks or months — how much would they pay? And they say, Well, don't hold us to it, but perhaps we could offer a $5000 advance, maybe a little more or less depending on how good the material is.

You now have a loose commitment from a couple of editors, so you turn your thoughts to the other half of the package, the writer. You contact one you know and tell him your idea and offer him a little money to develop it. What kind of money? Oh, maybe $500 for an outline and another $2000 for the completed manuscript, plus a percentage of any profit you may make, such as the advance, royalties, and subsidiary income, after you have recovered your investment and taken what you consider to be your rightful share for the work, money, time, brains, and energy you put into the project.

So, the writer does the book for you for $2500, and you take it to one of the editors you spoke to and sell it to him for $5000, a 100 percent profit on your investment. You are now a book packager. Since you acquired the manuscript from the writer, you can't really call yourself an agent. Agents don't sign book contracts, authors do; but when the time comes for the contract on this particular book to be signed, you will sign it as owner of the work, as if you were the author. So there's the critical difference: Whereas literary agents sell the work of others on consignment, packagers purchase the work of others and resell it for a profit.

There are many variations on this theme. Some literary agents, for instance, feel entitled to compensation beyond their normal commission if they themselves dream up the idea for a book and give it to a writer or if they edit an author's book so thoroughly as to be closer to collaborator than agent. This vested interest draws them closer to the role of packager because ownership is now involved: ownership of the idea, ownership of the editorial input.

Some packagers take more than 50 percent of the money paid by publishers, some less. Some buy the work outright from the author, then keep all the royalties and subsidiary income and pay the original author nothing further by way of profits. Some do a minimum amount of work on a manuscript and leave the editing and production entirely to the publisher. Others edit it, have it retyped, acquire illustrations if necessary, design and lay out the book, and present the publisher with a work ready to go to the printer. Indeed, some go even further and actually print the book, licensing to a publisher only the right to distribute it.

Some form elaborate companies consisting of writers, illustrators, designers and other production specialists, and subsidiary rights and marketing and advertising and promotion experts. These firms, instead of licensing to a publisher the rights to a work, will enter into a joint venture with a publisher in which they both share costs of developing, printing, distributing, and promoting the work, then share the profits in proportion to their investment.

The confusion, and sometimes resentment, that authors feel toward book packagers stems from their ambiguous position, which often breeds a degree of deceitfulness that is absent from the agent-author relationship. Few agents could in good conscience go to an author with a $5000 offer from a publisher and offer him only half of it. If the agent did want to keep half, however, he would have to pretend to the author that he didn't actually have a $5000 offer; rather, he'd pretend he was financing the $2500 purchase of the author's manuscript out of his, the agent's, own pocket. Or he might have to practice some deceit in his dealings with the publisher by representing himself as the originator of an idea or even as the author of a work when he was merely playing the agent's role.

Nevertheless, packagers make important contributions to the literary marketplace. In fact, if it were not for packagers, many authors would be out of work and publishers would lose a significant source of material. Book packagers often risk money to develop book ideas and projects that publishers cannot or will not invest in, and by becoming owners of literary properties they assume certain critical responsibilities and liabilities. And because high risk deserves high rewards, packagers should not automatically be criticized for getting rich.

The better book packagers pay their authors immediately or put them on salary or some other form of regular compensation, and, like agents, they pass royalties and subsidiary income along to their authors upon receipt rather than holding it to the end of six-month accounting periods, the way publishers do. These packagers understand a basic if lamentable truth: Writers would rather be paid

$1000 on time than chase a publisher to hell and gone for twice that amount. Packagers — at least, once again, the better ones — therefore offer writers reliability and security, something that neither an agent nor a publisher can do — an agent because he can't, a publisher because he won't. If packagers pay low, at least they don't pay late, and for that reason authors are less resentful than they might otherwise be to see their packager get rich.

Do agents sell to packagers? At first glance it would seem foolish for an agent to do so, and in some cases it is. From time to time a packager will approach me with a book idea that he would like one of my clients to develop but for which he has little or no money to pay. It would be silly for me to agree because I would, in effect, be putting the packager into competition with my agency, using my own client's material.

If, however, the packager were willing to pay my client a fair price for his work, and to agree to fair terms for further compensation if and when he resold the work to a publisher, I would consider him just like any other potential buyer. A packaging firm that offers an agent $10,000 or more to develop a client's book will usually get a respectful hearing. However, both in terms of psychology and economics, it is seldom that agents and packagers make good bedfellows. In due time the agent begins to resent giving the packager such a big slice of the pie. The agent's client does, too, and may also get sore at his agent for making a deal that nets the author less than 50 percent of the money paid by the publisher (remember, the agent takes a commission of 10 or 15 percent on the 50 percent he collects from the packager). And, since the author may view the packager as little more than an agent who takes an outrageous commission, the author may wonder why he needs an agent who sells his work to another agent.

Whether an author has an agent or not, the relationship between author and packager is often an uneasy one that grows in a soil of suspicion and all too often blossoms into hostility. Here's a scenario that more than a few authors may recognize:

John Q. Writer is approached by Irving Bookbroker with an offer of $5000 to write a book for him. Bookbroker further offers to pay John 50 percent of all advances, royalties, and subsidiary money earned on the sale of the book to a publisher. John writes a dandy book, and Bookbroker sells it to Pocket Books for $50,000. Bookbroker keeps $25,000 and pays John the other $25,000 ($20,000, actually, because he recoups the $5000 he originally paid John).

At first flush John is thrilled with his bounty and so grateful that he doesn't mind that Bookbroker made a 500 percent profit on his investment. In this atmosphere of good will, John signs an agreement to write two more books for Bookbroker, a painless task now that the packager has raised John's pay to $10,000 per book. Grins all around. And the grins broaden when Bookbroker turns around and makes a two-book deal with Pocket Books for $100,000 per book.

Then John gets to thinking, and the smile starts to fade from his face. He is writing two books worth a total of $200,000, but he will end up getting only $100,000 from them, less if he has an agent. Furthermore, John's contract with Bookbroker calls for Bookbroker to pay John only $10,000 per book and to remit any excess only on specific reporting dates that are six months apart, giving Bookbroker the use of large amounts of John's money for long periods of time.

Resentment begins to ferment in John's heart. John forgets that the packager gave him a great break, financing the writing of that first book and making John a star. All John can think of now is that Bookbroker is making an enormous profit on the sweat of John's brow and doing damn little to earn it. Oh, Bookbroker lightly edits the manuscripts and puts them in attractive submission boxes before sending them to Pocket Books — big deal! John begins casting an eye on that Pocket Books money and talking to his lawyer or agent about cutting Bookbroker out of his 50 percent, either on the present contract or when it expires. Quarrels erupt between John and the packager; the relationship bogs down and perhaps ends up in an acrimonious lawsuit.

Does this mean packagers are immoral and you should never deal with them? I don't think there is anything inherently immoral about them as long as they are candid with authors concerning their arrangements both with buyer and seller. But because, as I've said, packaging is an enterprise in which candor is often lacking, an author should be extremely cautious when entering into a relationship with a packager. Here are some tips.

**Don't write something for nothing.** If a packager approaches you with an idea for a book, insist on being paid for any work you do.

**Work out all contingencies in advance.** Negotiate your participation in any advances, royalties, and subsidiary rights revenue the packager may generate from the sale of your material.

**Insist on a contract.** Because many so-called packagers make up their deals as they go along, it's essential for your arrangements to be stated in writing for your mutual protection. The contract should include a schedule of payments the packager will make to you for each completed stage of the work you do (and make sure "acceptance" is defined as the *packager's* approval of your material, not the publisher's); the division of all proceeds from the sale of the work and exploitation of subsidiary rights (and make sure the packager furnishes you with copies of all statements); warranties and indemnifications spelling out who is liable for claims arising out of the work; the byline — under whose name will the book be published?; copyright — who owns it?; options on your subsequent work; termination of your arrangement with the packager; reporting procedures (insist on the immediate pass-through of your share of all monies the packager collects in excess of his advance to you); and any other procedures necessary to protect your interests.

**Look ahead.** Think the relationship through, not merely to the end of this first project but to subsequent ones as well. How will you feel when you see a large percentage of your income going into someone else's pocket, particularly if you don't feel that person has earned it? Will you want to tie yourself up for books beyond this one? Has your deal with your packager left you free to sell directly to the publisher eventually? How will you feel if your packager represents himself as being the creator of your work?

My experience is that most authors who get involved with packagers, even the good ones, enjoy the short-term benefits but find long-term relationships unsatisfactory both in terms of financial reward and emotional satisfaction. But when the packager is the only guy in town prepared to pay you for your work, you may have no choice about getting involved with him.

If you do, keep your eyes wide open.

# 21

# Auctions

A s I said in chapter 3, book auctions are extremely tricky affairs and are best left to professionals. Since the first edition of this book was published, however, many readers have asked me to describe what goes on in an agent's mind when he decides a literary property should be submitted simultaneously to several publishers. So let's talk about the whats, whens, and wherefores of multiple submissions, including the ultimate multiple submission: the auction.

Not all agents evaluate or handle properties the same way, so the approaches described here may be unique to my agency's style of doing business. But I'm reasonably certain that most agents, like me, separate manuscripts into roughly two categories: the kind that should be submitted to one publisher at a time, and the kind that should go out to two or more publishers simultaneously. What factors determine which way an agent handles the property?

**Is the book timely?** Some books have a currency that diminishes sharply with delay. As I write this I see on my bookshelf a biography of the late Jacqueline Kennedy Onassis issued only two months after her death. Two or three months is a remarkably short time for a trade book's production, but in terms of reader interest it may be the outside limit, beyond which book buyers shrug their shoulders and pass up a book about old news. I don't know the circumstances behind the selling of the book, but had I been the agent, it would have been dangerous for me to offer it to one publisher at a time.

Some books are drawn from ideas that are "in the air." At any given time, there are ideas floating about whose time has come. Authors, agents, and editors who think such ideas are theirs alone and develop them at a leisurely pace often wake up to find themselves scooped. The weapon called for when an agent takes on a book about a "hot" topic is a shotgun, not a single-action rifle.

**Does the book have universal appeal?** A manuscript that I'm confident will be bid on by nine of the ten publishers I'll submit it to is a good candidate for multiple submission. A novel like *Gorky Park* is one you know will elicit a feverish response from any editor you show it to. If, however, the book deals with some specialized topic, if I feel it will sell only to those editors who might be on the same narrow wavelength as the author — if, in short, I'm by no means sure I'll get an offer from any and every publisher I go to — I had better think twice about multiple submissions.

Sometimes, though, that's precisely the best time to do a multiple. If I have a manuscript I'm fond of but that takes a certain type of editor and I don't want to waste a year finding him, I might send the manuscript simultaneously to a dozen publishers in the hope of flushing out the one or two who are tuned to the author's wavelength. I have, using this approach, gotten eleven out of twelve submissions back with reactions ranging from indifference to dislike; the twelfth editor adored the book and was prepared to slash his wrists to get it. You can see why you shouldn't use this technique too often, however. An agent can't always afford to elicit eleven negative reactions in the hope of fetching one positive one.

**Does the book feel big?** Universality is an important trait because it assures an agent that the manuscript will sell. But it doesn't guarantee that it will sell for a high price. In order to do that, a book must have magnitude.

Unfortunately, many otherwise salable books are simply not big-money properties; they aren't good enough for an agent to expend all that energy, salesmanship, and, above all, credibility. If an agent blitzes publishers with every manuscript he takes on, he'll soon get the reputation for being a hype artist and the industry will begin discounting his judgment. Agents spend years and years establishing their credibility with editors. When an agent phones and says "This is good," the editor knows from experience with this agent that their definitions of "good" are similar. But if an agent calls something "fabulous" and it turns out to be dreadful, and does it often enough, he may find himself conducting auctions to which nobody comes. The agent who doesn't overplay every hand knows that when he at last has a manuscript that is indeed fabulous, he can make editors drop what they're doing.

Multiple submissions often turn into auctions, but the two aren't necessarily identical. An auction is a formally structured multiple submission with strictly defined bidding rules and a closing date. A multiple submission may not always stipulate a closing date or establish any other rules, and in some cases the agent doesn't even tell the publisher he's submitting the manuscript to more than one house at a time. Such multiples are more in the nature of fishing expeditions, using five or ten lines in the hope of boating one trophy. These loosely conducted simultaneous submissions can turn into auctions, however, if two or more publishers make offers and the agent begins playing the bidders off against each other. This is a spontaneous species of auction, and when it happens, the agent frequently finds himself making up the rules as he goes along, allowing the competitive offers to dictate the structure of the event.

In a more conventional auction, the agent submits copies of the manuscript to the editors he has selected, along with a letter defining the rights being offered, the rules of the auction, the closing date, and sometimes the minimum terms acceptable to the agent. "We are offering United States and Canadian hardcover rights, we will conduct two rounds of bidding, we will close the auction at 5:00 P.M. on Thursday, September 5, and we will consider no bid of less than $50,000 advance," such a letter might say.

By or before the closing date the publishers make their offers. In some cases their first offers are the only ones the agent will allow them; in others the agent makes the rounds of the editors, telling them the highest bid he has in hand and asking if they wish to top it. When everyone else has dropped out, the highest bidder wins the property — at least, most of the time. On occasion, an agent will award an auction to a lower bidder because he feels that that publisher will do a better job with the book than the house that bid higher. Or he will give the book to the publisher who offered a higher royalty, even though that publisher's advance was lower than somebody else's bid. In the long run, the book with a higher royalty will earn more than one with a lower royalty but a higher advance, the agent reasons.

In many auctions an agent will establish a "floor," the price already offered by one publisher as the minimum for bidding by other publishers. It gives the floor bidder an advantage: the right to match or top the highest bid and thus get the book.

How does the agent get this floor? Before making his multiple submission, he may show the book to one publisher, who likes it and makes an offer that is marginally acceptable but not as high as the agent hoped for. The agent therefore says to that publisher, in effect, "I'm loath to sell it to you at that price, but if you're willing, I'll use your offer as the floor for an auction of this book. If nobody bids higher than you, you'll win the book for the floor price you offered. If, however, other publishers top your floor price, I'll let them bid the book up until I have the highest possible offer. I will then inform you of the terms of that offer. You will then have the opportunity to match that offer [or top it by an agreed-on percentage, usually 10 percent], and if you do, the book is yours."

Suppose Doubleday has offered me a $50,000 floor with a 10 percent topping privilege. Let's say the bidding goes to $100,000, with Simon & Schuster making the high bid. I then ask Doubleday if it wants to top Simon & Schuster's bid by 10 percent. If Doubleday says yes, the book is theirs for $110,000. If Doubleday says no, it goes to Simon & Schuster for $100,000.

Auctions can be terribly exciting, but they are also fraught with great danger, for tempers can run high. If publishers feel the agent has not acted in good faith, they may never do business with him again, or might even sue him or his client for breaching the rules of the auction. For this reason, I advise unagented authors against conducting their own auctions.

# 22

# Of Taxes and the Writer

E arly in April a few years ago I got a call from a client who was preparing his income tax. This author wrote erotic fiction and wanted to know whether he could legitimately claim as a deduction his penicillin treatment for a little affliction he had contracted in the course of "researching" one of his novels.

I told him I imagined the treatment would probably fall under medical deductions rather than research expenses, but the story does illustrate that even the most untrammeled literary spirits have to pay their obeisance to Uncle Sam sooner or later. With more and more authors incorporating, purchasing expensive computer equipment, seeking shelters for their taxable income, and in general being more businesslike in their approaches to the art and craft of literature, the accountant is becoming as important as the literary agent in guiding the destinies of writers.

The chances of a writer being audited by the Internal Revenue Service are a little better than those of the average working stiff because most writers are free-lancers, and taxes on their income are not usually withheld as they are from persons on company payrolls. Thus, even though the odds that anybody will be audited are going down because of staff cutbacks at the IRS, a free-lancer's tax return may be more provocative than that of someone who works for IBM or Ford or AT&T. Your best defense, should the fickle finger of the IRS single you out, is a well-kept set of records, primarily your canceled checks, your receipts, and a journal or ledger recording details of every transaction for which you are claiming a deduction, particularly those for which receipts are not ordinarily given, such as taxis and public transportation, certain tips, and the like.

In general, an author is entitled to "write off," or deduct from taxable income earned from his writing, certain costs incurred in pursuit of that income. Among those costs are agent's commissions; rental of office space; editorial and secretarial assistance; purchase or lease of computers and other office equipment; office supplies, such as toner cartridges and paper; travel; the cost of entertaining editors, agents, producers, collaborators, and others related to his endeavors; and books and other research material.

Naturally, not all expenses are deductible; other expenses may be deducted over a period of years; others are only partially deductible; and still others are deductible only at your peril.

Because of the feast-or-famine nature of the free-lance life, you don't necessarily have to earn money in any given year in order to write off expenses. You may be working on a long-term project and a whole year or more may go by without income. Yet you may still claim the costs incurred that year and deduct them from whatever other income you received, such as interest or stock dividends, your spouse's income if you're married and file jointly, and the like. Even if you're not a professional writer at all but simply a would-be writer who has yet to realize a dime from his work, you may nevertheless write off your expenses for a period of years before these activities come under the definition of hobby, the costs of which are not deductible.

So much for famine. But there's also tax relief for those who feast. One form of it is the government-sponsored Keogh tax shelter plans, which are designed for free-lancers and other independent breadwinners who do not earn regular wages. By putting some of your income into a Keogh account, you in effect lower the amount of income you claim for that year and pay taxes on it only when you draw that income later in your life, at retirement age, when you will presumably be in a lower tax bracket. Meanwhile, your Keogh account will be appreciating through interest or dividends or (if you invest the money wisely) through capital gains on investments.

Another important money-saving technique for successful writers is income averaging. If you have a windfall year after several years of low or no income, the IRS permits you to combine your return for the big year with the returns from the four preceding years and pay the average tax on all five years. To simplify the rather complex formula, suppose you earned $5000 from your writing in each of the four previous years (all these figures are net, after deductions), then this year you struck it rich with $100,000. By adding the $100,000 to the income you earned in the four previous years, and dividing the total of $120,000 by five years, you get an average annual income of $24,000. So you pay taxes this year on only $24,000. Of course, you also pay *back* taxes on the $19,000 above the $5000 that you made in those four previous years. Even so, the total taxes you pay for all five years on an income-averaging basis are lower than the total you pay if you do not income-average — perhaps as much as $20,000 — and of course you save a lot of taxes in that windfall year.

✍

When it comes to taxes, the name of the game is deductions. Let's talk about some.

**Capital purchases.** Capital purchases are major items such as machinery and furniture. These might include your typewriter or PC, a desk, photocopier, file cabinets, a calculator, or fax. The government considers such purchases investments, and because investments are subject to depreciation, you are usually not permitted to deduct their purchase price in full the year you purchased them. Rather, you have to spread the cost out over several years for tax accounting purposes. Thus, if you buy a PC and a printer, you may only be able to "depreciate" it over five years; that is, deduct a portion of the price from your income each year for five years. On the other hand, you may be entitled to an "investment credit," a direct credit against your tax liability. Investment credits are a form of reward the government gives businesses for buying capital equipment. The principle is that such investments pump money back into our economy and keep it healthy, so investment credits encourage you to buy furniture and equipment.

**Straight deductions.** Most of the day-to-day necessities of the writing profession come under this category. Assuming you can furnish receipts, these are fully deductible, and deductible wholly in the year in which you pay them. They include paper and other stationery; pens and pencils, paper clips, rubber bands, and other office supplies; postage; messenger bills; photocopy bills; legal, bookkeeping, and accounting fees; dues and professional organization fees; editorial and secretarial assistance; agent's commissions and expenses; phone and cable costs; interest on loans; and certain state and local taxes, such as unincorporated business taxes, city rent or occupancy taxes, and the like.

Although many of these costs are indisputably business expenses and are seldom questioned by the IRS as long as you furnish solid documentation, some of them do fall into a gray area where eyebrows might be raised or IRS computers, programmed to seek variations from certain norms, might "flag" the questionable item. *Writer's Digest* is a pretty safe magazine subscription to deduct, but *Sports Illustrated? House Beautiful?* Well, if you can demonstrate that you wish to write for those markets or that the information they provide applies to a writing project you're developing, those subscriptions will be arguably legitimate. The same might be said of a television set. If you hope to write for television or consider TV a good source of information for your books, stories, or articles, you may be able to get away with depreciating the cost of the set.

The gray area gets even grayer with such deductions as travel and entertainment. At what point, if any, a dinner stops being social and starts being professional is often impossible to say, as is the point at which a vacation becomes a business trip. In order to legitimize these deductions, solid documentation is desirable in the form of receipts and canceled checks, a diary or journal, or other written evidence demonstrating intent and purpose. The IRS requires receipts for any claimed business meals of more than $25; for meals costing less (is there such a creature?), no receipt is necessary but a detailed journal entry or other memo is desirable. It should stipulate the date, place, persons involved, business purpose, and price. Home entertainment may be harder to document, since food and drink for business entertainment are often purchased with provisions earmarked for personal use, or food and drink already stocked at home may be used to entertain business guests. But here again, a combination of receipts and memoranda may at least convey to potential auditors the sincerity of your attempts to furnish good documentation. The IRS does assume that a certain percentage of a professional writer's or free-lancer's income is going to be claimed for entertainment, and within that range it may not raise any questions. But because entertainment deductions are usually among the most inflated found in the average return, any inordinate claims will usually trigger intense curiosity.

The same is true of travel. Business travelers are obliged to document the purpose of their trip and expenses, and even though such trips may in fact be 95 percent play and 5 percent work, orderly records will allow the benefit of the doubt to be given to the claimant. Indeed, no connection between the place visited and the place written about need manifest itself, for who is to say that you did not write a story about Acapulco that was rejected and never published, or that after spending a week in London researching a novel you did not decide to set the book in Paris instead? But there are limits to the government's credulity. The writer who flies with his family to Miami Beach during Christmas week may have a hard time convincing a gimlet-eyed IRS auditor that it was a research trip.

Probably the most common tax headache for a writer is what to deduct for the office in his home. If you have an office outside your home, you may claim the rent, utility, insurance, and related bills in their entirety. But what if your bedroom doubles as an office or you do your writing on the kitchen table? Until a few years ago, the IRS was liberal in its definition of office space in the home, but it has since become stricter, insisting that a room be set aside specifically and exclusively for professional use. If you have an eight-room home and use one room as an office, you may claim one-eighth of all your house expenses as deductible business expenses.

The telephone is another ambiguous item insofar as personal and professional uses are mingled on the same bill. In such cases you can assign a percentage of the bill to business use and note the long-distance charges for business calls. Perhaps the best way around the problem is to maintain a separate phone for business purposes.

A growing number of writers have become so businesslike about their profession that they have incorporated themselves. What benefits do they hope to derive? Is this something that every writer can or should do?

There are many financial, legal, and other good reasons for individuals to form corporations, but these are not always as clear for writers as they might be for manufacturing or service companies. One major benefit, for instance, is limited liability. With the threat of legal claims perpetually hanging over every writer's head, what author would not breathe easier knowing that the only assets he's in jeopardy of losing in a lawsuit are the rather meager ones of his corporation?

Unfortunately, it's nowhere near that simple. The law recognizes how easy it is for wrongdoers to hide behind the cloak of corporate immunity, and thus in the "discovery" process of a trial it may be ruled that the personal assets of the head of a closely held corporation (meaning that only you, or perhaps you and your spouse, hold all the stock) may be vulnerable to a claim. Furthermore, most publishers signing contracts with incorporated authors require them to furnish written "performance guarantees" that they will honor their contractual obligations and be responsible for the warranty and indemnification clauses of their contracts. After all, a corporation can't write a book — or, what is more pertinent in this case, it can't write a libelous, defamatory, obscene, scandalous, or privacy-invading book. Only individuals can do that, so authors must sign a document guaranteeing the contractual obligations of the corporations they own, and vice versa. This so vitiates the limited liability aspect of incorporating as to render it virtually impotent.

There are definite financial advantages for an author to incorporate, but these generally come into play only if that author is making a good deal of money, and making it consistently. Medical insurance can be paid out of before-tax income. A pension plan can be established, enabling you to shelter until retirement far more money than the government currently permits under Keogh plans. These pension plans usually have life insurance options, meaning that life insurance premiums may be paid out of before-tax income, a distinct advantage over the situation of unincorporated individuals. There are other benefits, too, but there are also disadvantages. The costs of starting and maintaining a corporation are not inconsiderable, and after you have paid legal and accounting costs, or spent so much time filling out and filing federal, state, and local withholding income tax, corporation tax, unemployment, Social Security, disability, pension, and other papers, you may find that you might have done just as well conducting your business as a plain old unincorporated human being. Besides, if the government feels you've established a corporation just to dodge taxes, you could get into trouble and end up paying heavy penalties and interest on back taxes. So before you start thinking about vying with Exxon for a place on the *Fortune* 500 list, consult your accountant.

# 23 ✍

# *Solidarity*

When are writers going to get organized?

Some years ago, I wrote a series of articles speculating on the prospects for an effective writers' union. In the intervening years, conditions for members of the free-lance writing community have actually worsened in many ways and the need for collective action has become more urgent. Yet, I'd have to conclude that the day when American writers can link arms to demand minimum contractual terms or the abolition of certain onerous publishing practices is scarcely closer than it was in 1980, 1970, or 1960.

As I originally pointed out, there is no dearth of organizations dedicated to improving the lot of writers. The issue, rather, is how large are the constituencies of those organizations and how effectively can the leadership act on behalf of its members.

Foremost among these organizations is the Authors Guild. Boasting a large and impressive roster of writers, the Guild through its excellent *Bulletin* airs many issues critical to the writing profession, offers a recommended book contract, aids indigent writers, and in recent years has taken some outspoken and aggressive positions on behalf of authors. One of its most impressive triumphs was a successful lobbying campaign to defeat a dreadful piece of federal legislation that would have caused authors crippling tax problems. Of late the Guild has instituted a plan to subsidize random audits of publishers' royalty statements.

The Guild is not a union, however, and thus by definition cannot undertake the kinds of actions for which unions are mandated — notably, strikes. We do have one true union, the National Writers Union, which in 1991 voted to affiliate with the United Auto Workers. Listing thousands of members, the NWU has pressured book publishers to institute reforms in such areas as timely payments, comprehensible royalty statements, nonrefundable advances, and arbitration of disputes. Though these activities have fallen short of strikes, the NWU has been particularly combative against newspaper and magazine publishers, persuading some of them to accept certain minimum terms, standards, and conditions. At this writing the union has instituted legal action to prevent publishers from exploiting electronic rights to material without compensation to writers.

Finally, there is a host of writers' organizations ranging in degree of political activism from truculent to indifferent. None of them has ever attempted anything remotely resembling a job action, strike, or boycott, their activities being limited pretty much to educating members on selected issues to help them take more effective individual action.

All this is light years away from the activities of the Writers Guild of America, the organization of motion picture and television screenwriters, whose work stoppages have brought the movie and television industries to their knees. The Guild is the sole and exclusive collective bargaining representative of movie and television writers. Its book-sized Basic Agreement defines the services performed by authors, then sets minimum compensation payable for those services. Waiting time for decisions and for remittance of payment are rigidly defined, and interest penalties are imposed on delinquent producers, studios, and networks. And the Guild has an elaborate system for hearing, settling, or arbitrating grievances. After reviewing the provisions of the WGA Basic Agreement in my *Locus* column back in the 1980s, I had to shake my head and muse whether those of us who boast about being activists are "living in some sort of aboriginal society at the farthest reaches of the civilized world."

Why can't free-lance writers achieve the same things? Well, first of all, they are not actual *employees* of their publishers as WGA members are employees of the producers, studios, and networks that engage their services. Free-lance writers are dispersed all over the country, as opposed to movie and television writers who in good measure are clustered in the Los Angeles area, an important factor when it comes to manning picket lines and rallying the troops. And it is far easier to demand a minimum wage scale for workers who all write half-hour sitcoms, say, than for those who write such widely differing categories as romances, westerns, mysteries, mainstream novels, histories, biographies, articles, and short stories. Thus divided, free-lance writers are conquered before they even begin to organize.

Another important hindrance to collective activity among book authors in this country is the power of literary agents. Writers have it pretty much fixed in their heads that (1) you can't get anywhere without an agent and (2) once you have one, you don't need an organization to help you improve your lot. For better or worse, there happens to be a lot of truth in those notions.

Luckily, the agents have an active trade organization of their own, the Association of Authors' Representatives. The AAR evolved out of the merger in 1991 of two major organizations of literary agents, the Society of Authors Representatives and the Independent Literary Agents Association. Consisting at this writing of nearly three hundred professional literary agents, the AAR is able to leverage the viewpoint of thousands of professional writer clients of these agents, to say nothing of countless other writers who are not represented by AAR agents or by any agents at all.

Because of the gentlemanly tradition of publishing and the close friendships of agents and editors, the style of the AAR and its predecessors has been relatively low-key. Issues are aired at meetings and recommendations discussed, arming the individual agent with sufficient information to take appropriate measures according to his or her lights. Small sorties of agents visit publishers to exert reason and quiet pressure to alter disagreeable practices and policies. The AAR initiated a newsletter, circulated not just among agent members but among influential figures in publishing and related industries as well, airing issues and concerns. These activities have succeeded in improving terms and conditions at a number of publishers. And, perhaps just as significantly, they have raised the consciousness of both authors and publishing people, narrowing the gulf of misunderstanding that has been a source of conflict in the past.

But of course, the agents cannot strike (*that* would certainly be interesting!), and because of the ever-present shadow of antitrust regulations they are prohibited from conducting any activities that restrict trade or competition. So there is only so much the AAR can do by way of collective action.

And collective action — a strike or boycott — is the name of the game; it, or even the implicit threat of it, is the source of any organization's power. Will any writers' organization be able to use those tactics?

Formal boycotts are illegal under current antitrade statutes. They may, however, be informally waged, such as a call by feminist groups to boycott Random House for publication of Bret Easton Ellis's slasher novel, *American Psycho.*

As for strikes, the National Labor Relations Act of 1933 permits labor unions of company employees to conduct strikes. However, independent contractors are specifically excluded from NLRA protection. That means free-lance writers. Bruce Hartford, in 1991 secretary-treasurer of the National Writers Union, told me in a letter that the U.S. government had come down very hard on violations of the Act: "In recent memory," Hartford wrote, "these same antitrust laws were used to slap a whopping fine on the Musicians Union for the crime of trying to set minimum rates for their members outside of the strict employer-employee relationship, the Dramatists Guild was found to have violated the Sherman Act by setting minimum fees for the rights to perform a play, and it cost the Graphic Artists Guild an enormous sum in legal fees to defend its promulgation of a standard rate book."

Bear in mind that strikes are by no means the only effective action that trade organizations may take to win concessions. Other kinds of pressure, particularly negative publicity, may achieve as much as formal job actions. When Pantheon's publisher resigned after Pantheon's parent company, Random House, pressured him to trim unprofitable titles from Pantheon's highly literary list, a number of big-name Random House authors, including James Michener, protested. Though Random House did not back down, the idea that this incident caused Michener to contemplate switching publishers sent bone-jarring shivers down the spines of Random House executives. And after the Professional Authors Network, an arm of the Romance Writers of America, published the results of a member survey of paperback romance publishers, the house that ranked lowest made a determined and successful effort to improve its image. One taste of the lash of bad publicity can often achieve more than a strike or a lawsuit.

And heaven knows it's a lot cheaper!

# 24

# Superstores

I t can be argued that the most dramatic change in the publishing environment during our lifetimes is the explosive rise of bookstore chains. As they expanded at express-train speed in the 1970s and 1980s, it looked as if the old-fashioned local bookshop would soon go the way of the stagecoach. In the mid-1990s, however, a resurgence of vitality brought independent bookstores back to fiscal health.

Analyzing this phenomenon, chain store executives countered with a variety of tactics designed to lure customers back. None is more impressive than so-called superstores, stupendous and elegant book emporia carrying a dazzling number and variety of titles. Taking their cue from the success of some mammoth independent single-outlet retail stores like The Tattered Cover in Denver and Powell's Books in Portland, Oregon, the chains have opened superstores in scores of locations around the country, and plans are afoot for innumerable more. The services and programs offered by these establishments cater to needs far beyond the simple desire to buy a book, making them libraries, museums, day care centers, theaters, and even cafés as much as bookstores. They point to some exciting new developments in the roles and responsibilities of bookstore chains, and a healthy upsurge in book consumption.

The enterprising executives who flung bookstore chain units into urban shopping centers and suburban malls were acting on some well-defined perceptions about book buyers. Their market research revealed, first, that most traffic in bookstores is casual: Potential customers walk into them impulsively, seldom have a specific book in mind, and make their selections on the basis of position on bestseller lists, word-of-mouth recommendations, placement of books in high-traffic areas of stores, and impressive promotional displays or events such as celebrity book signings.

A second conclusion reached by chain executives is that in order to make books profitable in shopping areas where other types of retail operations offer higher rewards to investors, brand names must dominate the merchandise. "Brand name" in the book business means star authors, notable bestsellers, backlist classics, and other works of broad or universal interest. That made it easier for chain store buyers operating out of a central headquarters to acquire titles on a countrywide basis with little regard for local variations in taste.

Third, computerization of sales information would furnish reliable profiles of books, authors, and categories of literature and how they were selling. This data would enable chains to focus ordering on the most popular and profitable merchandise, thus fueling the bestseller cycle.

Finally, the chain commanders decided to offer discounts, some of them quite deep. This was possible because the purchasing power of the chains allowed them to secure higher discounts on big-volume purchases from publishers.

These strategies succeeded in making bookstore chains such as Barnes & Noble, B. Dalton, Borders, and Crown the dominant factor in trade book publishing, for publishers were compelled to consider the purchasing might of the chains when deciding on which properties, and which types of properties, to acquire.

By the mid-1980s the chains had independent bookstores on the ropes and forced a number of them out of business. But all was not well with the chains and, quietly, things started to turn around. For one thing, the chains' discounting tactics began to backfire as margins thinned to a dangerous level. Also, a well-publicized antitrade lawsuit by a group of independent bookstores forced publishers to stop offering discounts that favored big chains at the expense of smaller stores or more modestly endowed chains.

Then, the glamor of chain bookstores began to wear off as consumer dissatisfaction made itself felt. The emphasis on bestsellers seriously cut down the variety of merchandise offered in chain store units. Not all customers fit the lowest-common-denominator profile for which the stores seemed to have been designed. Many customers sought backlist titles, classics, works of drama, essay collections, and poetry, or books that spoke to racial minorities, gays, and other special interests. Visitors to chain stores complained that the atmosphere there felt cold and antiseptic, more oriented to pushing merchandise and moving customers past the cash registers than to offering enlightenment and service. This impression was enhanced by clerical help that not only didn't love books but often seemed downright ignorant about them.

What is more, in their attempt to deliver cleanliness and efficiency, the managers of the chains had neglected those customers for whom books are precious treasures. Although the Tom Clancys, Danielle Steeles, and Stephen Kings are spectacularly profitable, not everyone who visits a bookstore seeks a bang-up read. A person in pain may seek consolation in a book of philosophy; travel books spirit one's imagination away on fantastic voyages; a volume of poetry can illuminate our most intimate experiences. But the Clancys, Steeles, and Kings were crowding these kinds of literature out of chain store doors.

The rich personal contact between customer and clerk, the elegant and civilized carriage trade ambiance, the charming disorder, so many of the things that had made bookshops abodes of exquisite discovery, had been sanitized in the new stores. Customers for whom these pleasures were important — and there were far more of them than chain store executives realized — took their trade back to the old places. And when the economy started to recede, the growth rate of shopping malls in which bookstore chains thrived flattened. Fewer customers flocked to malls, and those who did visit them elected to spend their money on necessities rather than discretionary items such as books. The chains staggered, and independent stores sprang back to life like new seedlings spring up after a forest fire.

It did not escape the attention of chain store executives that among the most successful independent stores were several giant outlets carrying a dazzling array of titles, in some cases more than 100,000 offered in tens of thousands of square feet of retail space. By contrast, a typical mall bookstore averages 3000 square feet and carries 15,000 to 20,000 titles. One of the most awesome independent superstores is Powell's, located on a hill near a brewery in Portland, Oregon. It stocks no fewer than one million copies of 550,000 titles in a spacious, well-lighted 43,000 square feet. Rather than rely on computers, it adheres to a manual card system to track inventory. But the 75 employees who preside over the sections (including 9,000 titles in poetry alone!) know their books. These factors combine to move some two million copies annually, many of them used books.

The odd thing is that instead of being overwhelmed by this multifarious selection, browsers at Powell's and similar marts thrive on it. Some fascinating quirk of human psychology was at work here for, instead of being dampened by such vast choice, the buying impulse seems to quicken and reach critical mass in the book-saturated reaction chamber of a superstore.

The chains realized they had to compete in this arena or continue to suffer flat sales. But stocking a lot of titles is not simply a matter of ordering one of everything from a publisher's catalogue. Small purchases lower the discount offered to stores, meaning lower profit margins. Freight costs for small orders are higher per book than those for large orders. And, if a store understocks a book that turns out to be successful, delays in received reordered copies can kill sales momentum.

Nevertheless, the destiny of the bookstore appears to be in big stores — roughly defined as those of 10,000 square feet or more — and between 1990 and 1995 they sprang up as fast as concrete could be poured. And not all of them were erected in the hearts of major cities. You can find a Bookstop superstore in Mesquite, Texas; a Tower bookstore in Citrus Heights, California; and a Barnes & Noble in Edina, Minnesota. And I am not including independent, single-unit superstores. If you are concerned about the decline of literature in our nation, this is very encouraging news.

Bookstores are expanding not only in size but in the variety of their merchandise. With the explosive growth of such software categories as audio, video, and computer games, bookstore owners have realized that they must accommodate consumers of those products. This is not merely a matter of good business but of survival, for video and consumer electronics store chains have begun to cast covetous eyes on bookstores. Futurists (including yours truly) envision media superstores with sections for audio, videocassettes, CD-ROM, computer software, and books — and a few examples have already made their appearances.

I recently had reason to visit a Barnes & Noble superstore in

Paramus, New Jersey, where I'd been invited to participate in Science Fiction Night. In a book-lined corner my co-panelists, author Barry Malzberg and agent Sharon Jarvis, and I discussed science fiction and related categories before an attentive audience of shoppers and aspiring writers. Our event was tied in with a book signing and a promotion of the store's extensive science fiction section.

The 17,000-square-foot Paramus store is simply gorgeous, bright, richly carpeted, and lined with dark walnut bookshelves flanking wide aisles. The selection, some 200,000 volumes of 100,000 titles, was overwhelming. It was not, however, paralyzing. In fact, I could not imagine leaving the store empty-handed, and I didn't. The clerical help was friendly and knowledgeable. Although I missed the amiable chaos of the old-fashioned bookstore, I would gladly trade it for modernity, efficiency, a thoughtful layout, and many welcome amenities. There were ramps for the handicapped, and child-sized tables and chairs in the juvenile section for little ones to pore over prospective purchases. Visiting this bookstore was a happy experience, and I understood firsthand what motivates a customer to purchase books by the stack and pay full price for them to boot.

Our little entertainment was but one on a crowded calendar of events offered at the store. In the month of September alone, visitors to the Paramus store could attend Poetry Night with readings by three leading poets; welcome best-selling novelist Sidney Sheldon (and have him autograph his latest novel); hear members of the Bicycle Touring Club of North Jersey discuss selecting and touring with a bike; marvel at an all-day demonstration of computer technology presented by Amiga; or hear your devoted correspondent espousing his latest crackpot theories about how life imitates science fiction. There is Children's Story Time every Wednesday morning at 10:00 A.M., and a create-your-own-bookmark contest for young artists conducted on a Saturday. While these events are obviously designed to attract customers and get them to buy books, they are also pleasant and positive activities that play up the bookstore's potential to become a community center offering cultural, educational, and entertainment benefits.

Only the grouchiest chain-basher would begrudge these corporations a profit reaped in the pursuit of such socially uplifting activities. You owe it to yourselves to visit a superstore soon.

# 25

# Titles,

*or My Life in Titles, or The Title Game, or Adventures of a Title Maven, or Titles: The Writer's Indispensable Tool, or What's in a Title?, or The Principles of Titling, or My Kingdom for a Title, or . . .*

Among the immortal literary classics to be found on the bookshelves of every civilized person are such books as *Trimalchio in West Egg*, *My Valley*, *Pumphre*, and *Tom-All-Alone's the Ruined House*.

Do you mean to say you've never heard of them?

Actually, they *were* the titles before the author or publisher thought better of it. You undoubtedly know them as *The Great Gatsby*, *East of Eden*, *Babbitt*, and *Bleak House*.

It's hard to know whether those novels would have endured despite their dreadful original titles, but it does make us wonder. In fact, book editor and author Andre Bernard wondered so much about titles that he produced a whole book about them, *Now All We Need Is a Title: Famous Book Titles and How They Got That Way*.

The first problem most authors face when commencing a book or story is what to call it. Many writers cannot start writing until the question of title is settled, for among its many functions, the title helps an author focus on the point of his tale, its theme, its mood, its tone of voice, and the nature of the audience that will be reading it. Each version of the title of this chapter represents a different solution to the challenge of how to approach this subject. Do I play it straight or cute? Grimly academic, pedantically classical, or cleverly metaphorical? Luckily, for purposes of illustration, I was able to use all of them. I doubt if we shall see such an opportunity again in our lifetime.

I am a connoisseur of very few things, but I do consider myself one on the subject of book titles. It is certainly not a form of expertise I deliberately set out to develop. But even if you have a tin ear, over a period of thirty years of immersion you do become something of a maven in this sub-sub-sub-species of literary endeavor.

There are worse things one could be. The first impression you form of a book is the one evoked by its title, and its impact on you is no less significant than the one you form upon first setting your eye on a stranger. Your bond with a book commences with its title: Your mind and heart are subliminally conditioned by a title to anticipate the book's message and respond to its contents.

The title of a book is its most important sales feature; you are often attracted or repelled by its title long before you see its cover, study its jacket blurbs, or browse through its contents to decide whether or not you want to purchase it. It is therefore not hyperbolic to suggest that many consumers make their decision to buy a book or pass it up on the strength or weakness of its title.

Little wonder, then, that authors, editors, and agents spend an inordinate time seeking les mots justes for the titles of their books. I keep a file of terrific titles for which no books have yet been written, and when a client complains about being stumped for a title, I haul out my list and see if I can make a match. Late in the 1960s I collaborated with Elizabeth Hogan on a Doubleday book describing the dangers of nuclear power plants that were then beginning to proliferate in the United States. We took our title from Robert Frost's poem "Fire and Ice": *Those Who Favor Fire*. We thought it was a brilliant choice.

Doubleday's sales reps didn't. Every publishing company sales department has a Vice President in Charge of Rejecting Great Titles and Substituting Mediocre Ones, and that's how our book ended up being called *Perils of the Peaceful Atom*.

The original title went into my Terrific Titles file, however, and when, years later, Marta Randall turned in an apocalyptic novel for which she lacked an appropriate title, I resuscitated *Those Who Favor Fire* and suggested it to her, and this time it passed muster.

Actually, it's not fair to make fun of the sales reps, for it is they after all who have to go out and sell the book to the accounts. If a sales rep is not confident that your title makes an immediate and forceful impact on the buyers — which translates into lost commissions for him — he is going to lobby his publisher to get it changed.

And what for authors is an inspired title may be seen in a very different light by the sales grunts slugging it out on the front line. Among the most common complaints publishers hear from sales reps are vagueness ("What the hell does *Attitudes* mean"?), insipidness ("*Alien Attackers* sounds like a million other science fiction novels"), and inappropriateness ("*Zen and the Art of Motorcycle Maintenance* sounds like it should go in the how-to section of a bookstore"). Sales reps are therefore the conservative party in any publisher's legislature, and they usually control a majority vote. But if I love a title enough I will fight like a devil for it, even with my own authors. In 1984 my clients psychiatrist Stanley Turecki, M.D., and co-author Leslie Tonner delivered to Bantam Books a contracted book advising parents how to understand and manage particularly difficult children. The authors and I had spent a long Saturday poring over Bibles, *Bartlett's*, and other reference books, and had at last distilled a splendid title drop by drop: *Parents Under Siege*.

It did not pass muster with Bantam's Vice President in Charge of Rejecting Great Titles, and we ended up with — well, what else? — *The Difficult Child*. Talk about difficult children, I was so bitterly disappointed I almost threw a tantrum. But the sales department felt that there are times when a title should simply state, without poetic flourish, what a book is about, and this was one of them. We ultimately acceded to this line of reasoning, and a dozen or so hardcover printings later I must grudgingly admit that Sales had a good point. But if you've written a book for which the title *Parents Under Siege* is appropriate, take it, it's yours.

Brilliant titles are not always desirable, however, and may actually hurt sales if they point the potential book buyer in the wrong direction. This is particularly true in genre fiction. Every category of books has what might be described as its own characteristic title "profile," a word or phrase that blatantly declares the book's genre. An obvious example is detective fiction, where you have *The Case of the . . .* or something with the words "murder" or "death" in it. Although these catch phrases have become clichés, they help everybody down the line, from editors to bookstore buyers to consumers, to immediately classify the book and make the selection process easier. The title, in other words, is a key element of the package, and guarantees the slot in which the book is to be displayed. A title that deviates too far from its appropriate genre can be a liability, no matter how clever or mellifluous it may be. If you don't think you've been mentally conditioned to respond to titles, take any mainstream title and marry it to a genre formula one and you'll see what I mean. Pretend you're a bookstore clerk and determine in which department you would display the following:

*The Valley of the Dolls Sanction*
*The Dragons of Valley of the Dolls*
*Dollsworld*
*Showdown at Valley of the Dolls*
*Mistress of Dollsvale*
*Love's Virginal Valley of the Dolls*
*The Dollsdale Horror*
*A Woman of Uncertain Valley of the Dolls*
*Murder on the Rue Valley of the Dolls*

It works for nonfiction, too:

*The Valley of the Dolls Syndrome*
*Tighten Up Your Valley of the Dolls*
*The Thirty-Day Valley of the Dolls Slimdown*

Even in mainstream literature, titles can give confusing and misleading impressions, and the results can be funny. *Zen and the Art of Motorcycle Maintenance* really did get placed on how-to shelves, and recently the *New York Times* ran an apology for referring to Evan Connell's biography of Custer, *Son of the Morning Star*, as a novel. If you didn't know better, you might very well place on the wrong shelves such ambiguously titled books as, *Exit the Rainmaker*, *White Mischief*, and *The Dancing Wu Li Masters*. It's no laughing matter when these mix-ups cause lost sales, however.

Like everything else in modern culture, titles tend to go in and out of fashion. The revolutionary '60s temporarily loosened strictures against long titles and book authors took their cue from the stage. Plays like *Oh Dad, Poor Dad, Momma's Hung You in the Closet and I'm Feelin' So Sad*, and *The Effects of Gamma Rays on Man-in-the-Moon Marigolds* had lengthy runs despite jawbreaking titles, and authors and publishers tried the same on books. Which is how we ended up with titles like, *Been Down So Long It Looks Like Up to Me*. The problem with titles longer than five words, however, is that they crowd the cover and must be reduced to an unacceptably small typeface. The counterrevolution restored short titles, and today such best-selling authors as James Michener, Stephen King, Janet Dailey, and Danielle Steele have been employing one-word titles to good effect.

Juvenile and young adult titles have become particularly inventive in the last few years, and it seems that the wackier they are, the more the kids love them. No more *Treasure Island* and *Little Women* for today's boys and girls. They want *Jelly Belly, There's a Boy in the Girl's Bathroom, Jacob Two Two Meets the Hooded Fang, Hershell Cobwell and the Miraculous Tattoo, How to Eat Fried Worms, Wonder Kid Meets the Lunch Snatcher, Can You Sue Your Parents for Malpractice?, The Alfred G. Graebner Memorial High School Handbook of Rules and Regulations*, and the like.

Every publisher's dream is to have a book that sells by the truckload on the strength of its title alone. Of course, it's impossible to know with any accuracy what attracts buyers to a book. After reading *The One Minute Manager* or *Swim with the Sharks*, you may wonder whether the contents lived up to the brilliance of the titles. But you probably plunked money down at a bookstore to find out.

Most lucrative of all is the title that starts a copycat fad, such as *101 Uses for a Dead Cat, Real Men Don't Eat Quiche*, and *Thin Thighs in Thirty Days*. For years after publication of those books, publishers brought out variants on the titles to take advantage of the public's infatuation. Imitation being the sincerest form of flattery, the rip-off titles merely fueled the success of the original ones. Patricia Matthews's romance *Love's Avenging Heart* launched a veritable flood of *Love's Something Somethings* that did not subside for years.

Nonfiction writers are luckier than novelists because they often get a second chance in the form of a subtitle. If your title is a bit poetic or obscure, don't worry, your subtitle will correct any ambiguities. What does *Final Cut* mean? It could signify anything until you couple it with author Steven Bach's subtitle: *Dreams and Disaster in the Making of "Heaven's Gate."* Similarly, Merle Miller's *Plain Speaking* doesn't give one a clear idea of his book's contents until you couple it with its subtitle, *An Oral Biography of Harry S. Truman.* Note that after you read the subtitle, your attention returns to the basic title, and you are now able to understand and appreciate it much better.

For authors struggling to come up with a good title, I advise you to make a long list of words and phrases that have any bearing, however remote, on your story. Some of these may come from the text itself: a description of your hero or heroine, a reference to the plot, theme, or action. Mix and match words until you arrive at the precise formula. If your title doesn't jump out at you, go through your thesaurus for related words that might be more felicitous than the ones on your list. Or use the index of your *Bartlett's* to locate passages in classical literature that succinctly, cogently, and lyrically evoke the appropriate image of your book.

Titling is an essential element of the writer's craft and requires as much thought as plotting and characterization. Some authors do have a special genius for it, however. I have, for instance, always admired Gregory Benford's ability to select monumental titles that capture the stupendous profundity of his stories of time and space: *In the Ocean of Night, Beyond the Sea of Suns, Timescape, Against Infinity*. You read his titles and you know this writer is grappling with nothing less than imponderables, immutables, and ultimates. If you are a romance fan you may find Janelle Taylor's titles fatally irresistible: *First Love, Wild Love, Whispered Kisses, Sweet Savage Heart, Passions Wild and Free*. The titles of Father Andrew Greeley's books guarantee that you will be witnessing the torments of sinners: *Thy Brother's Wife, Patience of a Saint, The Cardinal Sins*. And John Saul's titles portend suspenseful tales of creepy kids: *Suffer the Children, The Unloved, The Unwanted, When the Wind Blows*. Some authors get a lot of mileage out of a title. Lawrence Sanders has been going through all the deadly sins for his titles, and Harry Kemelman's mystery titles lured readers from one day of the week to another, starting with *Friday, the Rabbi Slept Late*.

Our love of great books is often enhanced by the great titles that go with them. *How Green Was My Valley, From Here to Eternity, East of Eden, Crime and Punishment, One Hundred Years of Solitude, King Solomon's Mines, Forever Amber, The Magic Mountain, Lord of the Flies* — how often are unforgettable titles married to unforgettable books!

If, try as you may, you simply can't come up with an apt title for your book, don't despair, you're in good company. Margaret Mitchell had a hard time coming up with anything more engaging than *Tomorrow Is Another Day* for her novel of the Civil War. Luckily, a better one did occur to her before the book went into production.

# 26

# Let's Have Lunch

When the time comes for me to lay down my sword and armor and cross into the Great Beyond after a lifetime of combat with venal publishers, crooked movie producers, treacherous lawyers, and kvetchy authors, it is my fondest hope that the gods will reward me with perpetual publishing luncheons. What fardels would I not bear knowing that such a treat awaited me on the other side! Some agents and editors feel lunches are tedious obligations at best and duck out of them whenever they can. I find them incredibly exciting, frequently dramatic, and always enlightening: I have never come away from one without having learned something useful. And, if everything comes together perfectly, the occasion can be a transcendental experience both culinarily and literarily, a sublime blend of art, commerce, and hedonism.

Most outsiders (such as authors) have a dim or distorted idea of what is involved in publishing lunches. To them, these affairs are as mysterious as royalty statements and discount schedules. So come perch on the right lobe of my brain, which in agents is the segment devoted to luncheon dates, and observe the process from the ringing of the phone (which automatically makes me salivate) to the final, discreet burp.

First, you should know that it is usually the editor who extends the invitation, selects the restaurant, and pays the check. Exactly why that is, I'm not sure, for it is clear that both parties stand to benefit equally from the occasion. (Mind you, I'm not complaining!)

Because it's the editor who proposes and disposes, any agent who reverses roles and offers to take an editor to lunch is apt to earn many bonus points on the editor's scorecard. When I worked for Scott Meredith, he never permitted his staff to allow editors to treat them to lunch, I think because it implied a dependency that tarnished the agency's image. I thought that was great, and I still do, but few agents can afford a steady diet (pardon the pun) of paying for editors, and if letting an editor pick up the tab suggests that the agent is dependent on him — well, in truth he is.

Editorial calendars tend to be filled for weeks and even months ahead with other lunches, editorial meetings, business trips, vacations, conferences, and conventions. So it is by no means unusual for lunch dates to be made far in advance, with the parties exploring dates for fifteen minutes before finding an open one. This practice makes one keenly and often disconcertingly aware of the rapid passage of time. A flip of your calendar, as you and your would-be luncheon partner seek an agreeable date, and you realize that another season has passed, another year. Here it is August, blazingly hot and swelteringly humid, and you are contemplating warm, heavy food, sweaters and furs, and talk of ski trips and Christmas books; in February, as bitter winds whistle past your windowpanes, you set a lunch date for a day when cherry and magnolia blossoms will strew the selfsame streets now carpeted with yard-high snowdrifts. It's a strange feeling. Red-letter days in the publishing calendar signal another year fled from our lives: "I can't make it in October, that's the Frankfurt Book Fair"; "November's no good, we have sales conference"; "Forget the last week in May — I have to get ready for the ABA convention." The seasons cycle inexorably and you wax philosophical about the rolling years. *Have I achieved anything important? Have I fulfilled my youthful goals? God grant me just one* Jane Fonda Workout Book, *just one full selection of the Book-of-the-Month Club, before He takes me away!*

Although your luncheon may be on some absurdly far-off day, the restaurant and precise hour are seldom selected until that very morning. Then, sometime around ten-thirty or eleven, your host or hostess calls you with the traditional phrase, "Are we on for today?" The time and place are then agreed upon. But not always easily. To wit:

"How does Italian sound to you?"

"Had it last night. Mexican?"

"I'm on a diet. There's a great fish place around the corner from my office."

"But that's all the way on the other side of town from me. Well, okay, but can we make it twelve-thirty? I have an author coming up to my office at two."

"That's bad for me. I'll be in a meeting all morning."

And so it goes.

Sometimes there is more to these negotiations than two busy people trying to find common ground. Nothing serious, just a subtle game of chicken, like waiting till twelve-fifteen before phoning to confirm the lunch date, or jockeying for who is going to come to whose side of town: *I am more powerful than you because I made you come to my side of town at an inconvenient hour and eat a cuisine that gives you heartburn.*

Occasionally lunch dates are canceled, and canceled at the last minute. The reasons range from "I forgot to mark it in my calendar" to "I have pneumonia." One morning, after waiting till noon, I phoned an editor to see if we were still on for lunch. "I'm afraid not," she said. "I was just fired." I told her I thought that was a very poor excuse for canceling a date and I took her to lunch myself.

As the cancelee of today may be the canceler of tomorrow, we all accept cancellations with a certain degree of equanimity. They can, however, prove frustrating. I can all but guarantee that on the day I don my best suit and most expensive silk tie in anticipation of a Lucullan orgy at a four-star restaurant with an editorial kingpin I've been wooing for months, the date will be canceled and I'll end up glomming a ham and Swiss on rye at my desk — and getting mustard on my tie to boot. Conversely, the days one wears jeans and a T-shirt to the office are inevitably the days one gets an impromptu invitation to Grenouille or Caravelle.

Your luncheon companions range from the most eminent and powerful editor to the callow rookie who has just been given a title and expense account and told to go meet agents. Some agents, particularly the more prominent ones, disdain invitations from freshman editors. Why waste time with subalterns without clout when you can pick up the phone anytime and get the head of the company? I personally find that attitude shortsighted. New editors are often the most enthusiastic, ambitious, and industrious, best attuned to trends to which the older guard may be oblivious — new music, hot electronic games, rising young film stars, embryonic fads, and so forth. There's another reason for cultivating young editors: In this turbulent age of musical chairs and sudden upward mobility, the green kid I dine with in March may be a department head in April.

Where you eat is a function of many factors: the age, seniority, and expense account of the editor; location; the amount of time available; dietary considerations; the importance of the host; the importance of the guest; the importance of the business at hand. Obviously, for example, young editors must entertain more modestly than senior ones. Yet many senior editors, having seen the inside of every restaurant in New York City after decades on the luncheon circuit, are just as happy to grab a burger at a coffee shop or munch a sandwich in the park. One of the most memorable lunches I ever had was with Robert Gottlieb, then editor-in-chief of Alfred Knopf. It consisted of vanilla yogurt, nuts and raisins, and an orange, eaten in his office — eaten, indeed, on the floor of his office, for every horizontal surface therein including the couch was covered with manuscripts. Gottlieb had courageously taken himself out of the luncheon game, professing it to be too time-consuming, expensive, and fattening. All of which is true, agents and editors remind each other as they study their menus and debate trading off the appetizer for dessert.

When a senior editor is courting an agent in the hopes of capturing a big-name author, you can expect a Drop Dead, Pull Out All the Stops, No Prisoners Taken luncheon, the kind most authors think occurs every day but which in fact happens quite rarely. Such affairs reverberate in memory till the end of time. I remember one laid on for a major client and myself at the Four Seasons. Every course from the quail egg appetizer to the ethereal flan dessert had been prearranged by our publisher-host. Captains and waiters, obviously tipped off to the preeminence of the guests, attended us with obsequies usually reserved for caliphs and maharajahs. Our host had but to nod and the staff was galvanized into action. And, as the presentation of a check would have been a base intrusion of crass mercantilism into so elevated an occasion, it was never brought out. I assume it was simply forwarded to the publisher's accounting department for review at some later date.

While sumptuous repasts are certainly incomparably exciting, and the author unaccustomed to "the treatment" may well feed off the memories till he's old and gray, I am far from convinced that they make much difference in influencing authors and agents. Such feasts seem much more appropriate for celebrating the closing of a major deal than for softening up reluctant objects of a publisher's affections. Which is not to say they should stop trying.

Authors have a misconception that lunches are the time when deals are made. In my experience most deals are made on the phone; the lunches are devoted more to getting acquainted with editors and their companies. Although I used to feel that some kind of business should be accomplished during lunch or a short time afterward, I've come to realize that friendships struck at lunch may not pay off for years. Nevertheless, there is something theatrical about presenting an editor with a manuscript at the luncheon table.

I remember one occasion when I brought a bulky manila envelope with me to a restaurant. Throughout lunch, the editor shot intrigued glances at it, and at last, toward dessert, she ran a covetous hand over it. "Is this something for me?"

"Oh Lord, no," I said with a gulp, realizing I had inadvertently led her on. "These are shirts going back to Bloomingdale's!"

Another common belief is that publishing lunches are rather boozy affairs. In truth, the dominant beverages for the last ten years or so have been wine and sparkling soda, and even the hallowed Marys are as apt to be Virgin as Bloody. On occasion, hard liquor is ordered, but sipped in moderation. As for the fabled two-martini lunch, I can truthfully say that in the last decade I can recall only one luncheon companion who ordered martinis, but since he was a confirmed alcoholic, the more he drank the more coherent he became. Because drunkenness is, among other things, a breach of manners (and manners are largely what publishing lunches are all about), editors and agents are extremely careful not to drink too much. I have seldom seen an editor become so much as tipsy at lunch. I wish I could say as much about authors, though in mitigation it must be said that they are usually a little nervous, unaccustomed to banquets on so lavish a scale.

Just what is ordered depends on the circumstances. Almost every editor in town has a diet book on his or her list and is experimenting with its advice. So there has been a distinct trend toward simple, highly nutritious cuisine, even in the elegant watering places where high-rolling publishing potentates hang out — all those places beginning with La and Le and Il. Exotic cuisines are usually avoided unless the editor and agent are old lunching companions and are willing to drop their guards a bit. With them I hit the Mexican, Brazilian, Thai, and Indian joints, drink beer instead of wine, relax protocol and manners, and exchange confidences seldom heard at high table.

Although the agent-guest is encouraged to order anything he wants, if the editor is decidedly junior it is an act of cruelty to order the most expensive items on the menu, but I do know some agents who, if they are mad at a publisher, will take their petty revenge by hitting the company up for a five-course extravaganza with champagne, brandy, and cigars.

Not all foods are suitable for business luncheons. Though I adore sloppy items like lobster and ribs, it is usually inappropriate to order them, for there is no way one can be cool and nonchalant while sucking the liquid out of a lobster claw or picking a sparerib clean with fingernails and incisors.

Like those in other industries, publishing luncheons have a rhythm and flow that follow Aristotelian dramaturgical principles, from the quiet exposition through the developmental passages and on to the stirring climax. While the talk at the outset is small — the weather, the latest Big Apple catastrophe, your life story, "How I Got into Publishing" — it is seldom unrevealing to one alert for clues to one's companion's literary interests, status in the company, industry clout, negotiating skill, and other traits that may prove useful in future intercourse. Above all, there is gossip.

New York trade publishing is a very small town. Although *Literary Market Place*, the industry's directory, contains thousands of names, my own short list of key contacts contain no more than three hundred names or so, and anything that happens to one of them is bound to affect my clients' interests. Promotions, firings, resignations, romances, divorces — all are grist for the agent's information mill in the perpetual process of assessing who's got the power, who's spending money, which way the market's going, what the next hot trend is.

Thus, in due time talk drifts toward serious business. What good authors and projects is the agent handling? What's the editor looking for? There is scarcely anything you can say that doesn't serve as a springboard. The birth of my son inspired luncheon discussions leading to at least three books my agency subsequently developed; let that be a lesson to anyone asking me to produce wallet photos of my kids.

Here, then, is what I love best of all about luncheons, for within seconds the conversation can shift from idle chatter to immense profundities, only moments later to shift again to money talk as the parties try to place a dollar value on the ideas under discussion. Listen:

*Agent:* Whew! Have you ever seen weather like this?

*Editor:* This is the third mild winter in a row. Do you think the climate is permanently moderating or something?

*Agent:* Possibly. This meteorologist I've been corresponding with thinks the pollutants in the air are seriously affecting world climate. The planet is overheating. The ice caps are melting.

*Editor:* Really? This meteorologist — um, is he writing a book perchance?

*Agent:* Funny you should ask. He's halfway through one. He's got great credentials and he's promotable as hell. Looks a little like Robert Redford.

*Editor:* I'd be interested in a book like that.

*Agent:* Would you be interested twenty-five thousand worth?

*Editor:* Ten thousand worth, maybe.

*Agent:* Ten! The guy's been on *Oprah* twice, for crying out loud!

Lunch is over. The editor pantomimes a scribble toward the captain, the time-honored gesture of summoning the check. There is no quarreling. The inviter pays, the invitee says thank you, and that's usually that.

Goodness, it's five minutes before three! Got to get back to the office. Loved every minute of it. Let's do business. Let's stay in touch. Let's have lunch again soon.

# APPENDIX
## *Is It a Good Deal?*

Below are summaries of the key elements of three kinds of publishing deals: hardcover, trade paperback, and mass-market paperback. They are intended for use as handy reference guides when immediate action is called for. I've broken each category of book into three ratings: poor deal, fair deal, and good deal. It is depressing to note that the advance prices have not changed by a single dollar since the first edition of this book was published in 1983. When you calculate the decline in the dollar's value due to inflation, you will realize that today's authors are writing for approximately half the price they wrote for then.

But your first sale should not be a depressing experience. So, practice reading the information below with one hand cupped over the telephone receiver while your family jumps up and down shrieking, "They're buying the book! They're buying the book!"

## Hardcover

### A Poor Deal
Publisher gets world rights in all languages.
Publisher controls movie, television, and multimedia rights.
Advance under $5000.
Royalties under 10 percent on first 5000 copies sold, 12 ½ percent on next 5000, 15 percent thereafter.
Publisher gets more than 25 percent of British and translation licensing revenue.
Publisher gets more than 10 percent of first-serial, movie, television, and multimedia revenue.

Publisher gets more than 50 percent of reprint, book-club, and other primary subsidiary-rights revenue.

## A Fair Deal

Publisher gets English-language rights in United States, its territories and possessions, Philippine Islands, and Canada.

Publisher does not control movie, television, and multimedia rights.

Publisher may control first-serial, British, and foreign-translation rights if author has no agent. Otherwise, these are reserved by author.

Advance between $5000 and $10,000.

Royalties at least 10 percent on first 5000 copies sold, 12 $\frac{1}{2}$ percent on next 5000, 15 percent thereafter.

If publisher does control first-serial rights, he gets no more than 10 percent of revenue.

If publisher does control British and foreign-translation rights, he gets no more than 25 percent of revenue.

Publisher does not participate in movie, television, or multimedia revenue.

Publisher gets no more than 50 percent of reprint, book-club, and other subsidiary-rights revenue.

## A Good Deal

Publisher gets English-language rights in United States, its territories and possessions, Philippine Islands, and Canada.

Publisher does not control movie, television, and multimedia rights.

Publisher may control first-serial, British, and foreign-translation rights if author has no agent. Otherwise these are reserved by author.

Advance over $10,000.

Royalties better than 10 percent on first 5000 copies sold, 12 $\frac{1}{2}$ percent on next 5000, 15 percent thereafter.

If publisher does control first-serial rights, he gets no more than 10 percent of revenue, and passes author's share to author upon publisher's receipt.

If publisher does control British and foreign-translation rights, he gets no more than 25 percent of revenue, and passes author's share to author upon publisher's receipt.

Publisher does not participate in movie, television, or multimedia revenue.

Publisher gets less than 50 percent of reprint, book-club, and other primary subsidiary-rights revenue, and passes author's share to author upon publisher's receipt after publisher has recouped advance.

## Trade Paperback

**A Poor Deal**

Same as poor hardcover deal, except royalties are less than 6 percent on first 10,000 copies sold, 7 ½ percent thereafter.

**A Fair Deal**

Same as fair hardcover deal, except royalties are at least 6 percent on first 10,000 copies sold, 7 ½ percent thereafter.

**A Good Deal**

Same as good hardcover deal, except royalties are better than 6 percent on first 10,000 copies sold, 7 ½ percent thereafter.

## Mass-Market Paperback

**A Poor Deal**

Same as poor hardcover deal, except royalties are less than 6 percent on first 150,000 copies sold, 8 percent thereafter.

**A Fair Deal**

Same as fair hardcover deal, except royalties are at least 6 percent on first 150,000 copies sold, 8 percent thereafter.

**A Good Deal**

Same as good hardcover deal, except royalties are better than 6 percent on first 150,000 copies sold, 8 percent thereafter.